THE PROSE OF MALLARMÉ

THE EVOLUTION OF A LITERARY LANGUAGE

The prose of Mallarmé

THE EVOLUTION OF A LITERARY LANGUAGE

PG
2344
Z5
K7

JUDY KRAVIS

LECTURER IN FRENCH AT UNIVERSITY COLLEGE, CORK

CAMBRIDGE UNIVERSITY PRESS

CAMBRIDGE

LONDON · NEW YORK · MELBOURNE

Published by the Syndics of the Cambridge University Press
The Pitt Building, Trumpington Street, Cambridge CB2 1RP
Bentley House, 200 Euston Road, London NW1 2DB
32 East 57th Street, New York, NY 10022, USA
296 Beaconsfield Parade, Middle Park, Melbourne 3206, Australia

© Cambridge University Press 1976

First published 1976

Printed in Great Britain by
W & J Mackay Limited, Chatham

Library of Congress Cataloguing in Publication Data

Kravis, Judy, 1947–
The prose of Mallarmé.

Bibliography: p. 233
Includes index.
1. Mallarmé, Stéphane, 1842–1898 – Style. I.Title.
PQ2344.Z5K7   841'.8   75–22977
ISBN 0 521 20921 8

CONTENTS

CONTENTS

INTRODUCTION

The prose of a poet usually commands some degree of critical attention, often on the tacit understanding that it may help the reader understand his poetry. He may also expect to find revealing comments about other writers, about the state of the art and its future. Last but not least, there is always a degree of curiosity regarding the poet himself, whom one might expect to find appearing 'in person' in the prose works. Were these the only reasons for considering a poet's prose, it would be surprising that Mallarmé's has been so neglected. The lacuna appears even more serious when we remember that Mallarmé's reputation is that of a difficult poet. If ever explanation – of the kind the poet himself rather than the critic gives – were needed, it is surely here. However, most of Mallarmé's prose is circumstantial in nature; it seems to bear the mark of a poet–schoolteacher forced, for entirely un-literary reasons, to confront the public world. How then, the reader may wonder, could it form even an interesting point of departure? Is it not merely a public episode in the private life and works of the poet? I propose to show in this study that Mallarmé's prose is far more than a public episode or literary embarrassment, that it does indeed have intrinsic merit. Furthermore, I consider it important not simply as an explanation of Mallarmé's poetry but as an aid to the understanding of any poetry.

Mallarmé is known to many as the poet who wanted to 'donner un sens plus pur aux mots de la tribu' (70),[1] and the words are commonly taken only to mean that Mallarmé wrote for an élite and did not want 'la tribu' to understand his work. While it is true that Mallarmé as a young man had little patience with any form of 'reportage', it would be a mistake to consider his attitude simply élitist. We should distinguish between the common artistic predilection for élitist rather than popular approval, and the necessity, in the artist's view, of a certain kind of expression. If an easily apprehensible 'reportage' will not do justice to

---

[1] All figures in brackets in the text refer to Stéphane Mallarmé, *Œuvres Complètes* (Paris, Gallimard, 1945).

his notion of literature, then the poet must use a more elaborate and apparently defensive language. When Mallarmé says in the early essay 'L'Art Pour Tous': 'Toute chose sacrée et qui veut demeurer sacrée s'enveloppe de mystère' (257), he is stating a fact of his art as well as a fact of his defiance. Furthermore, if 'mystère' constitutes a stumbling block to the average reader, there is no reason to suppose that it was so to Mallarmé. Indeed, the intricate analysis of literary expression that we find in some of the 'Variations' tells us that what looks like deliberate mystification is not so at all. If the younger Mallarmé felt the temptation of artistic arrogance, he also understood what was involved in writing about the expressiveness of words – those of 'la tribu' included. Mallarmé's aim of purifying words involves recognizing language in its own right rather than as tool of everyman's trade. Thus in the alarmingly ordinary modes of literary and dramatic criticism, translation, fashion journalism, philology and public tribute, Mallarmé's language appears in the process of revealing its purity and discovering itself. What the reader may see as a certain strangeness in the writing is the result of his following the emergence of a creative language out of various public circumstances, instead of confronting it as a 'fait accompli' in the form of poetry.

Mallarmé's prose writing is an investigation of the inner liveliness, the curious, often compelling relationship of language with reality. This may at first set the reader at a certain distance; he has to learn to 'read the language', instead of remaining at the more passive level where he gets to know the author or the author's opinions. Paradoxically there is a clue in the personality and reputation of Mallarmé. Tactful and polite, neither recluse nor bohemian, Mallarmé was a modest leader of the so-called Symbolist Movement, and an urbane host at his Tuesday evening gatherings in the Rue de Rome. Close friends and respectful guests came to talk, but more, to listen to the 'Maître'. One might almost say that he was a poet whose reputation lay in the reverent incomprehension of his many adherents. However, if he was thought an inaccessible but undoubted genius, it was often remarked[1] that he was a consummate performer of language. If it was not easy to understand immediately or remember exactly what he said, the very fact and flow of his language was memorable as a work of art in itself, like that 'calme bloc ici-bas chu d'un désastre obscur' (70) which Mallarmé saw in Poe's work. Within that apparently slight fact of reverence – that one should remember the performance as a whole and not the details that

---

[1] See, for example, the testimony of Camille Mauclair in *Mallarmé Chez Lui* (Paris, Bernard Grasset, 1935), pp. 65–6.

hold it together – lies a clue to our understanding of Mallarmé's written language. It must be seen as a performance, as a language in action whose ultimate achievement is to be what it says. Thus we can only appreciate and learn from it as we might from watching other people playing a somewhat unfamiliar game, and not from studying a set of rules and instructions on how to play it.

The reader of poetry is of course familiar with these attitudes: a poem cannot be paraphrased, often defeats translation, and cannot, like even the worst joke, withstand explanation. He does not anticipate finding a detachable meaning in what he reads; he knows what the game is and how it must be played. In other words, he can cope with a degree of difficulty in the language because he knows how to take it, because he recognizes from the start that what he has before him is 'un écrit', a map of words across which he has to make a personal, if not quite pioneering journey. He knows that poetry operates according to laws that do not necessarily play a part in the ordinary, quotidian patterns of prose. There is only one mistake in such an attitude, and Mallarmé's prose shows us clearly where it lies: it is not poetry which has special laws, but written language itself.

Hence a primary hurdle of readerly disquiet can easily be overcome. If prose can centre our attention upon the fact of the word on the page, and upon the singular expressive richness of it, then it will make the terms 'prose' and 'poetry' merely convenient, almost historical categories. Furthermore, such a revelation will help to bring into proper focus some of the problems the reader may have with Mallarmé's poetry, such as: 'What exactly is Mallarmé talking about in "Ses purs ongles"?' Mallarmé is 'talking about the same thing' in both prose and poetry; it is our expectations which often blur that fact. Poetry is traditionally held to be language at its apex of expressiveness, where words may operate differently, and may even mean something different. That poetry was, by the mid-nineteenth century, a sort of autonomous realm with almost a lexicon to itself meant that attention was deflected from poetry as language in favour of poetry as a crypto-mythical entity. The result of that is essentially that poetry looks like another form of 'reportage', simply transporting the reader to another realm. If generations of readers have found Mallarmé's poetry difficult, it is probably because it is disconcerting. The reader is not transported anywhere at all. It is simply not possible to read the poems according to the rules of poetry's 'other', Elysian realm.

The same is true, though in a different way, of the prose. Naturally we can read much of it as simple communication of fact; we can learn

3

that Mallarmé thinks highly of Verlaine, less of Wagner and little of Rimbaud. But in order to appreciate it fully, we have to extend the word 'reading' to mean something like 'seeing from within the words'. Returning for a moment to the famous 'difficulty' of Mallarmé's writing, we can now see the purpose it serves. We cannot go through the words as if only intent upon capturing a sense and making it ours. The degree of difficulty – though perhaps 'strangeness' would be a better word – demands a special attentiveness on the part of the reader, not unlike that which we give to music. The attention is completely involved, yet discerning; we feel at once that we are inhabiting a world beyond articulate meaning, yet feel none the less that something both precise and human is being communicated. Words, unlike music, have a clear link with everyday life; indeed most of the words ever spoken or written have more to do with banal human dealings than with poetry. Thus another part of our attentiveness has to cope with accommodating, on top of all the commoner uses of language that we know, this one too.

It is an autonomy rather than a simple use, and it is this, more than anything else, that makes it difficult for the reader. Few people see the world as a book or the word as a creative artefact; or rather, few are able to see that the special qualities of words arise out of their distinct and not subservient relation to reality. It may be easy to forget any number of facts learned, but it is not easy to forget an attitude towards language which is so far-reaching a fact of human life that we have almost ceased to notice it. How perplexing then, when we not only have to notice it, but actually see the whole system the other way around. Mallarmé's world is seen through his language. There is no way of understanding it from the outside, from the standpoint of any theory of literature.

The titles of the prose works show us quite clearly what we should *expect*. The 'Médaillons et Portraits', written at different times throughout Mallarmé's life, form the most predictable part of the prose. They are literary appreciations, superficially of the kind that any well-known writer might be expected to produce out of reverence or sheer friendship. There is some translation work, apparently a peripheral task with little interest for the creative writer. Yet we find that translation is not necessarily a tedious or problematical exercise, that it demands a novel confrontation between writer and language. The articles that make up 'Crayonné au Théâtre', and the lecture 'La Musique et les Lettres', look at first like the 'poet's view' of other domains of art. However, the language that sets out to say what theatre is, or what music is, can actually explain itself as well. 'La Dernière Mode', a fashion journal entirely written by Mallarmé himself, is certainly the most surprising of all the prose works. Nothing could appear more distant from the concerns of the poet, and yet we discover that its interest is other than a poet's whimsical holiday from literature. Then, in 'Les Mots Anglais', another surprise: the philology text-book contains a mine of insights for the reader of literature. Finally, the series of articles collected under the title 'Variations sur un Sujet', are perhaps the only part of the prose that one might have expected Mallarmé to produce. They are rich, often dense pieces, clearly the work of a writer who is both mature and famous enough to appear in his authentic colours even in a magazine column. Completing the prose works, there are a few prose poems, some occasional pieces written in honour of people or events, and one inchoate story, 'Igitur'. The whole has the air of a collection rather artificially made, as if to form a picture of the poet's ordinary, if eccentric existence. It is, of course, also an accepted homage now to create out of the discrete elements of a life's work, the 'Œuvres Complètes' or final apotheosis.

Mallarmé's own comments on his prose do not really help the reader either. His statements of aims or intentions are nearly always either grandiose or over-modest – the former in youth and the latter in maturity, as one might expect. In an early letter of 1866, for example, we find: 'J'ai voulu te dire simplement que je venais de jeter le plan de mon Œuvre entier.'[1] This is what Mallarmé says in a letter to a friend, and neither confidence nor grandiose planning is lacking. Indeed that confidence forms an interesting contrast to the rather daunted tone of the early poetry, where Mallarmé confronts the prospect of an unattainable 'Azur'. The reason behind that confidence can perhaps be seen in the series of notes that were written around the year 1869. Here Mallarmé writes of 'le langage se réfléchissant', and later expands this:

> Dans le 'Langage' expliquer le Langage, dans son jeu par rapport à l'Esprit le *démontrer*, sans tirer de conclusions absolues (de l'Esprit). (853)

Bearing in mind these very sure and specific remarks, one can see that Mallarmé did indeed have a plan for his 'Œuvre', and that it was not exactly what it at first appears to be.

Mallarmé twice makes the assertion that 'tout, au monde, existe pour aboutir à un livre' (378), and this statement, together with the fact that he often uses the word 'Œuvre', seems to suggest that he did have in mind a work on the scale of Dante's *Commedia*. It is quite possible that Mallarmé himself, at any rate in his youth, had such an image, and

---

[1] Stéphane Mallarmé, *Propos sur la Poésie*, ed. Henri Mondor (Paris, Editions du Rocher, 1946), p. 70.

5

it is certainly true that his elusiveness as a writer and as a person led admirers to believe that he was always working on a secret and definitive 'Livre'. However, the very idea of a work in one mode would not do justice to the broad scope of Mallarmé's understanding of language. It is only by working towards the 'Œuvre', through various modes and situations of language, that Mallarmé is able to encompass the whole gamut of possibilities that language has. Poetry is the 'Œuvre' in microcosm; it is the sharp and memorable glitter of the diamond. But it is prose which collects the facets of the diamond and allows us to know its nature. Thus it is no idle whim which makes Mallarmé write:

> Je m'occupe de l'armature de mon œuvre qui est en prose.[1]

It is the prose, the 'armature', which runs the whole length of Mallarmé's 'Œuvre', showing us 'le langage se réfléchissant' in many different situations. With the deftness one might expect of a born showman or a mythical chivalrous knight, Mallarmé takes on the challenge of language in all its modes: rhapsodic, analytical, public and private. The very fact that we are conscious of neither challenge nor struggle already indicates the breadth of his success.

Mallarmé's language, both 'se réfléchissant' and reflecting each of its tasks, has at once the immovable quality of a fact and the impregnable quality of a private world. It can only be entered by progressive and sensitive acquaintance; hence its only analogue would be a living creature, a human being. Furthermore, just as human love fulfils both the lover and the loved one, so a deepening acquaintance with language is a joint performance between words and reader, demanding the full extension of the faculties of each. It is because the distinctiveness of Mallarmé's language does not exclude the reader but prompts his complete participation that we feel we are in the presence of that which is in the process of making itself, and is therefore at the heart of both the human and the literary enterprise.

The human analogue can be taken further if we consider the case of the spoken word. We do not usually notice that the speaker's face and voice influence our understanding of his words. Similarly, we may not notice in prose that our reading is partly based upon our reaction to the equivalent 'voice and face' of the words. Curiously enough, the most obvious elements of speech are those least noticed. But in Mallarmé's writing it is difficult to be so unobservant. When we read it, we are looking at books, theatre, fashion or music through language, and the voice we listen to while we are looking is that of language.

---

[1] Mallarmé, *Correspondance*, vol. ii (Paris, Gallimard, 1965), p. 248.

Hence there is nothing arid about the experience. It is easy to see that the listener could be both entertained and informed by a speaker who communicated a performance rather than just a set of facts. (A case in point is surely the peculiarly American oratorical skill of saying very little with a marvellous flourish of words.) The notion is not really over-flippant in connection with Mallarmé. His enjoyment of the tasks set for language – its different 'faces' – is often evident, especially in 'La Dernière Mode', and the enjoyment plays a part in the contact between Mallarmé and his language. Objects appear all the more transformed into objects of language, parts of an artefact. And, paradoxically, they appear all the more visible. This applies to word, page and book, just as it applies to the famous absent 'fleur' of the Mallarméan bouquet.[1] Gabriel Josipovici tells us, in *The World and the Book*, that:

> We are, in fact, two people, one who has the experience of the sunlight on water, and one who expresses this in such terms as 'What a lovely day!'[2]

In order to articulate the first and avoid the expressionless language norm of the second, it is necessary to *see* more intensely, so that language supersedes the overworked currency of 'What a lovely day!' or 'une fleur'.

This of course brings us to the commonest of all tags attached to Mallarmé's name: symbolism. Is the absent flower a 'real' one, or a symbol? It is neither one nor the other; it is the creature of words. It would be inept to explain Mallarmé's achievement in terms of symbolism. The very word implies a divisiveness which is quite contrary to both the aims and the effects of his writing. However, going back to the hypothetical reader faced by what looks like a difficult piece of writing, it is easy to see that if the opportunity of understanding words as 'reportage' is removed, the next rationalization of the strangeness would be to see the words as signs hiding a secret and greater significance. Such an attitude towards words is probably as old as the practice of literature and the recognition of the artefact. But it is impossible to do justice to Mallarmé's use of language by explaining it in this way, for symbolism implies a rational 'third man' holding the key to words and writer alike.

I have found it more convenient, as well as more revealing, to structure

---

[1] Thus it appears that the artefact in words is not necessarily unreal, that in fact quite the reverse is true if one accepts the idea – so distasteful to nineteenth-century realism – than an artefact is *different* from reality, not a second-best version of it.

[2] Gabriel Josipovici, *The World and the Book* (Macmillan, 1971), p. 258.

this study according to circumstance rather than chronology. Many of the pieces in, for example, the 'Médaillons et Portraits' were written at different times. On the other hand, 'La Dernière Mode', written roughly in the middle of Mallarmé's career, is so different from anything else in the prose that it is hardly illuminating to place it chronologically. The most important question posed at each stage of this study is: 'What happens when Mallarmé's language confronts this situation?' It is only by collecting the reactions to this question that we can sense the evolution of Mallarmé's language and arrive at an understanding broad enough to encompass the final stage. Here language considers literature without the intermediary of any situation. It is impossible to understand – even to see – the result of an experiment such as this one without having traced its different stages. It is likewise difficult to see the significance of a 'language of literature'. I have used this phrase, not because I think it one that Mallarmé would necessarily have approved, but because it is probably the only way of indicating the 'subject' of Mallarmé's later prose. In the 'Variations sur un Sujet' and 'La Musique et les Lettres', for example, we do not exactly find a piece of literature; we find the language of which literature is, or might be, made. The only justification for cavilling about 'language' or 'literature' here must lie in the difference of attitudes towards the experience: where we might admire literature, we are involved in language, following a process or experiment whose 'result' appears desultory beside its 'déroulement'.

Mallarmé's is a very single-minded experiment, all the more so for appearing to make even frivolous deviations now and then. Indeed it is probably this unity of approach which explains why Mallarmé's name is so often mentioned in connection with language in recent years, even though current linguistic speculations have very little to do with what he wrote. Mallarmé may have been one of the first writers to consider language in its own right, but this does not automatically – or even interestingly – make him ancestor to the whole range of twentieth-century language studies. He was a creative writer, and used language to express what he saw, what he felt language to be, not in order to prove a point. Thus we must not expect to sift out any formulae from Mallarmé's writing; indeed to do so would be to fail entirely as readers. For, as Mallarmé himself recognized very early on:

> Il faut toujours couper le commencement et la fin de ce qu'on écrit. Pas d'introduction, pas de finale. Tu me crois fou. Je t'expliquerai un jour que là n'est pas ma folie...[1]

[1] *Propos*, p. 39.

Mallarmé himself gives no introduction or finale to what he wrote; his language is essentially a process which we as readers can complete. But we should do so on the understanding that such a completion would be but a prelude to the future creativity of other reading or writing. One might then, describe Mallarmé's prose as a vast and complex handbook, composed with rare demonstrative skill, about the art of creative writing.

▲ 1 ♥

'Médaillons et Portraits':
the language of
admiration and tribute

For Mallarmé the moment of considering other writers' work is but a different form of the basic situation in which the writer confronts his own language. Instead of entering a free creative field, his words are prompted by others already existing. Unusual directions are opened up, though sometimes restricted by the critic's duty to react tactfully as well as sensitively to their possibilities. Conventional forms of tribute can appear to disguise or even dissolve evidence of real feeling, approbatory or otherwise. Yet Mallarmé's literary criticism hardly bears the mark of these limitations; indeed they bring one unexpected freedom, that of being able, without any need for circumlocution, to write about writing. Thus, despite the need for tact, and despite the constraints of writing what are often circumstantial pieces, there is no doubt that the Mallarmé of 'Brise Marine', arrested by 'le vide papier que la blancheur défend' (38), is no less dramatically impressed by pages inscribed with the writing of others.

It was once common practice for the student painter to spend much of his time making copies of the great masters, in order to understand their techniques and to develop new ones. Would-be writers, on the other hand, usually content themselves with reading the works of those they admire, rather than attempting to copy or imitate them. In the 'Médaillons et Portraits' and other allied writing, Mallarmé borrows the form of the painter's apprenticeship. He does not make copies, he formulates reactions; but the exercise still has the effect of teaching the artist his craft. Also, Mallarmé does not restrict himself to writing about the works of great masters. Many of the 'Médaillons' deal with writers who were little known then and less so today. However, Mallarmé's reactions to their work shows us that it is not less, and may be more valuable for the artist to consider the work of those who are not yet and may never be great masters. Another important factor to consider is that the critic – or eulogist, as he often is – has a public task to do, and often a public language with which to do it. Convention demands a measure of

10

pastiche as homage to the great, and pastiche is not interesting in itself unless pursued to the lengths achieved by Proust, or Queneau. Nonetheless, even in limited use, pastiche is not a copy but an imitation of style, and so allows for elements of both original and imitation to be present simultaneously. In other words, it allows Mallarmé to carry out his own experiment while appearing to abide by the conventions of the critic's rôle. By taking note of Mallarmé's fluctuating respect for convention the reader can discern something more than the predictable literary homage or judgements. Conventional form is a gauge, in Mallarmé's writing, by which we can measure his own achievement; it enables us to see, through his different reactions and criteria, the shaping of his language.

The tributes naturally vary in their degrees of praise. But, where one might expect the famous to receive generous homage and the lesser-known only generous advice, in fact Mallarmé does something quite different. The tributes to famous writers, such as Verlaine, Banville or Tennyson, are all characterized by fairly conventional language. The tributes to lesser writers, on the other hand, are almost all examples of Mallarmé's own voice. Thus it seems as if those who carry the torch of the art are not those who, for Mallarmé, keep it burning. The fact of achievement in literature obviously fascinated Mallarmé, partly because of the extraordinary contrast it forms with its actual making.

One might say then, that Mallarmé's language of admiration and tribute moves between two poles. One is a grateful, if formalized, discerning of a public entity, Literature, within whose shape and tradition the writer moves, and which in some measure protects what he writes. At the other extreme, Mallarmé writes of minor works, giving them greater scope than they actually have by situating them as new initiatives within that shape of Literature. And, naturally, in order to do so he must use the full weight and expressiveness of his own language. On the one hand we see the status and impact of established literature; on the other hand, the sheer force of the young writers' efforts towards their vision of the art. But that vision never appears compatible with the one which established literature provides. Moving thus between different visions of creativity and the fact of having achieved it, Mallarmé's, language has the effect of a complete and essentially mobile entity, governing an area of the possible and the achieved, without settling, by virtue of its form, in either one or the other. Freed from the possible constraints and fears of creative writing, and not succumbing to either passive assessment or simple admiration, Mallarmé's writing itself forms a contribution to the discovery of literature.

Early literary criticism

If we look at a few examples of Mallarmé's early literary criticism, we see that what might look like a deliberate or perverse policy of avoiding judgement stemmed from an intuitive discovery. The early tributes to Baudelaire, Gautier and Banville, all reverential in the extreme, are only poor instances of Mallarmé's own language. When he writes of Des Essarts's poetry, on the other hand, he has freedom to consider the actual situation of paying literary tribute, and comes to some interesting conclusions. For example, in the first of two articles, he writes:

> Je crois qu'on risquerait fort de revendiquer chez son auteur des qualités qu'il ne devait pas montrer, de demander des violettes à un églantier, si, pour apprécier une œuvre, on fondait sa critique sur les seuls principes de l'art; et qu'il faut, au contraire, passer du poète au poème et juger ce qu'il a fait par ce qu'il a songé à faire. (249)

Not only is the twenty-year-old Mallarmé chary of applying any literary theory to his appreciation of poetry; he also takes care to situate the work in question within, so far as he can sense it, the author's image of poetry. The critic's writing is thus more attuned to that of the poet, and also has the effect of extending its scope. In the second article, we see another instance of the way in which the critic both appreciates and develops the work he is writing about:

> Comme notre vie n'est qu'un désir permanent de tremper curieusement les lèvres dans la coupe de toutes les sensations, après m'être enivré de cette volupté de proclamer des vers amis la veille de leur naissance, je veux savourer celle de les applaudir au milieu de leur marche rayonnante, cependant que l'éditeur Malassis monnaie en écus leur étoile. Une troisième volupté serait de les défendre sous forme d'oraison funèbre. (254–5)

Mallarmé circles the life-span of the literary work – its roots, its present and its future – but without setting it upon a static pedestal. He also mentions, where another might not, the banal fact of the book in its financial aspect. For, as he recognized in another early article entitled 'L'Art Pour Tous', ordinary terms of homage do little justice to the work of art:

> Comme tout ce qui est absolument beau, la poésie force l'admiration; mais cette admiration sera lointaine, vague, – bête, elle sort de la foule. (257)

A great achievement in any art does, in this sense, force admiration; hence the best tribute is often silence. But in the case of Des Essarts's poetry, silence is not appropriate. Mallarmé acknowledges its authenticity and its imperfections by viewing it from all sides, even looking ahead to the time when he will be able to write its 'oraison funèbre'. Even at this early stage, Mallarmé appreciated that more interesting demands were made on his own language as a critic when it attempted to focus upon the quality of that which shows potential rather than on that which is already established in the hierarchy of literature. He also warns us not to expect in his literary criticism any *a priori* theory of literature, only evidence of confrontation with literature itself. Similarly, the reader impatient to know 'what Mallarmé's "Livre" is', should take warning from the attitudes shown here, that it is not likely to be summarized at any point, but will be sensed, in its turn, by the reader's confrontation with Mallarmé's words.

Verlaine

Mallarmé's writing on Verlaine can be divided into two kinds: first, expressions of friendship and sympathy, and second, admiration for what he wrote, largely in the form of loose imitation. The piece entitled 'Sur Verlaine' (874) consists entirely of reminiscences concerning Verlaine as a 'confrère' of Mallarmé the unwilling English teacher, and shows Mallarmé's language at its most straightforward and light-hearted. The 'Enquête sur Verlaine' (873–4), written a year earlier in 1896, is largely a discussion of Verlaine's place in the tradition of literature. Mallarmé and Verlaine were considered 'leaders' of 'opposing literary schools', yet Mallarmé makes no direct mention of this. It is obvious that he is concerned with the larger fabric of literary tradition and not with considerations of status as imposed by the public.[1] The 'Enquête' does place Verlaine within the tradition of literature, but also pays homage 'au type permanent impersonnel dont se réclame quiconque fit de beaux vers'. (873) As an instance of the Poet, Mallarmé finds Verlaine to be without equal, not because he complied with the conventions of the Parnassian poets and not because he created entirely new forms to rival them:

L'antérieur Parnassien eut suffi à une carrière et une renommée; et même, peut s'isoler, depuis, qu'avec sa survivance ont joué, subitement, comme seules, des orgues complexes et pures. Quant

[1] Mallarmé's view of 'literary schools' can be seen in the piece entitled 'Solitude' (405–9) in the 'Variations'.

à la nouveauté de ces quinze ans, ceci l'annonce, seulement. L'essentiel et malin artiste surprit la joie, à temps, de dominer au conflit de deux époques, une dont il s'extrait avec ingénuité, réticent devant l'autre qu'il suggère; sans être que lui, éperdument – né d'un moment littéraire indiqué. (873–4)

Verlaine's emergence from the Parnassian tradition does not re-instate him in any other school, but places him in the succession of Poets, as one whose 'doigt a été mis sur la touche inouïe qui résonnera solitairement, séculairement'. (873)

It is this achievement which invests Verlaine, for Mallarmé, with the status of a Poet:

> Mais le père, le vrai père de tous les jeunes, c'est Verlaine, le magnifique Verlaine dont je trouve l'attitude comme homme aussi belle vraiment que comme écrivain, parce que c'est la seule, dans une époque où le poète est hors la loi: que de faire accepter toutes les douleurs avec une telle hauteur et une aussi superbe crânerie. (870)

It is as such a figurehead of literature that Mallarmé most admires Verlaine. The poet as inspiration to younger writers is very different from the poet as figurehead of a school whose existence depends upon argument and dogma. The former emphasizes the notion of the writer as part of the fabric of tradition, punctuating it by his 'Œuvre' and perpetuating it by the encouragement that his work and his personality are to others. But any discussion of the latter must take the critic further from what Verlaine wrote. If Mallarmé's admiration is led away from the substance of Verlaine's writing it is in order to emphasize his position as an independent and autonomous milestone in the tradition of literature. References to what he wrote are only indirect. For example, the text written for Verlaine's funeral contains a number of reverent pieces of pastiche:

> Aussi, de notre part, à plus menant un deuil fraternel, aucune intervention littéraire: elle occupe, unanimement, les journaux, comme les feuilles blanches de l'œuvre interrompu ressaisiraient leur ampleur et s'envolent porter le cri d'une disparition vers la brume et le public. (510)[1]

---

[1] It is incidentally significant that Mallarmé's romanticizing of the function of newspapers here stands in marked contrast to comments elsewhere concerning their content, or 'reportage'. The view of newspapers here arises partly out of the influence of writing about Verlaine, but also indicates the extent to which the *notion* of something like a newspaper can, for Mallarmé, overlay the reality of its existence and function.

'Les blanches feuilles de l'œuvre' and 'une disparition vers la brume et le public' are phrases very much in keeping with the atmosphere of Verlaine's writing in their melody and their wistful kind of romanticism. In the same piece, Mallarmé writes: 'Paul Verlaine, son génie enfui au temps futur, reste héros.' (511) His dramaticizing of Verlaine's influence indicates both politeness and a belief in the importance of the notion. The idea that Verlaine's genius should vanish into the misty future of later writing is an apt formulation of tribute as well as a contribution to Mallarmé's own thought.

This should not suggest that Mallarmé had only a limited admiration for Verlaine's writing, but that he saw Verlaine's work chiefly within a scheme of literary development. The attitude demonstrates at once a high degree of egoism and a high degree of admiration: it shows egoism because, by writing of Verlaine as a landmark in literature and by stressing the importance of his influence on young writers, Mallarmé suggests that one of the greatest values of his work is that it will be superseded – if by no means entirely over-shadowed – by the work of later writers. It is clear, on the other hand, that admiration for such an achievement would be genuine and unflawed.

Gautier and Banville

Verlaine's work both punctuates and propels the tradition of poetry. That of Gautier and Banville, for Mallarmé, both guarantees it and invests it with splendour. His admiration is directed towards the atmosphere of their writing .This can best be described as a generous indulgence in a generalized sensation of poetry such as it is traditionally conceived. For example:

> Bientôt une insensible transfiguration s'opère en moi, et la sensation de légèreté se fond peu à peu en une de perfection. Tout mon être spirituel, – et le trésor profond des correspondances, l'accord intime des couleurs, le souvenir du rythme antérieur, et la science mystérieuse du Verbe, – est requis, et tout entier s'émeut, sous l'action de la rare poésie que j'invoque, avec un ensemble d'une si merveilleuse justesse que de ses jeux combinés résulte la seule lucidité. (262)

This is a great tribute to the sensation of reading Gautier, but says nothing of his use of language; admiration is reserved for the perpetuation of the sensation of poetry.

As for the tributes to Banville, it is interesting that the later piece, written in 1892, does not significantly alter the sentiments of the 'Symphonie Littéraire', dating from 1864. In many ways, the terms of Mallarme's early rapture are entirely suited to his more mature understanding:

> mon poète, c'est le divin Théodore de Banville, qui n'est pas un homme, mais la voix même de la lyre. Avec lui, je sens la poésie m'enivrer – ce que tous les peuples ont appelé la poésie, – et, souriant, je bois le nectar dans l'Olympe du lyrisme. (264)

When Mallarmé writes of Banville, he does not exactly write praise of what he wrote, but in praise *that* he should have written 'ce que tous les peuples ont appelé la poésie', and that he should be recognized as 'Maître', as a poet meriting public speeches and a monument in the Jardin du Luxembourg.[1] Banville's writing is seen as of a kind which is easily identifiable by young writers – and by the public – as an indisputable example of 'La Poésie, ou ce que les siècles commandent tel' (521). It is a clear and admirable landmark, summarizing the past rather than revealing how language 'becomes' poetry. Evidence of the distinct-ness of the 'landmark' can be seen throughout Mallarmé's tribute. For example:

> Affection à part, si, parlant poèmes, se peut omettre le souvenir de l'auguste tête fine que le buste instauré éveille pour le promeneur et ami, je vouai à Théodore de Banville un culte. L'exceptionnelle clarté où je l'admire, trait unique et comme absolu, s'aidera de la brièveté de ma causerie. (520)

Banville was, early on, a cult figure for Mallarmé, but when Mallarmé himself had developed as a writer, Banville's work aroused an admiration so clear that it needed few words to express it. It is therefore possible to infer a certain limitation in Mallarmé's admiration.

> Non que n'importe de signaler des dons excessifs, divers; mais je les confonds en tant qu'éléments d'un miracle. (520)

If we see Mallarmé's main concern as the gradual elucidation of the nature of literary language, it will be apparent that a writer whose work arouses such clear admiration will actually have less to offer to the

---

[1] Banville's reaction to the 'Symphonie Littéraire' is interesting in that it recognizes the element of over-generous admiration for the traditional notion of poetry: 'Si je ne puis m'empêcher de voir que vous me louez mille fois trop et d'en être confus, je me rassure en songeant que je suis là seulement un prétexte, grâce auquel vous chantez d'une façon merveilleuse un des plus beaux aspects de notre chère et sainte poésie.' (1544)

development of Mallarmé's own language.¹ If Banville's achievement is in some sense the consummation of a form of poetry, it is also a dead end to the aspiring poet – who can then only imitate, in the shadow of an acknowledged miraculous achievement – and to the critic who may well find it almost suspicious, given that the imperfections of language are so commonly seen, that such a miracle can have taken place. It is not that the clear and decided quality of Mallarmé's tribute in any way rings false (except perhaps in some of the early tribute), but that the very elements which he praises in Banville's work are far *too* clearly manifest to have a place in Mallarmé's far more complex notion of language. For example:

> *La divine transposition*, pour l'accomplissement de quoi existe l'homme, *va du fait à l'idéal*. Or, grâce à de scintillantes qualités, épanouies aux deux siècles français aristocratiques dont Banville résuma la tradition en ce mot: *l'esprit*..., nous eûmes cette impression d'extrême, de rare et de superlatif. (522)

There is no doubt that such perceptions are within the ambit of Mallarmé's preoccupations; yet they are relatively limited and do not advance the expressiveness of Mallarmé's language. The first part of the quotation above is a general statement which the reader takes to apply to Banville, but the second part suggests that Banville only made a contribution to this general process, and accomplished the transposition with such a masterly air that this air becomes more important than the detail of exactly what he transposed into what.

Thus Mallarmé's tribute speaks its own lack of depth: the writer for whom he would have the highest admiration would probably not be a Banville, since such an admiration would merit either the form of poetry, or else a form of Mallarmé's prose which takes language nearer the expressive heights associated with poetry. Yet if admiration is qualified here, it is still coupled with a sense of genuine gratitude towards one who 'représente, à travers les somptuosités, les ingénuités et les piétés, l'être de joie et de pierreries, qui brille, domine, effleure'. (523)

Rimbaud

If Mallarmé is more than just towards Banville, he is less than just towards Rimbaud. The reasons for this spring both from what Rimbaud wrote and from his position in literary history. Of Banville, Mallarmé

---

¹ There is no perverse ingenuity in this judgement. Mallarmé would welcome not resent the miracle should it appear, as we can see from his tributes to Poe.

can write: 'La riante immortalité d'un poète résout les questions, en dissipe le vague, avec un rayon' (519). Though the statement is sufficiently general, he would not have used it of Rimbaud, since it is obvious from the beginning of the tribute that he is uncertain where to place Rimbaud:

> le nom soudainement d'Arthur Rimbaud se soit bercé à la fumée de plusieurs cigarettes; installant, pour votre curiosité, du vague. (512)

Although this piece was written for an American journal, 'The Chap Book' and thus called for a certain amount of biographical detail, the manner in which Mallarmé deals with his subject reveals a high degree of uncertainty:

> Quel, le personnage, questionnez-vous: du moins, avec des livres *Une Saison en Enfer, Illuminations* et ses *Poèmes*, naguères publiés en l'ensemble, exerce-t-il sur les événements poétiques récents une influence si particulière que cette allusion faite, par exemple, on se taise, énigmatiquement et réfléchisse, comme si beaucoup de silence, à la fois, et de rêverie s'imposait ou d'admiration inachevée. (512)

The Mallarméan trait of noting the correspondences between abstract considerations and the physical space in which they are made, appears here despite an obvious unwillingness to give a decided view. Mallarmé's hesitations about Rimbaud involve two factors: first, the substance of Rimbaud's work, and second, his sudden and brief career.

Mallarmé recognizes the 'Bateau Ivre' as a masterpiece, acknowledges that Rimbaud is the author of 'de beaux vers', but otherwise concerns himself with the strangeness and exoticism of Rimbaud's life. He seems unable to detach the content of Rimbaud's writing from the life he led.

> Menus faits, quelconques et, du reste, propres à un, ravagé violemment par la littérature le pire désarroi, après les lentes heures studieuses aux bancs, aux bibliothèques, cette fois maître d'une expression certaine prématurée, intense, l'excitant à des sujets inouïs, – en quête aussitôt de 'sensations neuves' insistait-il 'pas connues' et il se flattait de les rencontrer en le bazar d'illusion des cités, vulgaire: mais, qui livre au démon adolescent, un soir, quelque vision grandiose et factice continuée, ensuite, par la seule ivrognerie. (514)

It is clear that, as a friend and admirer of Verlaine, he cannot help seeing

18

Rimbaud as a social and literary black sheep. Rimbaud's tendencies towards the exotic only serve to set him at a distance from the more mature and urbane Mallarmé. Rimbaud essentially wanted to transcribe what his imagination had *already* transformed; he wanted his intensity of living to find itself re-instated in language. Such an aim would seem to negate even the simple 'transposition du fait à l'idéal' that Banville's writing operates. For Rimbaud, life itself operates the transformation, and language merely holds it, as it were, in place, by evoking it as clearly as possible. So it might be said that Rimbaud saw language as something smaller than life, whereas for Mallarmé it was always an *equal* to life.

Had Mallarmé at first thought that the precocity and brevity of Rimbaud's literary achievement required some considerable change in his own scale of literary values, he was, in a way, saved by Rimbaud's eventual desertion of poetry in favour of lived adventure. It appeared to Mallarmé that Rimbaud was in a way conquered by language, that he laid his brief and brilliant siege, produced its explosions and dazzling flashes, derived moments of beauty in his writing, but could not sustain it. In his article on Rimbaud, Mallarmé makes frequent references to the suddenness and brevity of Rimbaud's achievement. For example:

> Eclat, lui, d'un météore, allumé sans motif autre que sa présence, issu seul et s'éteignant. (512)

Rimbaud appears 'Maître d'une expression certain prématurée' (514), and his adventure that of a child:

> trop précocement touché et impétueusement par l'aile littéraire qui, avant le temps presque d'exister, épuisa d'orageuses et magistrales fatalités, sans recours à du futur. (518)

Sprung from nowhere, Rimbaud's work can have no 'recours à du futur'. When Mallarmé considers the classic question of 'what Rimbaud might have written', he does not display his usual interest in the potential development of the writer, but says:

> J'estime, néanmoins, que prolonger l'espoir d'une œuvre de maturité nuit, ici, à l'interprétation exacte d'une aventure unique dans l'histoire de l'art. (518)

There is here a detectable suspicion that had Rimbaud gone on writing, he might indeed have developed literary tradition to the point of over-throwing it, and this, for one who believed that literature is a development and not a meteoric explosion, would be revolutionary. But, since

Rimbaud did not explore the 'épanouissement' of his first brilliant literary explorations, Mallarmé is able to say safely:

> Tout, certes, aurait existé, depuis, sans ce passant considérable, comme aucune circonstance littéraire vraiment n'y prépara: le cas personnel demeure, avec force. (512)

Mallarmé clearly does not intend high praise, yet he does give such praise indirectly. Had Rimbaud been any *less* original Mallarmé would have admired him more; but Rimbaud's visceral refusal of the past and defiance towards the future arouse a unique reaction of disquiet and distrust in Mallarmé. If, superficially, he has little to say about Rimbaud, if he is unable to place him within the tradition of literature, this is tribute in itself. We have seen the ease and readiness with which Mallarmé praised Banville, and how his admiration seemed qualified by the fact that its terms in no way permitted any development of Mallarmé's own language. There is, however, no question of Mallarmé's language encompassing Rimbaud's achievement. This itself acknowledges the exceptional strength and wealth of Rimbaud's language.

Whatever Mallarmé's misgivings, there is, strangely, a similarity between his own writing and Rimbaud's, which may have blinded Mallarmé to the merits of his younger contemporary. This critical 'blind spot' concerns the degree of importance that language has for the writer. Rimbaud wanted language to restore and perpetuate the richness of sensation; because he wanted so much from language and could not accommodate himself to its limitations, he abandoned literature. It is possible that Mallarmé saw Rimbaud as one who succeeded in breaking the laws of literary reality, by actually saying his intensity of living out loud. Dismayed by the law-breaker, he would fail to see that Rimbaud's intensity was also of language. Wallace Stevens makes the observation:

> In both prose and poetry, images come willingly, but, usually, although there is a relation between the subject of the images there is no relation between the images themselves. A group of images in harmony with each other would constitute a poem within, or above, a poem.[1]

It is in the realm of 'a poem above a poem' that Rimbaud and Mallarmé could be said to meet. They both create in language a palimpsest over that language, though strangely the poems 'within or above' the poems are in each case like a mirror image of the other, almost literally a mirror image in the sense that one has within the poem on the page what the

---

[1] Wallace Stevens, *The Necessary Angel* (Faber, 1960), p. 78.

other has in palimpsest outside it. Obviously this is not a notion that either poet would necessarily have supported, neither would it be true for every reader. But if there were a kind of magnet that could pick up quality of atmosphere, it would very likely appear that the fragile tremulous quality that appears in Mallarmé's poetry, and in the best of his prose, could equally be found, not on the page, but in the aftermath of a reading of Rimbaud's last works: and vice versa. Naturally this would not apply to every page, but Rimbaud's presence as magician/controller of clouds that 's'amassaient sur la haute mer faite d'une éternité de chaudes larmes'[1] is surely an ideal, almost a necessary complement to the scintillating absence that governs the pages of Mallarmé.

Younger contemporaries

The younger and lesser writers whom Mallarmé discusses constitute a rich moment in the 'Médaillons et Portraits', since their work is not yet seen as a finished monument in the tradition of literature; they are still forging that position, as they are forging their language. The special situation of young writers in France at the end of the nineteenth century, as Mallarmé saw it, was that despite, or even because of traditional literary education, young poets recognized fewer and fewer restrictions (without, for the most part, going as far as Rimbaud did, and abandoning them altogether).

> Nous assistons, en ce moment...à un spectacle vraiment extra-ordinaire, unique, dans toute l'histoire de la poésie: chaque poète allant, dans son coin, jouer sur une flûte, bien à lui, des airs qu'il lui plaît; pour la première fois, depuis le commencement, les poètes ne chantent pas au lutrin. Jusqu'ici, n'est-ce pas, il fallait, pour s'accompagner, les grandes orgues du mètre officiel. Eh bien! on en a trop joué.... (866)

The alexandrine had enjoyed such pre-eminence that it had finally become recognized as the sum and limit of poetry itself; and the very existence of such a convention gives added force to 'une flûte bien à [soi]'. But the innovations of young poets, probably for reasons of limited powers as well as of reverence, do not entirely dispense with the alexandrine:

> Le vers officiel ne doit servir que dans des moments de crise de l'âme; les poètes actuels l'ont bien compris; avec un sentiment de réserve très délicat, ils ont erré autour, en ont approché avec une

[1] Arthur Rimbaud, *Poésies* (Paris, Garnier, 1960), p. 256.

singulière timidité, on dirait quelque effroi, et, au lieu d'en faire leur principe et leur point de départ, tout à coup l'ont fait surgir comme le couronnement du poème ou de la période! (867)

The 'sentiment de réserve très délicat' is exactly that of Mallarmé when writing of the acknowledged literary masters of his time. It is true of the tribute to Banville, and also of the tribute to Leconte de Lisle, in which Mallarmé writes:

> Le maître dont apparaît l'œuvre comme une cité exclusive ou grandiose de palais et de temples, devait par un beau droit présider au banquet, où s'asseoient les poètes. (864)

Such 'palaces and temples' stand behind new literary attempts, not as reproach or defiance, but simply as a clear moment in the development of literature, a point around which the young writer can create 'une sorte de jeu courant pianoté autour...ne permettant au vers officiel de sortir que dans les grands occasions'. (870)

There is, in the ease with which Mallarmé outlines the contemporary state of poetry, a note of subtle supremacy, as of one who is actually capable of seeing so clearly the state of affairs. As Jules Huret notes:

> un charme puissant se dégage de l'homme en qui l'on devine un immarcescible orgueil, planant au dessus de tout, un orgueil de dieu ou d'illuminé, devant lequel il faut tout de suite intérieurement s'incliner, quand on l'a compris. (866)

The tactfulness of such supremacy, in the situation of literary tribute, could give rise to conventional forms of politeness, but in Mallarmé it stimulates subtleties of language:

> Après la toujours éblouissante et certaine parole de notre aîné en art – Catulle Mendès –, je tends une coupe privée de mousse ou mieux, à vous, Kahn, simplement la main, y enfermant la ferveur qui suscite la salle vers votre vaillance spirituelle. (863)

The delicate placing of the two writers, one established and one a 'débutant', is hardly conventional in form, yet gives a just balance to the relative merits of the two writers: the dazzling status of one is complemented by the straightforward – 'privée de mousse' – enthusiasm of the other.

The limitations, indeed the necessarily unfinished nature of the works by Mallarmé's younger contemporaries, together with his freedom from any obligation to admire, leave Mallarmé an interestingly open field. The 'Frontispiece' written for a book by Tailhade contains a kind of writing which is almost interchangeable within the prose output of Mallarmé. Most of the piece is concerned with Tailhade's much publicized escapades, but the last paragraph takes the reader beyond the realm of scandal, and even beyond the realm of Tailhade's writing:

> Rien, malgré l'accident politique intrus en la pure verrière, je sais celle qui vous occupe, Tailhade, n'y périclita; cuirassée de fragilité à l'épreuve par le préalable bris plombant sa diaprure, dont pas un enflammé morceau d'avance comme la passion le colore, gemme, manteau, sourire, lis, ne manque à votre éblouissante Rosace, attendu et par cela qu'elle-même d'abord simule dans un suspens ou défi, l'éclat, unique, en quoi par profession irradie l'indemne esprit du Poète. (527)

This paragraph, beginning with 'Rien', ending with 'Poète', is a 'Rosace' of Mallarmé's; it transforms the simple windowpane of earlier paragraphs into a literary entity, the 'Rosace', and constitutes a tribute to poetry as a whole rather than specifically to the writing of Tailhade. Since Mallarmé did not write directly of Tailhade's work, it is possible that he did not find it outstanding; yet the mere situation of writing a preface or tribute has its own charms, as Mallarmé recognized as early as 1862:

> il faut... passer du poète au poème et juger ce qu'il a fait par ce qu'il a songé à faire. De là j'eus toujours un grand amour pour les préfaces. A défaut de préface, quand on a la bonne fortune d'un livre aussi sincère que celui-ci [here, of Emmanuel des Essarts], on recherche l'idée dans le titre, qui la résume, et dans les épigraphes, qui la révèlent. (249)

In his tributes to younger writers, Mallarmé deals less with what each poet 'a songé à faire' than with what he, Mallarmé, finds important. He gives neither direct advice nor direct criticism. In the 'Préface aux Raisins Bleus et Gris' by Léopold Dauphin, he writes:

> Cet ami ne traite la versification en tant que complément à son spécial don mélodique, ainsi que doit l'essayer tout compositeur aujourd'hui et produire une écriture spacieuse, discrète de livret; non, il ferme sur le vol des inspirations frémissantes, d'abord son piano, ou reploie le trop d'aile; et... vise directement au chant parlé, tel qu'une intégrité résulte ou poème pur. (859)

The verb 'produire' goes with 'doit', but, because the 'doit' is not repeated, the reference becomes ambiguous. The point of reference is

23

not merely the pages of Léopold Dauphin, nor are the words explicitly prescriptive. The title of the piece does of course place the words in reference to Dauphin, and yet the distancing of them leaves the reference open. The opportunity of situating the writing affords Mallarmé a measure of protection: he can perform both the public task of paying tribute, and the private task of more general literary musing.

Admiration thus does not have to be concerned with ultimate criteria, only to recognize their possibility. Tributes to different writers involve different kinds of language, and so suggest to Mallarmé the possibility of a language which could ultimately account for and express the notion of literature he is shaping here. It is not a proof of Wittgenstein's theory (that a language B is necessary to write of language A, and so on) but rather that the way in which it is possible to write of different languages itself constitutes a language unique to, because transformed by, the individual writer. At a less important point along the scale of this transformation, we find writing of the kind that Mallarmé uses in the tributes to Dierx and Regnault. In the case of Dierx, Mallarmé is unusually explanatory, for reasons probably to do with the nature of his reaction to the other's writing, rather than to any desire to elucidate. If, in this case, Mallarmé does not find himself in the presence of a work that is truly great, he can still discern certain elements of which Dierx suggests the germ. He actually apologizes, in this article, for attempting to say anything about the bases of Dierx's work:

> Je demande pardon au rêveur d'avoir, par amour excessif de la symétrie, exposé à l'œil l'armature mystérieuse de son œuvre; et du fait ordinaire que ces impressions ne sont pas amassées, dans le sommaire précédent, sans affecter une ressemblance lointaine avec ce que représente à tout esprit la Poésie, j'infère cette indéniable vérité que nous avons affaire à une âme non commune de poète, et complète: car elle est à la fois logique et sensible. (690)

It is less important to see whether or not Mallarmé actually does reveal the 'armature mystérieuse de son œuvre', than it is to see how such an 'armature' can even appear to exist. One thing is clear from this piece: only 'une âme...à la fois logique et sensible' will be able to apprehend that 'armature'.

The 'Avant-Dire' to René Ghil's 'Traité du Verbe' is one of the most outstanding pieces in the 'Proses Diverses'. Mallarmé's response to the work is dramatic, not in the degree of approval or disapproval it shows, but in the level of language used. The preface is clearly a piece of writing 'for' the title, rather than 'about' the contents of the book. The scientific nature (and naïveté) of Ghil's enterprise makes it probable that Mallarmé would not have cared or might not even have been able, in the obvious sense, to say very much about it. Yet the book is patently about language, and thus is, in theory, very close to Mallarmé's concerns. So instead of writing a polite introduction to what he saw as a mistaken emphasis on an essential subject, Mallarmé writes a tribute to language itself, revealing an 'armature mystérieuse' of *words* rather than of a book.

The substance of this 'Avant-Dire', later placed at the end of 'Crise de Vers' in the 'Variations', is discussed later. It is interesting that such a piece should even exist as a preface, manifestly superior in style and subtlety to what it is prefacing. The 'Avant-Dire' may be seen as one of Mallarmé's most effective and expressive pieces of writing (not just in the prose, but in his work as a whole). It shows that it is not necessary for there to be anything, in the normal sense, 'to write about'. Mallarmé reacts to what amounts to an attempt to explain how language expresses, and himself provides a performance. The effectiveness of the 'performance' shows how the writer at his most creative only translates or transforms what the mind offers, and does not create, with language, a separate literary entity. In the 'Avant-Dire' Mallarmé offers his own 'translation' of Ghil's intention, and thus demonstrates the necessity of 'explaining' the nature of literary language *in* literary language. That literary language is seen, here as elsewhere in Mallarmé's writing, to be different from the rhapsodic or exotic virtuoso pieces that one might expect.

What Ghil does, to use Mallarmé's terminology, is to write something 'brut' about something 'essentiel'. In the introductory paragraphs of the piece, Mallarmé says:

> Tout, au long de ce cahier écrit par M. Ghil, s'ordonne en vertu d'une vue, la vraie: du titre Traité du Verbe aux lois par maints avouées à soi seul, qui fixent une spirituelle Instrumentation parlée. (857)

The wording of the second phrase is judicious, for it suggests that although the book 's'ordonne en vertu d'une vue, la vraie', it does not constitute a realization – or 'proof' – of such a view. If Ghil's writing is not in the category of 'reportage', it is certainly guilty, in its attempt to 'explain' language scientifically, of a grave misunderstanding of the transformatory powers of language. Yet the very clarity of Ghil's misunderstanding, his writing about 'the right thing' in what is for

Mallarmé 'the wrong way', prompts Mallarmé to write his own brief 'Traité du Verbe'. Had Mallarmé found Ghil's work more convincing, he would have felt obliged to admire it for what it was, rather than for its intention.[1] Most of the writing in tribute to younger writers expands particular aspects which Mallarmé finds sympathetic to the concept of writing and its traditions. Ghil's book is alone in its intention to explore Mallarmé's own field of interest, and that he found it misguided (much as he might have wished to admire it, for its purpose alone) is clear from the fact that his preface is so much a piece of his own writing, and not in any way derived from Ghil's ideas. One might conclude that the greater the admiration, the more derivative the tribute. Homage to an intention is free to be an instance of the language of Mallarmé and not an imitation of the language of Ghil, and it is this situation which, as in the confrontation between Mallarmé and the painters, contributes most to Mallarmé's elucidation of the quality of language.

A form of this situation can be seen in the 'Avant-Dire' to Reynaldo Hahn, where Mallarmé is moved by friendship as well as by sympathy towards an intention. The distance from Mallarmé's own vision of Ghil's 'Traité du Verbe' allowed for a corresponding distance from the norms of literary criticism and tribute in Mallarmé's writing. With Reynaldo Hahn a similiar distance exists, since Hahn was primarily a musician and not a writer; yet Mallarmé senses a sympathy in Hahn's work that allows for considerable scope in a tribute:

> J'annonce que vous n'allez pas, Mesdames et Messieurs, ouïr de la musique exclusivement; pourtant une très sûre musique. Le jeune compositeur l'estime sa façon de ressentir: à savoir que vibre, sur l'instrument d'accord au dedans, quelque émotion pareille aux objets, laquelle prélevée à part et essentiellement, dans leurs traits lumineux, en passion, en grâce, s'exhale par bouffée pure – comme si ces objets brûlaient, d'eux-mêmes, sur un trépied, vers la beauté. (860)

The 'instrument d'accord au-dedans' is not merely that of the musician; Mallarmé is referring to a process which every creative artist knows, usually at a subconscious level. His description of the process is elliptical, scant even; it is a series of emphases whose delicacy and imprecision reflect the inspiration of music. In order to indicate the mode of musical expression, Mallarmé has to use language which is as

---

[1] For a description of Ghil's (favourable) reaction to Mallarmé's preface, and his later split with Mallarmé, see René Ghil, *Les Dates et les Œuvres* (Paris, Crès et Cie, 1923) chapters 2, 3, 7.

creative. A little further on in the tribute, he openly makes the connection between music and literature:

> mais, outre qu'il tire le poème inclus en tout, le voici affronter, quelle audace, les poèmes existant dans le sens strict ou littéraire, et, précisément, y triompher; rien de plus, il perçoit le chant, sacré, inscrit aux strophes, il l'espace et le désigne, répandu par l'éternelle blessure glorieuse qu'a la poésie, ou mystère, de se trouver exprimée déjà, même si près du silence – oui, il en presse les authentiques lèvres pour un jaillissement nouveau. (860)

It is Hahn's sensibility which attracted Mallarmé, his innate sympathy towards the processes of art. That he expresses that sympathy mainly in music offers Mallarmé the opportunity of considering the effect of a 'sense of poetry' finding expression in musical form. Such a possibility in the case of Wagner – not only a great composer, but also a large-scale one – is scarcely even interesting. This is not to say that Mallarmé *preferred* minor to major artists, only that the indecisiveness of Hahn – alternating between expression in music and in words – seemed to offer a positive rôle to Mallarmé's language, even in the gesture he makes towards the attractiveness of such indecision. Wagner, on the other hand, is not merely decisive, but also presumptuous in his attitude towards the union of the arts of music and poetry.

Hahn was by no means a great composer, and appeared to Mallarmé a man who had a considerable sense of art, and perhaps only had recourse to music as one possible means of expressing it. Hahn's music is scarcely mentioned in Mallarmé's tribute. Similarly, in the brief paragraph about the singer Georgette Leblanc, we find few general comments about singing and much more about the artistic process itself. For example:

> A l'encontre de la loi que le chant, pur, existe par lui, rend l'exécutant négligeable, une interprète, de très loin, revient, avec mystère, s'y adapter... (861)

Mallarmé is thinking here of the nature of performance in general, and of the curious relation of performer to performance. He also considers the subtle solitude of the performer:

> L'étrange et passionante femme accentue la notion que l'art, dans ses expressions suprêmes, implique une solitude, conforme, par exemple, au mouvement, pour étreindre quelqu'un n'existant qu'en l'idée et vers qui le cri, de rabattre un geste ployé et le contact de mains sur sa poitrine à soi. (861)

27

The human voice, like the movement of language or body, resembles an embrace proferred to 'quelqu'un n'existant qu'en l'idée'. Mallarmé sees the singer as one who offers, by the quality of her singing, a warmth and a wealth which, as she acknowledges by the anxious gestures of her arms, appear only to come back to her and confirm her solitude.

Tennyson and Swinburne

The value of writing about someone like Hahn can be seen by comparing the tribute to him with that to a poet of great repute, Tennyson. Though Mallarmé uses terms of what seem like the highest praise about Tennyson, the general tenor of the fairly long passage is considerably less intense than that of the tribute to Hahn. Most of it is taken up by tentative comparisons between him and other writers. Mallarmé reacts to Tennyson's status rather than to what he wrote, and stresses particularly the idea of the poet laureate:

> Ce titre de lauréat, mal compris, en outre, suggérerait un exclusif fabricant pour orphéons, presque un confrère versifiant, et inférieur, à l'échotier. (528)

The fame of Tennyson, like that of Banville, lent support to the background of literature. That there should be a poet laureate is not in itself of great importance, yet it does contribute to the abstract and somewhat rarefied notion of the realm in which poets work. Certain traditions of painting favoured the use of generalized or Arcadian landscapes as background. In a similar way, Mallarmé sees literature against a background of tradition, in which public recognition is only necessary as a factor contributing both to the spread of influence and to the theatrical nature of literary existence. The public offices and public tasks of the 'littérateur' foster a consciousness that 'les Lettres' exist and are created, while writers themselves are reminded of the theatrical situation in which they operate. It is theatrical because of the great distance between the creation of a work of art and the public dimension in which it is distributed and appreciated. It could of course be argued that the public situation of the poet, as presented by the existence of the office of poet laureate and similar institutions, only give rise to the wrong sort of consciousness, and, in the general reading public as Mallarmé sees it, this is probably true. Yet the idea of tradition as a near-theatrical hierarchy is important to Mallarmé, not only because literature develops out of its past and gives clues as to its future, but also because it guarantees the activity of the writer. Mallarmé's respect for the status of the Poet, as seen in his attitude towards Banville, as well as towards Tennyson and Swinburne, appears to stem less from an actual respect for fame or status, than from a desire to see perpetuated the mythical status of the poet. Again, it would be easy to assume from this attitude that the mythical dimension of the Poet also involved a mythical, or unreal dimension in what he wrote. However, it is the achievement of Mallarmé's prose to show that it is not the workings of language which are unreal, but only their effect when considered as the works of such and such a writer. For example, in the piece on Tennyson, this appears very clearly:

> Le nom du poète mystérieusement se refait avec le texte entier qui, de l'union des mots entre eux, arrive à n'en former qu'un, celui-là, significatif, résumé de toute l'âme, la communiquant au passant. (529–30)

The writer's existence is identified with his work, and this combination appears mythical, unreal, a perfect theatrical setting for what the writer actually puts down on paper. That a poet is known primarily as 'the author of his works'[1] or as poet laureate, is a glory not merely for the man who writes poetry, but rather for something that has always been poetry –

> car, enfin, il faut bien que le génie ait lieu en dépit de tout et que le connaisse chacun, malgré les empêchements, et sans avoir lu, au besoin. (530)

Mallarmé's point is that it is better (for the present and future of literature) for a poet to be known as Poet, even without being read by most of the public, than to remain unknown. At least, this is what Mallarmé says when writing of a Tennyson or a Banville, but when he is no longer writing in a situation which is enhanced by the presence of a notional or public world of letters, there appear invectives, as powerful as Mallarmé ever utters, against the inability of the general reading public to fulfil its own function, which is knowing how to read.[2]

It is then less important to decide whether Mallarmé thought Tennyson (or Swinburne) a great poet, than to recognize the consequences of his vision of the status of Literature, as distinct from the activity of writing. In the tributes to Tennyson and Swinburne, we discern in Mallarmé's language a greater emphasis upon the public aspect of their

---

[1] As in the case of Beckford. See page 555.

[2] See the piece entitled 'Le Mystère dans les Lettres', in the 'Variations', p. 386.

achievement, and only a conventional response to what they wrote. For example, Mallarmé writes of Tennyson:

> Tout ce que la culture portée à l'état supérieur, ou d'art, avec originalité, goût, certitude, en même temps qu'un primordial don poétique délicieux, peut, en s'amalgamant très bellement, produire chez un élu, Tennyson le posséda, du coup, et sans jamais s'en départir à travers l'inquiète variété: cela n'est pas commun. (530)

The very generality of these terms suggests also a very general admiration, not so much for Tennyson's work as for the qualities that make 'un élu'. The very suddenness and emphasis of this 'éloge' to Tennyson by no means recall the presence of literature (as did many of the tributes to younger and lesser-known writers). The rhythm of the piece makes it more reminiscent of the drum roll before an important announcement than a true instance of 'beauty awakening beauty'.

Similar reservations are to be made about the apparently whole-hearted comments in the piece on Swinburne:

> Quiconque ouvre un livre pour *chanter au-dedans de soi*, le vrai lecteur de vers a, depuis dix ans, en Angleterre, comme avant ce temps, en France, il le fera, emprunté pour son âme le déploiement d'ailes de chacune des stances de l'œuvre lyrique de Swinburne. (702)

The elaborate syntax and its 'précieux' effect suggest that Mallarmé is writing publicity rather than tribute. He also shows rare evidence of the author in some haste to finish:

> A trop grands traits écrite et hâtive, telle (un peu) l'impression causée par l'ensemble. (702)

Mallarmé's experience of reading Swinburne is chiefly characterized, at least according to this article, by a strong awareness of musical qualities. When he does write directly of the contents of Swinburne's work, as opposed to its exalted status, he records, rather than expresses, its qualities:

> Je signale aussi dans des proportions parfois inconnues, le silence: profond, divin, gisant dans l'âme des lecteurs. (702)

Although this is obviously a domain in which Mallarmé himself is able to write, he does no more than point to it here, suggesting either that Swinburne's writing did not really provide confirmation of his intuitions concerning the virtual creation of silence by words, or else that the writing itself was less important to Mallarmé than the fact that it should exist, as one of the imprecisely known, but apparently sympathetic planets that form the Mallarméan 'Constellation'.

Edgar Allan Poe

But if tact, friendly interest, and concern for the public 'theatre' of literature might legitimately extend as far as Tennyson and Swinburne, this is not the case with Poe, who stands in Mallarmé's work as the supreme example of the writer whom Mallarmé *wanted* to see. It is this apparently unlikely fact which alone can elucidate what appears to be evidence of strange taste in Mallarmé. Failing to understand Rimbaud, yet conferring every possible mark of honour upon Poe suggests something more than a mere quirk of taste. If Mallarmé is to be in any way 'rescued' from the heavy hand of opinions such as that of Henry James – that 'an enthusiasm for Poe is the mark of a decidedly primitive state of reflection'[1] – we have to consider not only what Poe wrote, but also the complex of his life, works, and status.

From what we have already seen of Mallarmé's image of Literature, it is obvious that it will be of considerable use to him to be able to recognize one writer as upholder of its mythical status. Poe's life and work certainly show a concern far beyond the ordinary with both the myth and the reality of literature. We must take into account first, Poe's written theory of poetry, of a kind certainly more sympathetic to Mallarmé than Ghil's 'Traité du Verbe'; second, the content of his poetry; third, the juxtaposition of these two, and the way in which they operate in Poe's stories. All this amounts to an 'Œuvre' of proportions beyond those of any other contemporary writer Mallarmé had read. It is also important to remember Poe's situation in the world of literature: he was little known in his own country before his death, and, largely because of Baudelaire's translation of his stories, became a cult figure in France. In the light of all that has been said concerning the public image of the poet, it is not hard to see, in theory, why Mallarmé should have chosen Poe as a 'cas littéraire absolu'. (531)

It is interesting that much of the fascination with Poe lies in the juxtaposition of theory and practice, between the theoretical writings and the poetry, rounded off with the unreal image of the 'Poet' as he is designated after his death. Mallarmé's reaction to Poe is at once emotional (a reaction to the figure of the Poet), and theoretical (reacting to

---

[1] Cit. Louis Broussard, *The Measure of Poe* (Norman University of Oklahoma Press, 1969), p. 18.

what Poe said in his theoretical and poetic writing, and also to the fact that he should have undertaken both). It is as if Mallarmé is saying: we have this given collection of circumstances and achievements, therefore they must, even if only by dazzling, by sheer force of evidence almost, add up to a 'cas littéraire absolu'. It is not hard to see that the discovery of such a writer must have been startling enough to cause a degree of obscured if not blind admiration for what Poe actually wrote. This must be considered further in connection with Mallarmé's translations of the poems. At this point it is more important to look at Poe as poet 'par excellence': to see the elements in his theoretical writing which corresponded roughly to those of Mallarmé, and to see, above all, why it did not matter that the theory in no way corresponded to the quality of the practice.

The importance Mallarmé attaches to the fact that Poe wrote about his own writing, not only emphasizes Mallarmé's belief that great writing is not a matter of intuitive chance, but rather a conquering of chance, the true product of 'une âme...à la fois logique et sensible' (690). It also underlines the values of Mallarmé's own writing, which is, far more consistently than that of Poe, *about* writing. In the 'Scolies' attached to the translations of Poe's poems, Mallarmé writes:

> A savoir que tout hasard doit être banni de l'œuvre moderne et n'y peut être que feint; et que l'éternel coup d'aile n'exclut pas un regard lucide scrutant l'espace dévoré par son vol. (230)

The last phrase is judiciously worded, perhaps more so than Mallarmé intended, since to many readers, the theoretical writings of Poe do indeed 'devour' the space they traverse, to the extent that they can appear to preclude altogether the possibility of the creative writing itself. However, if Poe's writing is lacking in subtlety, it is not lacking in atmosphere. Indeed, in terms of what Mallarmé might write in tribute to Poe, it does not even matter that it should be lacking in subtlety. If the general scheme is clear, then the field is actually more open for Mallarmé's response. Consider, for example, these extracts from Poe's theoretical writing:

> Ideality is indeed the soul of poetic Sentiment.[1]

> A poem, in my opinion, is opposed to a work of science by having, for its *immediate* object, pleasure, not truth; to romance, by having for its object an *indefinite* instead of a *definite* pleasure.[2]

[1] Edgar Allan Poe, *Selected Works* (Penguin, 1967), p. 396.
[2] *Ibid.* p. 385.

Although such writing is crude even before it is asked to bear comparison with the writing of Mallarmé, it clearly expresses sentiments which, at both a superficial and a profound level, would attract Mallarmé. The sum of Poe's achievement was such that it is likely that Mallarmé would read his theoretical writing less in order to find it 'right' or 'wrong' in attitude or expression, than with gratitude towards one who attempted such a thing at all. Such is his gratitude that he is willing to overlook, even condone, the alcoholism in Poe's life as:

> sa chance unique d'arriver à certaines altitudes spirituelles prescrites mais que la nation dont il est, s'avoue incapable d'atteindre par de légitimes moyens. (226)

Yet in Rimbaud's case as precocious truant in the annals of literature, the poet's way of life comes in for strong criticism. (514–15)

For evidence of the seriousness inherent in what might appear to be Mallarmé's over-dramatized judgement of Poe, the reader should look at the short note sent to Charles Morice (872), in which, in terms that altogether outstrip Poe's accomplishment, Mallarmé evokes what he sees as the fundamentals of Poe's writing. The faculty of writing to which he pays tribute here is his own rather than Poe's. Yet that he should want to recognize it in someone else testifies to his modesty and tact, as well as to a desire to understand writing of the kind at which he constantly aimed as operating not in a vacuum of personal solitude – although this is how, necessarily, the writer must operate[1] – but in a notional, partly invented theatre of literary existence. There is, thus, a kind of literary impunity in what Mallarmé has to say about Poe. If the life and works of Poe are an approximation, far above the average, of Mallarmé's image of the Poet, there is reason enough for Mallarmé to dispense with the facts and consider only the notion that these facts suggest.

> Cependant et pour l'avouer, toujours, malgré ma confrontation de daguerréotype et de gravures, une piété unique telle enjoint de me représenter le pur entre les Esprits, plutôt et de préférence à quelqu'un, comme un aérolithe; stellaire, de foudre, projeté des desseins finis humains, très loin de nous contemporainement à qui il éclata en pierreries d'une couronne pour personne, dans maint siècle d'ici. Il est cette exception, en effet, et le cas littéraire absolu. (531)

Forgetting Poe for a moment in order to consider a hypothetical 'cas littéraire absolu', such as Mallarmé might have conceived, one is more

---

[1] See the essay 'Solitude' (405–9) in the 'Variations'.

likely to imagine a Shakespeare, a man who can write in every mode, who can theorize about the unutterable, then utter it without any appearance of betrayal, who is known to the world as a Poet above all else, and is, preferably, no longer alive. Poe shows that he is capable of some of this, and does fulfil, after his death, the last two requirements. Thus, perhaps more than any of the other writers with whom Mallarmé was familiar, Poe provides both a moment in literature (an 'Œuvre' which stands out clearly as a moment in the tradition of literature) and an intuition of the movement of literature. The two sides of the writings in tribute could be divided, if crudely, into writing about those who provide an intuition of such a moment, and writing about those who provide an intuition of the movement of literature. Into the first category one could put Banville, Hugo, Wagner, and into the second the younger poets, together with Maupassant, Beckford and Villiers, who, in his tribute, Mallarmé puts on equal footing with Poe. (494)

Wagner

The rather remote phrase 'le cas littéraire absolu' suggests the practical impossibility, alongside the desirability of imagining that it could be possible. The best way of seeing Mallarmé's judgement of Poe in true perspective is to compare it with his attitude towards one who himself claims to have already created a *Gesamtkunstwerk*, rather than allowing Mallarmé to sense its possibility. The naïve juxtaposing of theory and practice in Poe's work allowed Mallarmé to see clearly the important relation between the two activities. Wagner on the other hand shows a different kind of naïveté; he claims that his own work actually comprises all the possibilities that art offers. Faced by such a claim, Mallarmé ought, classically, either to join the faction or oppose it. Ultimately he does oppose it, but that is less interesting than the details of his reaction to 'le Monstre-qui-ne-peut-être'.

There appears, from the very beginning of the 'Rêverie' about Wagner, an element of unusually obvious enjoyment in Mallarmé's writing. Mallarmé himself described the piece as 'moitié article, moitié poème en prose' (1592), and points out the difficulties involved in writing of a work with which he was not very familiar. When he wrote the 'Rêverie' he had seen none of Wagner's work, and his later acquaintance was restricted to the extracts that were played at the Lamoureux concerts.[1] However, the cult of Wagner was so widespread that

---

[1] For details of Mallarmé's introduction to Wagner's works, see Suzanne Bernard, *Mallarmé et la Musique* (Paris, Nizet, 1959), p. 24.

Mallarmé could not fail to learn about Wagner's theories and intentions. If Mallarmé appears to enjoy writing about Wagner, it is partly because he was writing about theory and not about practice. His private hesitations are at first overshadowed by the public splendour in which Wagner's achievement bathes:

> Un poète français contemporain, exclu de toute participation aux déploiements de beauté officiels, en raison de divers motifs, aime, ce qu'il garde de sa tâche pratiqué ou l'affinement mystérieux du vers pour de solitaires Fêtes, à réfléchir aux pompes souveraines de la Poésie, comme elles ne sauraient exister concurremment au flux de banalité charrié par les arts dans le faux semblant de civilisation. (541)

The radical difference in 'éclat' on the world between Mallarmé and Wagner gives Mallarmé great certainty in plotting out the course of the 'Rêverie'. In the first few paragraphs there is a considerable sense of his 'accepting a challenge', a sense that is manifest in the use of capital letters: 'Poésie, Culte, Monstre-Qui-ne-peut-Etre, Initiation', in the use of exclamation marks, and in the general tone of the short paragraph:

> Singulier défi qu'aux poètes dont il usurpe le devoir avec la plus candide et splendide bravoure, inflige Richard Wagner! (541)

The emphatic tone of 'défi – usurpe – bravoure – inflige' gives a strong sense that Mallarmé, having scented the challenge, is now accepting it.

> Le sentiment se complique envers cet étranger, transports, vénération, aussi d'un malaise que tout soit fait, autrement qu'en irradiant, par un jeu direct, du principe littéraire même. (542)

It is the very ground of Mallarmé's interest – 'le principe littéraire même' – which seems to be in danger; yet just two paragraphs earlier Mallarmé had written of 'la Danse seule capable, par son écriture sommaire, de traduire le fugace et le soudain jusqu'à l'Idée' (541). Not only does Mallarmé momentarily place the expressiveness of the dance above that of language, but he also obviously has no serious anxieties concerning Wagner's usurping the ground of literature. As he notes in a piece in 'Crayonné au Théâtre', any anxiety is soon dispelled by the very act of writing about Wagner's achievement:

> O plaisir et d'entendre, là dans un recueillement trouvé à l'autel de tout sens poétique, ce qui est, jusque maintenant, la vérité; puis, de pouvoir, à propos d'une expression même étrangère à

nos propres espoirs, émettre, cependant et sans malentendu, des paroles. (323)

It is immediately 'suspicious' in terms of Mallarmé's conception of what can be written, that it is not only possible, but even easy to write about Wagner. There need be no 'malaise que tout soit fait'.

However, the magnitude of the threat that Wagner might have appeared at first to present is reflected in the seriousness of much of the 'Rêverie'. The fact that Mallarmé had never seen a Wagner opera did not limit what he could say; the mere idea that Wagner 'effectua l'hymen' of 'le drame personnel et la musique idéale' (543) is as fascinating as the performance would be:

> Le tact est prodige qui, sans totalement en transformer aucune, opère, sur la scène et dans la symphonie, la fusion de ces formes de plaisir disparates. (543)

The somewhat remote opening of the sentence appears to suggest that Mallarmé is actually withholding judgement on whether or not Wagner did achieve what he claims. There are similar intonations of a judgement withheld in the phrase that appears a little earlier: 'à l'aide d'un harmonieux compromis' (543). Even if a compromise can often work to good effect, it strikes a slight discordance with the theory of one who claims to create a total, hence absolute, art work.

The long piece on Legend and Hero, the substance of which must be considered alongside Mallarmé's theatrical writings, reveals a basic difference between Mallarmé and Wagner, and also constitutes, by its lofty tone, an apparent gesture towards the greatness of Wagner's work. Legend, the 'ruisseau primitif' which Mallarmé considers basic to Wagner's art, is not compatible, as Mallarmé sees it, with 'l'esprit français';

> Si l'esprit français, strictement imaginatif et abstrait, donc poétique, jette un éclat, ce ne sera pas ainsi: il répugne, en cela d'accord avec l'Art dans son intégrité, qui est inventeur, à la Légende. (544)

Art prefers, Mallarmé thinks, the greater abstraction of the Fable 'celle inscrite sur la page des Cieux' (545) since that is the product of the imagination and the sensibility and not in any way a national heritage. Fable is unspecific; like the notion of theatre, it is 'dégagé de person-nalité' (545). Wagner's music dramas, with their basis in legend, succumb to the temptation of containing or describing ideal situations.

Far more appropriate to Mallarmé is this concept of the human drama:

> L'Homme, puis son authentique séjour terrestre, échangent une
> réciprocité de preuves.
> Ainsi le Mystère. (545)

As a comment on the basic operation of art, this is typical of Mallarmé in its combination of generality and suggestion of a very specific process. Also, if the 'réciprocité de preuves' between man and his experience results for Mallarmé in a sense of the mysterious, it follows that any presentation of that mysteriousness via Art cannot be direct. As Mallarmé says elsewhere: '*Nommer* un objet, c'est supprimer les trois quarts de la jouissance du poème qui est faite de deviner un peu: le suggérer, voilà le rêve'. (869)

The final paragraph of the 'Rêverie' presents a noticeable *flow* of language reminiscent of the beginning of the piece. The earlier sense of enjoyment is replaced by one of relief that the theoretical basis of Mallarmé's apprehensions has been in some measure elucidated, and that he can then say:

> Voilà pourquoi, Génie! moi, l'humble qu'une logique éternelle
> asservit, O Wagner, je souffre et me reproche, aux minutes
> marquées par la lassitude, de ne pas faire nombre avec ceux qui,
> ennuyés de tout afin de trouver le salut définitif, vont droit à
> l'édifice de ton Art, pour eux le terme du chemin. (546)

Such humility and deference on Mallarmé's part can only be taken as tongue-in-cheek after his more serious writing of the preceding pages. With the problems of defence now largely accounted for, Mallarmé can at last give judgement; and indeed the judgement that he gives is far more decisive than most of those in the tributes. Wagner's impact, both as person and as theoretician, was such that Mallarmé was actually forced to take sides, while the strength of Wagner's apparent challenge to the art of literature gave rise to valuable perceptions on the nature of the theatre. Although Mallarmé admits that he cannot count himself among those who recognize Wagner as the summit of 'la montagne sainte', he does say:

> Au moins, voulant ma part du délice, me permettras-tu de
> goûter, dans ton Temple, à mi-côté de la montagne sainte, dont
> le lever des vérités, le plus compréhensif encore, trompette la
> coupole et invite, à perte de vue du parvis, les gazons que le pas
> de tes élus foule, un repos: c'est comme l'isolement, pour l'esprit,

de notre incohérence qui le pourchasse, autant qu'un abri contre
la trop lucide hantise de cette cime menaçante d'absolu, devinée
dans le départ des nuées là-haut, fulgurante, nue, seule: au-delà
et que personne ne semble devoir atteindre. Personne! ce mot
n'obsède pas d'un remords le passant en train de boire à ta
conviviale fontaine. (546)

There is an unusual degree of something bordering on malice in this
piece, as well as a faintly perceptible note of triumph in one who seeks
only 'un repos' where others find 'le terme du chemin'. Clearly, in the
interest of the supremacy of language, Mallarmé cannot afford to see
Wagner's music dramas as absolute, especially when that absolute status
is chiefly assured by the presence of all forms of art: music, drama,
poetry and ballet. Such an absolute is for Mallarmé 'la *trop* lucide
hantise' (emphasis mine). It is the result of wanting the absolute form
too much (as Mallarmé did in his early poetry), and of presuming that
it can be assembled out of the union of all the elements of art with the
help of some sort of magic arithmetic. There is a considerable distance
between Wagner's assertions about the *Gesamtkunstwerk* and Mallarmé's
references to the 'Œuvre'. Wagner claims to have achieved it;
Mallarmé does not say that it is not possible, but, as a writer, he cannot
see it as a 'harmonieux compromis' between different elements of art.
For one who believes that 'tout, au monde, existe pour aboutir à un
livre' (378) Wagner can only be seen as a challenge, and, had his
challenge been any less great, it would have been possible for Mallarmé
to give a less biased assessment of Wagner.

Villiers de l'Isle-Adam and William Beckford

In the public sense, Villiers was certainly a smaller figure than
Wagner or Poe, but, both as a writer and as a person, Mallarmé greatly
admired him. Throughout his long tribute Mallarmé shows a constant
and spontaneous sympathy towards one who may have been only a
'figurant' in the theatre of literature, but whose qualities appeared to
Mallarmé just as valuable as those of the more grandiose participants.
Those qualities revolve around the notion of Villiers the dreamer, the
eccentric, obsessed with his aristocratic origins and taking refuge in the
consolation of a literature of dream, aspiration, mysticism and humour.

There is much obviously genuine sympathy in Mallarmé's tribute (see
pp. 496-9), partly stemming from Mallarmé's strong impression of
Villiers as a person. Indeed the pathos of Villiers's dependence on the
rarefied atmosphere that language can create offers Mallarmé a unique

opportunity of writing about an author as, in a way, the figuration of his work. Villiers sought to live out in his literary existence the aristocratic dream-world of which he was deprived. His dependence upon it was so strong that it was revealed even by his presence:

> Tant de feu en son silence et l'impossibilité d'aborder le millier des propos, comme les flammes distantes entre elles et mobiles du gaz. Son vêtement, avec la brusquerie d'un livre ouvert – *il était, lui, ce folio authentique, prêt toujours* – apparaissait, aussi, de quelque profondeur de poches la candide réalité d'un papier. (485) [Emphasis mine.]

When he met Villiers, Mallarmé felt 'une présence de l'éternel et palpable germe du chef-d'œuvre en train' (485); and after he had left:

> on restait, lui parti, certes étonné comme par la grandiloquence d'*un texte en suspens*. (484). [Emphasis mine.][1]

Within the context of a tribute such strong analogies are not out of place. If Mallarmé sees Villiers as a 'folio authentique' to which both his work and his presence contribute, then he will see, notionally, that 'folio' as one in which he, Mallarmé, and other later writers will make their mark. Furthermore, the very impressiveness of Villiers's presence must have made him appear close to the embodiment of the 'théâtre littéraire', combining pathos, humour, a measure of both achievement and possibility, to form a real Harlequin or Baptiste, accessible as all spectacle must be. Yet the very pathos of Villiers's life, as distinct from the impalpable and invaluable 'life' of his mere presence, makes him a tragic and distant figure:

> Sa vie – je cherche rien qui réponde à ce terme: véritablement et dans le sens ordinaire, vécut-il? (482)

The doubt whether Villiers actually lived as opposed to dreamed his life may be a disaster in human terms, but it is certainly an advantage in literary terms. Villiers has no bridge to cross from life to art. He may not be a great writer, but he is manifestly 'made for' literature.

> Je voudrais, et aucune violation à l'égard d'écrits comportant le désarroi de hasards où ils se produisirent – faire, enfin, voir la plus parfaite symétrie d'âme qui fut jamais, ou cette dualité (l'éloge a cours) d'un songeur et d'un railleur! (502)

---

[1] It is interesting to place side by side the 'chef-d'œuvre en train' and the 'texte en suspens', suggesting that Mallarmé's notion of the 'chef-d'œuvre' had to do with a notionally and indefinitely suspended text.

The qualities of 'songeur' and 'railleur' form a distancing that perfectly complements Mallarmé's view of literature as a mode of language set apart from the norm of 'reportage'. The trio of dream, joke and poem, ill-matched as they may look, are united by their distance, sometimes obvious, sometimes subtle, from reality.

Another form of distancing, or rather of the 'texte en suspens', appears in the notion of the outcast, of which Poe was the supreme example to Mallarmé. The concept is strengthened in the case of Villiers because he saw literature as a more or less adequate replacement for the world to which he thought he belonged, and from which he was excluded: the world of the nobility. Villiers depended on the distinction that only the sonority of his own name could give him; as Mallarmé says, Villiers

> venait conquérir tout avec un mot, son nom, autour dequel déjà
> il voyait, à vrai dire, matériellement, se rallumer le lustre. (492)

Thus the distinction of being misunderstood as an artist was also apt:

> l'impression restait, au ramas, d'un extatique ou d'un halluciné et,
> à part cette profanation, la jouissance goûtée par l'admis s'avivait
> de l'incompréhension de tous, à mesure que resplendissait, en
> rapport avec la majesté de la veillée, dans ce café, l'entretien.
> (487)

In a sense it was inevitable that Villiers should be misunderstood since:

> Ce qu'il voulait, ce survenu, en effet, je pense sérieusement que
> c'était: régner. (489)

He wanted more of literature than it could give him; as well as the personal 'soulagement' afforded by the powers of language, he wanted 'la seule gloire vraiment noble de nos temps, celle d'un grand écrivain'. (489). Mallarmé saw that Villiers was not in the ordinary sense 'un grand écrivain', yet as one who played to the full the rôle of writer, Villiers merits this apotheosis:

> car ce n'est pas contemporainement à une époque, aucunement,
> que doivent, pour exalter le sens, advenir ceux que leur destin
> chargea d'en être à nu l'expression; ils sont projetés maint siècle
> au-delà, stupéfaits, à témoigner de ce qui, normal à l'instant
> même, vit tard magnifiquement par le regret, et trouvera dans
> l'exil de leur nostalgique esprit tourné vers le passé, sa vision
> pure. (496)

It is not simply the content of the achievement, as in the case of Villiers and of Poe, that prompts Mallarmé's admiration, but the possibility of seeing (and then writing) a vision of which Villiers and Poe could not truly be conscious. Evidence of Mallarmé's own distinction tacitly lies in his ability to see 'maint siècle au-delà', to confirm the strangeness and the genius of Villiers's and Poe's involvement with the age in which they lived, and, in doing so, to construct a monument to their memory which is not merely nostalgic in its reverence, but also forward-looking in its form.

In his tribute to Villiers, Mallarmé makes extensive quotations, and his comments on them often refer to the atmosphere of dream and mysticism that characterizes Villiers's writing. For example:

> Quels parfums, subtils, versent, dans leur aparté, à toute raré-faction adéquate, les phrases. (502)

The world of spiritual and fantastic 'aparté' is found again in Mallarmé's preface to Beckford's *Vathek*, and it is possible to see in this preface how unimportant it was to Mallarmé that Villiers should have been so concerned with a quasi-mystical quest, and how indeed such an enterprise, carried out with the intention of finding or revealing a mystical truth, might be illuminating in the very aberration of its conviction. The atmosphere of the quest, mystical or mythical, is perfectly compatible with the atmosphere of poetic language, for both are concerned with a transformation rather than an illumination of the real world. The world of Villiers's fiction and drama, in keeping with his delusions of nobility, is the world of fantasy and dream, and, like the writing of Beckford, it constitutes a necessary and richly enjoyable other side of literature, perhaps all the more enjoyable to Mallarmé in that it does not *appear* to have anything to do with his deeper interests (as 'La Dernière Mode' appears at first irrelevant to the considerations of the poet).

The 'Préface à Vathek' is chiefly taken up by discussion of the circumstances of the writing and publication of the story, but the beginning of the preface shows why Mallarmé undertook the task. He considers first the reasons for the apparently extinct fashion for oriental stories:

> La cause: mainte dissertation et au bout je crains le hasard. Peut-être qu'un songe serein et par notre fantaisie fait en vue de soi seule, atteint aux poèmes: or le rythme le transportera au-delà des jardins, des royaumes, des salles; là où l'aile de péris et de djinns fondue en le climat ne laisse de tout évanouissement voir que pureté éparse et diamant, comme les étoiles à midi. (549)

41

It is above all the atmosphere, as described in those last few phrases, that attracts Mallarmé; as he admits, 'je voudrais auparavant séduire le rêveur' (549):

> L'histoire du Calife Vathek commence au faîte d'une tour où se lit le firmament. (550)

That in itself, to the general reader, and with respect to the concerns of the narrative, is insignificant. It is only an introduction leading to the more important – so far as the development of the story is concerned – events that take place in the tower. But to the reader of Mallarmé, the peculiar delight or contentment inherent in the sentence is clear. Without any pretence or complicated allegorical allusions, Mallarmé is able to say something which almost all his readers will pass over without noticing anything more than its content – nor is it essential to him that they should react otherwise. Meanwhile he has the odd pleasure of writing about diamonds and firmaments in a context that is literal in one way, and yet, if one stops and thinks, this fully blossomed fantasy is more ambitious than any of Mallarmé's own 'obscurities'. The same sense of near-indulgence is even more marked in the translations of the 'Contes Indiens', where Mallarmé does not merely comment, but is actually involved (if at one remove, in the exercise of translation) in the formation of such fantasies.

In the 'Préface à Vathek', as in the translation of the 'Contes Indiens', Mallarmé is confronted by the 'Architecture magistrale de la fable et son concept non moins beau' (550). The 'architecture' of the fable, fairy story or 'conte fantastique ou oriental' is such that it cannot be separated from the content. In such stories, it is not what happens that is important, but the atmosphere, amounting to imaginative autonomy, in which it happens. The language of such stories is usually simple, and so is the plot; but the effect is for Mallarmé:

> Une poésie (que l'origine n'en soit ailleurs ni l'habitude chez nous) bien inoubliablement liée au livre apparaît dans quelque étrange juxtaposition d'innocence quasi idyllique avec les solennités énormes ou vaines de la magie: alors se teint et s'avive, comme des vibrations noires d'un astre, la fraîcheur de scènes naturelles, jusqu'au malaise; mais non sans rendre à cette approche du rêve quelque chose de plus simple et de plus extraordinaire. (550–1)

The great apparatus of myth and magic which figures so prominently in the oriental tale contains a story that is often extremely simple. The magical aspect alone, or the story alone, would be of little interest to Mallarmé, but the juxtaposition of the two constitutes an 'approche du rêve' which typifies the entire situation of poetry. There may be little originality in comparing poetry with dream, but what creates the state of dream is interesting. It arises out of a combination of precise factors not out of a vague desire; it is thus compelling as the result of a process and not as a 'fait accompli'. Dream thus becomes inseparable from 'ce qui fait rêver'. Similarly, in poetry it is not ingenuity of subject matter nor rarefied language which move the reader; it is rather the interplay between form and content, resulting in an atmosphere or dream which can ultimately be ascribed to neither.

If Mallarmé does not say much about the content of 'Vathek' beyond the first paraphrase of the plot, it is probably because the story 'révèle chez qui l'écrivit un besoin de se satisfaire l'imagination d'objets rares ou grandioses' (549), while the distinctive features of such stories remain unimpaired either by the author's inadequacies or personal needs. Thus, although one might expect the question of the language of 'Vathek' to be of primary concern, Mallarmé only says:

> Tout coule de source, avec une limpidité vive, avec un ondoiement large de périodes; et l'éclat tend à se fondre dans la pureté totale du cours, qui charrie maintes richesses de diction inaperçues d'abord. (565)

It is the tradition of the oriental tale that speaks for 'Vathek', regardless of Beckford's linguistic skills,[1] and assures its position for Mallarmé as both autonomous and magical: retaining in its aura if not in its language some of the grandeur that belongs also to the activity of writing.

Writing resembles the world of myth and fable in that neither relies upon a great accumulation of apparent wealth, but on evidence of a world apart, or imaginative autonomy. Two pieces in the 'Variations sur un Sujet', 'Or' and 'Magie' make this point clear. The notion of gold is both grandiose and suggestive, but:

> L'incapacité des chiffres, grandiloquents, à traduire, ici relève d'un cas; on cherche, avec cet indice que, si un nombre se majore et recule, vers l'improbable, il inscrit plus de zéros: signifiant que son total équivaut spirituellement à rien, presque. (398)

The accumulation of gold as a currency 'équivaut spirituellement à rien, presque'. It is impressive in quality not in quantity. Thus is not the

---

[1] Mallarmé sees that Beckford is not a gifted translator, but this does not detract from Mallarmé's enjoyment. See note on p. 565.

grand total of either economic or linguistic currency that is valuable, but its distinctiveness. Language does not have the solidity and worth of gold or the 'pierre philosophale', it conveys those qualities which make gold and alchemy (and legend too) distinctive and slightly forbidding. In the 'Enquête sur l'Evolution Littéraire' Mallarmé says:

> L'enfantillage de la littérature jusqu'ici a été de croire, par exemple, que de choisir un certain nombre de pierres précieuses et en mettre les noms sur le papier, même très bien, c'était *faire* des pierres précieuses. (870)

Beckford, and more especially Villiers, may have been seeking the assurance of this kind of illusion, but the authenticity of their aspiration allows Mallarmé to see their created 'precious stones' as suggestion, not as finalized creation. Thus despite their shortcomings, according to the ideal scale that Mallarmé sees, Beckford and Villiers do afford a glimpse of the compatibility of manner between myth and language.

At the end of the essay 'Magie' Mallarmé points explicitly to the parallel:

> Je dis qu'existe entre les vieux procédés et le sortilège, que restera la poésie, une parité secrète; je l'énonce ici et peut-être personnellement me suis-je complu à le marquer, par des essais, dans une mesure qui a outrepassé l'aptitude à en jouir consentie par mes contemporains. Evoquer, dans une ombre exprès, l'objet tu, par des mots allusifs, jamais directs, se réduisant à du silence égal, comporte tentative proche de créer. (400)

Compared with this vision of language Villiers's and Beckford's works are minor attempts to convert reality into dream. Here we see how precisely Mallarmé envisages the process. Myth seems to suggest a hidden reality, but language seems to create it. Under 'le sortilège' of poetry, the hidden reality is none other than the 'objet tu', transformed by the allusive powers of language. Dream has become reality as it is transformed by language.

Beckford and Villiers leave a literary monument as compelling as it is unreal. In the 'Préface à Vathek' Mallarmé comments that Beckford's work seems to be compiled out of all that was rarefied and exotic in his life, much as the rich of that period thought it suitable for the education of the young to undertake a journey in which the traveller collects, even unearths, things that are rare and unusual. Their tour has subsequently a mental shape, derived from the arrangement and impressiveness of these finds. In the same way the writer arranges the most memorable of his experiences:

44

Ce genre, le Voyage, fut du coup porté au même degré de perfection que chez plusieurs de nos poètes par un style égal au leur: le collectionneur se procurant les mots brillants et vrais et les manient avec même prodigalité et même tact que des objets précieux, extraits de fouilles. (555)

In the tribute to Villiers, his work is characterized thus by Mallarmé:

Mais quel tombeau et le porphyre massif et le clair jade, les jaspures de marbres sous le passage de nues, et des métaux nouveaux: que l'œuvre de Villiers. (502)

When we see Villiers's works as his 'tombeau' we also see that the assurance he sought in literature does appear, if posthumously, in the overall splendour of his achievement. The legacy of Beckford, on the other hand, apparently less prestigious, is that of being known as 'l'auteur de Vathek' (555), thus contributing to the notional union of an author and his work, a union which both assures the distinction and autonomy of the literary world, and constitutes a reminder that a writer is not an extraneous character who presents a work, but one whose language is his world and the form of his legacy.

Maupassant and Zola

There is in the work of both Villiers and Beckford an element of 'aparté' which is attractive to Mallarmé and related to his own notions of language. In the work of Maupassant we see the real testing-ground for Mallarmé's reaction to the pure story-writer, for there was little in Maupassant's work that could have inspired in Mallarmé any reflections on language. Indeed the tribute to Maupassant is written in a fairly direct style, and the high points of Mallarmé's enjoyment in writing it are derived from the public impact of Maupassant's work rather than from the way he used language. One of the reasons for the popularity of Maupassant's stories was certainly the ease with which it was possible to read them. To a writer like Mallarmé, concerned above all with the way language conceals rather than presents its objects in order to reveal its own qualities, the great gamut of wisdom and ingenuity in the plots of Maupassant's stories must have been nearly dazzling. 'Igitur', Mallarmé's only attempt at what might be called a story, contains no plot other than that of language attempting to reach the absolute. Maupassant's stories, by comparison, are down-to-earth and uncomplicated:

Un cas, ordinaire à ces déités de terroir, éclate ici, que quiconque

45

lit, peut les lire et à la suite tout lire. Haussant subitement à leur degré le simple et l'initiant, loin: c'est restituer aux lettres la vertu d'une fonction originelle et inapprise, qui me frappe comme un dessein français. (524)

If 'déités de terroir' and 'la vertue d'une fonction inapprise' seem faint praise, the reader should remember the extraordinary distance from Mallarmé's work of Maupassant's writing:

foulant, selon la mystérieuse perfection attachée à sa nature, avec virginité, ce qui, pour tous, est la route où l'on peina. (524)

It is perhaps the sense of this difference that allows Mallarmé to pay genuine tribute to such an achievement, and to perceive also certain important features of writing as accessible as that of Maupassant.

Maupassant provides an opportunity for a valuable confrontation with the world of journalism in the work of one whose constant antagonist was the writer (and reader) of 'reportage'. Mallarmé describes Maupassant as 'le plus admirable des journalistes littéraires de ce temps' (525), perhaps because the source of his journalistic accessibility is not so much reality as fiction, in its greatest diversity. That Maupassant's stories usually resemble reality is of little concern here, for the total of the stories provides a far greater 'éclat' than that of newspapers, and indeed, as Mallarmé is delighted to see, Maupassant's works competed with newspapers and periodicals on the bookstalls. Maupassant's works appear to Mallarmé as an unofficial spectacle of the world of the newspaper, now relieved of the possibly disturbing (to literature as well as to the reader) truths that news stories contain. Maupassant's contribution is the provision of:

un concours énorme pour la fondation du Poème populaire moderne ou tout au moins de Mille et Une Nuits innombrables où cette majorité lisante soudain inventée s'émerveillera. (525)

Just as Scheherazade's stories constituted a delaying action, so Mallarmé sees those of Maupassant as a kind of 'staving off' of the world by means of fiction, effected in such a way that the reader does not notice how it is done or even that it is done. Maupassant's language is not that of a poet, it is, to Mallarmé, that of a showman in its ingenuity, in the spectacle, of its persistence in keeping up the 'fête' that is neither life nor language, for so long. If the reader can 'lire et à la suite tout lire', he is less involved in the expressiveness or resonance of language than in its spectacle. From such writing Mallarmé sees that poetry 'restera exclue' (525), but:

Comme à une fête, assistez, vous, de maintenant, aux hasards de
ce foudroyant accomplissement. (525)

Mallarmé only comments on the ease, amounting almost to hypnotism,
which this 'fête' confers on language. The fact that Maupassant is little
concerned with those questions of style that preoccupy Mallarmé actually makes the experience more valuable. One might compare his only
comment on Flaubert, the greatest ironic story-teller of the day, as well
as one of the greatest stylists: 'J'isole Gustave Flaubert, parmi plusieurs
absolus.' (524) It seems as if, for Mallarmé, Flaubert could not be considered alongside Maupassant precisely because he *did* play with the
form of the story in order to say something about the nature of stories
as well as about the nature of the world. Flaubert may have had a greater
hold on his world and on his language, but the limitations of Maupassant
reveal more clearly the charm of straightforward story-telling. His work
is 'the best that Fiction can do'; it has none of the disquiet arising from
personal doubts and aspirations that plays so great a part in the writing
of Villiers, and none of the explicit moral emphasis found, for example,
in the work of Zola. If Maupassant's stories contain valid social comment
or personal doubts, it is scarcely obvious, and the reader takes in rather
than takes hold of any intended message. Hence it is possible for Mallarmé, reading Maupassant, to remain at the simplest possible level of
reading; the reader need only dwell upon language 'juste le temps
d'épuiser un état d'âme opulent et bref' (as Mallarmé says of certain
'courts récits' by Villiers (505)). Mallarmé's final comment on Maupassant's achievement goes to the unique miracle, however limited in vision,
of 'ce talent savoureux, clair, robuste comme la joie et borné comme elle
au don (seul enviable, il suffit)' (526).[1] Perhaps the showman must have
that limited vision if he is to avoid encroaching upon the gravity of the
moralist or the obscure exaltation of the poet.

The work of Zola, and Mallarmé's tribute to him, illustrate this well
enough. In Zola's work there is none of the delight, but all the moral
seriousness that cannot quite be imputed to Maupassant. Admiration
for Zola cannot be admiration for his showmanship, but something more
massive and solid. Berlioz writes that on seeing the pyramids he felt that

[1] It is interesting to compare Henry James's comment about the gift of
Maupassant: 'What makes M. de Maupassant salient is two facts: the first of
which is that his gifts are remarkably strong and definite, and the second
that he writes directly *from* them, as it were: holds the fullest, the most
uninterrupted – I scarcely know what to call it – the boldest communication
with them.' Henry James, *Selected Literary Criticism*, ed. Morris Shapira
(Penguin Books, 1968), p. 121.

they were alive by their sheer mass.[1] This reflects the willingness of humanity to submit to the spell of the immense, of the grandiose. Zola certainly gives his readers the grandiose in human terms, and Mallarmé only finds the imaginative space to write that he has 'une grande admiration pour Zola' (871). Significantly, when he does write in more detail of what he admires in Zola, he qualifies it immediately:

> J'ai une grande admiration pour Zola. Il a fait moins, à vrai dire, de véritable littérature que de l'art évocatoire, en se servant, le moins qu'il est possible, des éléments littéraires; il a pris les mots, c'est vrai, mais c'est tout. (871)

Maupassant and his accumulation of stories do not move exactly in the realm of literature, but their brilliance and showmanship are qualities which distinguish literature from 'reportage'. Zola, on the other hand, moves, via literature, with intent to guide and educate. Hence Mallarmé's admiration can only be the almost dutiful admiration for the record-breaker, recognizing the discrepancy between the record shot and the means that achieved it. The case here is something like that of the admiration of the hurdler for the man who breaks the record at caber-tossing, a dutiful admiration logically derived from the notion of beating records and attaining distinction. Zola's achievement is:

> L'œuvre d'une organisation vraiment admirable! Mais la littérature a quelque chose de plus intellectuel que cela; (871)

he adds, gently and substantially understating the case.

The Impressionist painters

The writing of tributes to fellow writers is a task which requires infinite tact, since Mallarmé is using the same means of communication – language – and can thus be prey to reproaches of imitation or diffidence. The other mode of such tribute is the poem written in homage. In many ways this must be the highest tribute, since poetry is traditionally assumed to be the high point of expressiveness in language. The mere situation of writing in tribute does seem to demand such 'pompes suprêmes' and Mallarmé did compose sonnets in tribute to Poe, Baudelaire (who receives little mention elsewhere), Verlaine, and Wagner.

With the Impressionist painters Mallarmé has much greater freedom, since he is not writing about another *writer's* work, and there is no

---

[1] Jacques Barzun, *Berlioz and the Romantic Century* (Columbia U.P. 1969), p. 565.

48

diminution in the level of achievement considered. There can be no sense of his either equalling or surpassing the achievement of the painters. The writer is able to admit, freely and fully, the attainment of the painter, since, in absolute terms, neither can see what the other intends. Yet Mallarmé can see in the work of the Impressionists a progression from the aims and techniques of earlier painters (and even the mass of contemporary painters), and can respond to those elements which appear to echo the distinctiveness of his own achievement in his own field. Henri de Régnier remarked[1] that Mallarmé had been little interested in painting until the time of his friendship with Manet, but it needs little more than a brief acquaintance with the paintings of Manet and the other Impressionists to see why Mallarmé should have been so attracted by them. Furthermore, what might have seemed a pretentious or presumptuous tribute (that of a writer to a painter) is made both simple and accessible by the easy compatibility between Impressionist painting and Mallarmé's writing.

Mallarmé says in a brief passage about Zola:

> les choses existent, nous n'avons pas à les créer; nous n'avons qu'à en saisir les rapports; et ce sont les fils de ces rapports qui forment les vers et les orchestres. (871)

It is a relationship of this kind, as perceived by the eye of the painter, which distinguishes Impressionist painting, and it is the ways in which the Impressionists alter traditional depictions of objects and scenes which Mallamé discusses in his tributes, and which enable him to speak of painting as 'poétiser par art plastique'. (536) The chief reasons for this very considerable tribute lie in the subtlety of the Impressionist vision of reality, and, importantly, in the movement which their painting in general conveys.

In the piece written in defence of Manet's paintings in 1874, Mallarmé is writing in a situation that almost demands a degree of invective. He is eager to defend Manet's paintings, and his language is suitably direct:

> La simplification apportée par un regard de voyant, tant il est positif! à certains procédés de la peinture dont le tort principal est de voiler l'origine de cet art fait d'onguents et de couleurs, peut tenter les sots séduits par une apparence de facilité. Quant au public, arrêté, lui, devant la reproduction immédiate de sa personnalité multiple, va-t-il ne plus jamais détourner les yeux

[1] See note, p. 1619.

de ce miroir pervers ni les reporter sur les magnificences allégor-
iques des plafonds ou les panneaux approfondis par un paysage,
sur l'Art idéal et sublime. Si le moderne allait nuire à l'Eternel!
(696)

Mallarmé's argument against traditional representational painting, is
that in depicting reality so faithfully it obscures the *means* of art, 'fait
d'onguents et de couleurs'. Manet's impressionist technique may at first
appear to obscure reality, and Mallarmé shows no sympathy for those
who see it as no more than that and return with relief to the near-
photographic reproduction of their 'personnalité multiple'. Impressionist painting is, as he says in his tribute to Berthe Morisot:

> Poétiser, par art plastique, moyen de prestiges directs, semble,
> sans intervention, le fait de l'ambiance éveillant aux surfaces leur
> lumineux secret: ou la riche analyse, chastement pour la restaurer,
> de la vie, selon une alchimie, – mobilité et illusion. Nul éclairage,
> intrus, de rêves; mais supprimés, par contre, les aspects commun
> ou professionnel. (536)

Impressionist painting does not resort to 'the dream' as a way of avoiding banality, but renders 'aux surfaces leur lumineux secret'. It is the
artist's particular impression of the surface of things, not his ability to
transcribe in detail their substance, which allows a consciousness both
of the atmosphere of objects and of the medium of art.[1] As Mallarmé's
tributes often show, such an attitude by no means constitutes an obscuring of the object; on the contrary, the desire to convey by means of art
the particular atmosphere of an object leads to a far clearer (more real,
rather than more 'realistic') image of that object. Mallarmé writes of
Berthe Morisot's paintings:

> Ici, que s'évanouissent, dispersant une caresse radieuse, idyllique,
> fine, poudroyante, diaprée, comme en ma mémoire, les tableaux,
> reste leur armature, maint superbe dessin, pas de moindre in-
> struction, pour attester une science dans la volontaire griffe,
> couleurs à part, sur un sujet. (536)

The suggestion of immediacy in the 'griffe' is a tribute to the sensation
of direct experience given by impressionist painting, and points clearly

---

[1] Cf. the comment by Ortega y Gasset, cit. in Suzanne K. Langer, *Feeling and
Form* (Routledge, 1953), p. 54. 'The majority of people are unable to adjust
their attention to the glass and the transparency which is the work of art:
instead they penetrate through it to passionately wallow in the human
reality the work of art refers to.'

to its impact. That, as Mallarmé sees, is not the result of a vague or merely colourful impression of reality but of a sure, perceptive and even learned art. The word 'griffe' also appears in the tribute to Manet:

> Cet œil – Manet – d'une enfance de lignée vieille citadine, neuf, sur un objet, les personnes posé, vierge et abstrait, gardait naguères l'immédiate fraîcheur de la rencontre, aux griffes d'un rire du regard, à narguer, dans la pose, ensuite, les fatigues de vingtième séance. Sa main – la pression sentie claire et prête énoncait dans quel mystère la limpidité de la vue y descendait, pour ordonner, vivace, lavé, profond, aigu ou hanté de certain noir, le chef-d'œuvre nouveau et français. (532-3)

The terms that Mallarmé uses here do not merely suggest an enthusiastic first impression or a generalized appreciation; a number of detailed points come across very clearly. First, Mallarmé sees a quality of freshness which is not simply that of the precision found in representational painting. As he says:

> Toute maîtrise jette le froid: ou la poudre fragile du coloris se défend par une vitre, divination pour certains. (535)

The freshness and immediacy of Impressionist painting comes not from a 'maîtrise' over subject matter, but from a constant sense of being in contact with the subject, and more importantly, with the means of communication. Another essential point lies in the phrase 'dans quel mystère la limpidité de la vue y descendait'. The word 'limpidité' involves the senses far more than the word 'clarity'; it suggests greater depth (supported by the use of the verb 'descendait') hence another dimension, a medium like water, more mysterious looking. The result is thus, to Mallarmé, a fascinating combination of the clear, the mysterious and the sensuous – 'vivace, lavé, profond' – and also a close analogue to the possibilities of language with its constant interplay of sense and atmosphere.

In these tributes, Mallarmé makes clear the distinction between the purely dreamlike[1] and the mysteriousness that results from a very precise seeing of reality. Impressionist painting shows 'la hantise de suggestions, aspirant à se traduire en l'occasion' (536), rather than a purely imaginative vision, and shows too the quality that colour can have. Mallarmé's general comment on Berthe Morisot's paintings is:

> Ici, que s'évanouissent, dispersant une caresse radieuse, idyllique,

[1] There is in impressionist painting, Mallarmé notes: 'Nul éclairage, intrus, de rêves.' (536)

fine, poudroyante, diaprée, comme en ma mémoire, les tableaux.
(536)

The words 'caresse...poudroyante, diaprée' give a strong sense of
physicality, even activity; while the first line of the tribute – 'Tant de
clairs tableaux irisés, ici, exacts, primesautiers' (533) – contrasts the
lightness of that movement with the sense of exactness and clarity that
can be had from the apprehension of such strongly felt movement. In
the article in defence of Manet, Mallarmé writes of the 'gamme délicieuse
trouvée dans les noirs' (698). The simple possibilities of the colour black
become, in the hands of Manet, a noticeable range, a scale, of such a
kind that the painting 'veuille comme sortir de la toile' (698). It is certainly a feature of highly representational painting that it seems to 'have
life'; but in the case of the Impressionist painters, it 'comes to life', and
only when elements such as the 'gamme délicieuse' have been seen and
felt. The spectator cannot instantly 'read' Impressionist painting, but
as Mallarmé often says it has, when the vision has been apprehended, a
poise and fragility that could not exist in a painting that had been
instantaneously 'read':

> il y a entre tous ses éléments un accord par quoi elle se tient et
> possède un charme facile à rompre par une touche ajoutée...
> (698)

A touch more might bring too much explicitness, might make Manet's
paintings into near-photographic landscapes, and Mallarmé's poems into
mere descriptions of swans or darkened décor. One essential point that
arises from this degree of obscurity, or rather reticence or ellipsis, is that
the spectator must become much more actively involved in what he sees;
he cannot look and instantly 'take away' the subject of the painting, just
as the reader often cannot do this with Mallarmé's writing. The combination of lightness and depth, precision and 'diaprure' demands col-
laboration; the eye must move across what appear at first to be obscure
patterns. The spectator of Impressionist paintings, like the reader of
Mallarmé, becomes involved in a transformation of reality, which, as an
observer, he appears to have helped create.

It is always obvious that Mallarmé is not writing about other works
of art in order to tell the reader 'what they are about'; indeed the reader
wanting this sort of information would certainly be disappointed. In
the case of the Impressionists Mallarmé is not in a position to write a
highly technical appreciation. He writes, instead, of those elements
of their work which attract him, and also evokes certain parallels

between painting and writing. When writing of other writers, on the other hand, there is far more technical discussion, and fewer instances where the reader feels that Mallarmé has been genuinely impressed by the writing he praises. In all the tributes Mallarmé's writing is most expressive when the work in question seems to contribute to his own notion of art, when what we read appears to be rather the result of an impact than of an informed investigation. Hence the conventional exercise of tribute reveals a private 'texte en suspens', a series of different gestures towards those elements which are constant in art. One of those elements, which might be described as the uniqueness and authenticity of contact between the artist and the world, is clearly seen in the work of the Impressionist painters. Another element, often noted both directly and indirectly by Mallarmé in the course of the 'Médaillons et Portraits', is the way in which the work of art supersedes the past and contains a germ of the future. Art thus has, on the one hand, a close relationship with reality and, on the other hand, an immunity to its laws.

One might also say that Mallarmé in his tributes reveals a range of characteristics which would, if removed from the situation of tribute, constitute the literary language which always appears in view yet never quite in sight. But Mallarmé's apparent delaying tactics in his exploration of literary language do provide insights essential to the writing of the eventual text itself, so that occasionally, without declaring it, he may begin to write that text. Each expression that results from a confrontation with a different work of art, even if superficially it only manifests 'une humilité de guide vers l'édifice' (504), thus constitutes a valuable moment in Mallarmé's own 'œuvre'.

The prose poems and the translations

The 'Médaillons et Portraits' showed us that Mallarmé's experiment with language could be carried out in, and could indeed benefit from, an ostensibly non-creative situation. Language did not have to invent or copy, but transformed a given circumstance. At its most effective, it did not merely supersede the limiting factors of the situation, but achieved a form that bypassed traditional categories of poetry and prose. On the face of it, one might imagine that the prose poem would encourage a similar achievement since it appears to bridge two modes and hence offer the writer great freedom. However, it is also such an obvious-seeming gesture of reconciliation that it may seem bound to fail. Considering Mallarmé's achievement in what looks like a non-creative situation, one might view with some suspicion a form that attempts to reconcile two worlds. It also appears, in its nineteenth-century context, to be a bid for freedom from the alexandrine on the one hand, and from the realistic narrative of the novel on the other. However, its strangeness within Mallarmé's opus certainly lies in the fact that it temporarily reinstates two categories which Mallarmé elsewhere sees as false:

> Le vers est partout dans la langue où il y a rythme, partout excepté à la quatrième page des journaux. Dans le genre appelé prose, il y a des vers, quelquefois admirables, de tous rythmes. Mais, en vérité, il n'y a pas de prose: il y a l'alphabet et puis des vers plus ou moins serrés: plus ou moins diffus. Toutes les fois qu'il y a effort au style, il y a versification. (867)

Rash as it may be to declare that 'there is no such thing as prose', Mallarmé is probably one of the few writers who can declare it with any truth. The prose poems, and also *Igitur*, demonstrate the validity of the notion, yet they are the only works that are not circumstantial.[1] They are also among the least successful of Mallarmé's works. The translations

---

[1] Although the 'Variations' can scarcely be described as circumstantial, they were nonetheless written as articles for a journal.

on the other hand, despite their academic or prescribed appearance, offer Mallarmé a wealth of perceptions about language. This points to a curious fact concerning the circumstance of writing. Mallarmé saw even poetry as appropriate to certain circumstances, moments of ceremony or a 'crise de l'âme' (867), while prose of course covers a whole patchwork of circumstances. The great advantage of recognizing, rather than trying to disguise the circumstance of writing, is that the circumstance, rather than just the words themselves, makes the first contact with the reader, just as the title of a poem or of a novel may prepare the reader for what he is about to confront. Circumstance thus crosses the bridge from reality to art, and language is set at a slight distance, with the immediacy only of an *other* reality. It does not have to cope with the initial strangeness, or at worst the battle, of words meeting the human consciousness. The first hurdle crossed, language can then operate with unexpected freedom, gradually detaching itself, when most successful, from the circumstance in which it arose. Mallarmé's early set of prose poems, written in 1864, scarcely achieves that detachment, and then autonomy, of language. The later group, written about twenty years later, begins to show that 'poetic anecdote', if compatible in content, does not altogether preclude an autonomy of language. In the late prose poems we have a paradigm of language gradually 'shedding its object' in order to 'reveal itself'.

The prose poems

Mallarmé's early prose poems, following the tradition set by Baudelaire, are highly emotional, highly anecdotal. The primary effort of language appears directed towards the evocation of an emotional atmosphere, and it is by the measure in which this is achieved that the reader judges the success of the poem. 'Plainte d'Automne', for example, evokes a certain state of mind, one which seems to demand 'la poésie agonisante des derniers moments de Rome' (270). The sense of indulgence in feelings of sadness is so strongly made in the first paragraph by the evocation of an absent love, the death of a well-loved cat, and by thoughts of all 'qui se résumait en ce mot: chute' (270), that the climax of the situation, the sound of the street organ, is more an event of the emotions than of language:

> L'instrument des tristes, oui, vraiment: le piano scintille, le violon donne aux fibres déchirées la lumière, mais l'orgue de Barbarie, dans le crépuscule du souvenir, m'a fait désespérément rêver.

Maintenant qu'il murmurait un air joyeusement vulgaire et qui
mit la gaîté au cœur des faubourgs, un air suranné, banal: d'où
vient que sa ritournelle m'allait à l'âme et me faisait pleurer
comme une ballade romantique? (270–1)

Though one would not want to doubt the authenticity of emotion here,
the poem is still a tribute to the tradition of the prose poem, rather than
a superseding of it. Language does not go beyond event and emotion; it
has little autonomy and so little truly 'poetic' value.

In the 'Démon de l'Analogie' the anecdote is about language itself,
yet when Mallarmé writes of his obsession by the phrase 'La Pénultième
est morte', the concern with language appears sterile. For example:

La phrase revint, virtuelle, dégagée d'une chute antérieure de
plume ou de rameau, dorénavant à travers la voix entendue,
jusqu'à ce qu'enfin elle s'articula, seule vivant de sa personnalité.
(272–3)

The point at which the writer is conscious of a word 'vivant de sa
personnalité' is valuable and creative, but here it is purely descriptive:
the word in question has reached in the writer's imagination what might
be called the point of creativity, but it is not developed. It is possible to
see here suggestions of Mallarmé's attitude towards language, but we do
not actually see it in action.

Another prose poem in which there are hints of the later developments
of Mallarmé's language, is the 'Frisson d'Hiver' (271). It is largely concerned with the evocation of an interior, with 'la grâce des choses fanées'
and their atmospheric quality. The paragraphs are interspersed four
times with parenthetical sentences referring to the poet's perception of
spiders' webs high up in the room, and this refrain underlines the
sadness and nostalgia of the occasion. It also ensures that the reader is
virtually transported into the room. He is given ample 'time' to situate
himself amongst the objects, to 'believe' in them, during the various
musings about the 'pendule de Saxe' and the 'glace de Venise'. The
strongly descriptive and nostalgic atmosphere denies the intermediary
of the writer as 'translator' of reality, since the language sets up little
imaginative distance from the situation described. In writing which is,
like this poem, largely descriptive and emotional, the words have only
a momentary existence as words, before guiding the reader back to
the emotional reality of the various events or scenes. In this sense,
language is subservient to reality. In some of the sonnets written in the
1880s Mallarmé uses an initial situation similar to that of 'Frisson

d'Hiver'. Both 'Quand l'ombre menaça' (67), and 'Ses purs ongles' (68) – especially the latter – are concerned to some degree with a still-life setting, but the elements of the still-life are so compacted and distilled that they force language into a position of far greater prominence than it has in 'Frisson d'Hiver'. In the sonnets it is no longer the physical and nostalgic background which matters, but uniquely the language. The point can in a sense be 'proved' by the fact that it is possible to read one paragraph of 'Frisson d'Hiver' and to gain from it the full weight of the poem's atmosphere; whereas in the sonnets it is the atmosphere derived from a reading of the whole which is both impressive and significant. As Mallarmé said as early as 1866, in a letter to François Coppée:

> ce à quoi nous devons viser surtout est que, dans le poème, les mots – qui sont déjà assez eux pour ne plus recevoir d'impressions du dehors – se reflètent les uns sur les autres jusqu'à paraître ne plus avoir leur couleur propre, mais n'être que les transitions d'une gamme.[1]

In order to appreciate the quality of words as 'les transitions d'une gamme' it is necessary for the reader to remain with the words, and not be 'delayed' momentarily by the physical or emotional reality behind them. Only then can language manifest its own reality.

'Un Spectacle Interrompu' was written in 1875, between the two main groups of prose poems, and it shows quite clearly the development of those elements of Mallarmé's language that it is necessary to read, rather than simply to associate with reality. Although the pattern of events is as strong in 'Un Spectacle Interrompu' as in the early prose poems, there are indications here and there both of a greater degree of difficulty in Mallarmé's language, and of a greater distancing of language from event. This distancing is even indirectly referred to:

> Artifice que la *réalité*, bon à fixer l'intellect moyen entre les mirages d'un fait. (276)

Reality of situation or event is here merely a means of fixing what appear to be the more important 'mirages d'un fait', and those 'mirages' are evident to a certain extent in this poem:

> Que se passait-il devant moi? rien, sauf que: de pâleurs évasives de mousseline se réfugiant sur vingt piédestaux en architecture de Bagdad, sortaient un sourire et des bras ouverts à la lourdeur

[1] *Propos*, pp. 74–5.

> triste de l'ours: tandis que le héros, de ces sylphides évocateur et
> leur gardien, un clown, dans sa haute nudité d'argent, raillait
> l'animal par notre supériorité. (276)

The sentence is rhythmically and dramatically built up, with a characteristic use of the colon in place of more cumbersome introductory
phrases. The phrases like 'de pâleurs évasives de mousseline' and 'dans
sa haute nudité d'argent' are obviously cases where Mallarmé follows
his own advice to 'peindre non la chose mais l'effet qu'elle produit'.
Their successful amalgamation with the mode of anecdote does indeed
suggest that Mallarmé's 'façon de voir, après tout, avait été supérieure,
et même la vraie'. (278)

It is in one of the late prose poems, 'Le Nénuphar Blanc', that we see
this 'façon de voir' valuably taken much further. Here language itself
plays such a significant part that it seems to transform situation and
anecdote almost entirely to its own needs. There is no question of the
poet's providing first a situation, and then a language at once suited to
it and going beyond it in expressive power. Stravinsky pointed out,
when asked whether the idea of music came before the orchestration of
it, that the idea *is* the orchestration of it.[1] The language of 'Le Nénuphar
Blanc' shows that this is no less true of language at its most expressive.
The evocation of reality is not necessarily a hindrance to the higher
concerns of poetry, and indeed an evocation in language of reality can so
transform that reality as to appear virtually to replace it, to place a
palimpsest over the scene or situation that is, nonetheless, more or less
adequately described.

There is one essential difference between the anecdote contained in
'Le Nénuphar Blanc' and those of the other prose poems: the others are
concerned with either scenes or incidents, but 'Le Nénuphar Blanc' is
concerned with an event that does not take place. Here is the clearest
possible instance of Mallarmé's language building up the atmosphere
that surrounds the absence of an object, so that the object only *is*
according to the manner in which the situation reflects its possible
presence. The mysterious neighbour exists only as the shimmering
afternoon on the river makes it possible to recall her nearness by the
consonance of its atmosphere and décor. The neighbour is undoubtedly
the subject of the piece, but it is not she who appears. The river, light,
warmth and radiance suggest not only the possibility of her appearance,
but also the fact that if she *did* appear, language would cede pride of
place to her outstanding, anticipated presence, forcing the reader to fall

[1] Igor Stravinsky, *Conversation with Robert Craft* (Penguin, 1962), p. 42.

58

back into the realm of 'what happens next' instead of being held, poised by language, in a state of possibility. The waterlily of the title is an obvious symbol, corresponding to the poetic tradition of circumlocution for the absent heroine. Yet the waterlily does not merely 'represent' the absent heroine and the curiosity of the poet, as can be seen in the following passage:

> Résumer d'un regard la vierge absence éparse en cette solitude, et, comme on cueille, en mémoire d'un site, l'un de ces magiques nénuphars clos qui y surgissent tout à coup, enveloppant de leur creuse blancheur un rien, fait de songes intacts, du bonheur qui n'aura pas lieu et de mon souffle ici retenu dans la peur d'une apparition, partir avec: tacitement, en dérament peu à peu sans du heurt briser l'illusion ni que le clapotis de la bulle visible d'écume enroulée à ma fuite ne jette aux pieds survenus de personne la ressemblance transparente du rapt de mon idéale fleur. (286)

Although in this extremely rich piece the waterlily is essential as an image of whiteness, and, above all, of possibility, it is the development of that sense of possibility which comes across most strongly. Mallarmé uses the waterlily less as a symbol than as a basic element of a situation in which the writer discovers the powers of objects – as in the occult – as they contain and distill their own situation and, by the application of language, that of language too. Thus although the waterlily, 'fait de songes intacts', is necessarily central, the chief effect of the passage is to preserve the sensation offered by the flower, not to elaborate its significance or its connotations. Mallarmé succeeds in making language sustain a sensation offered by the natural world, and creates a momentum of language which in every way equals that of nature. It is a subtle and effective feature of this piece that language should preserve the atmosphere of 'songes intacts' and counter it with the idea of 'du bonheur qui n'aura pas lieu', thus manifesting a perfect state of, perhaps, serenity rather than happiness, in the sensation given by the language. A simple anecdote thus works through the narrative, through the first impact of symbolism, to a new situation in which the language – and not the scene concerned – is able to take the reader on to a ground where all events appear to be events which language has brought about.

The reader can see from the language of 'Le Nénuphar Blanc' that symbolism or metaphor constitute only an initial stage in a process within which a presence of language is made manifest. The convention of poetic metaphor can often permit the reader to attain a level at which

reality is superseded by language, but it is only too easy for such transformations to send the reader back even more emphatically to reality.
But when the language of that metaphor has sufficient impact and
atmosphere, it does not refer to reality nor challenge its supremacy, but
moves parallel to its most attractive aspects. Language appears to transform reality by capturing its ephemeral sensations, while at the same
time transforming its own descriptive and denotative qualities and con-
firming Stravinsky's notion that idea and orchestration are one.

The varying achievements of the prose poems show Mallarmé's
progression towards this notion. The translations return the reader in
some measure to the situation of the 'Médaillons et Portraits', where
Mallarmé was writing against a background of literature; although in
translation the possibilities are somewhat modified, since Mallarmé must
abide very closely by the text he is translating. Yet it can be seen,
particularly in the case of the 'Contes Indiens', how a text that was
sufficiently attractive to Mallarmé can provide him with an opportunity
to 'orchestrate' in his own way, to such an extent that the orchestration
is itself a virtual melody.

The translation of Poe's poetry

In a sense none of Mallarmé's translation work is truly great,
perhaps because none, except the translation of Poe, was undertaken
for the usual reasons of reverence or interest. Mallarmé is often more
interested in the kind of work he is translating, rather than in its literary
value. Translation certainly is for him 'a literary mode', as Walter
Benjamin describes it,[1] but his own attempts at it fulfil only unevenly
that lofty concept. Benjamin says, in his essay 'The Task of the
Translator':

> Not only does the aim of translation differ from that of a literary
> work – it intends language as a whole, taking an individual work
> as a point of departure – but it is a different effort altogether. The
> intention of the poet is spontaneous, primary, graphic; that of the
> translator is derivative, ultimate, ideational. For the great motif of
> integrating many tongues into one true language is at work. [2]

These ideas are actually more suited to Mallarmé's work as a whole than
specifically to the translations, if we interpret the 'many tongues' as
the many modes and circumstances of Mallarmé's writing. However, the

---

[1] Walter Benjamin, *Illuminations*, trans. Harry Zohn (Jonathan Cape, 1970),
p. 76.
[2] *Ibid.*, pp. 76–7.

translation of Poe also belongs here, in its spirit if not in its quality. The translation of the 'Contes Indiens', however, is not literary but drawn from folk tales. There seems then, no question of grandiose or literary intention here. Yet in the 'Contes Indiens' Mallarmé does contribute to that integration of 'many tongues', only the 'tongues' are modes of action and narrative rather than actual languages. His enterprise is rather more selfish than idealistic; it is his own language he discovers. That this should become a part of the 'one true language' of which Benjamin writes is hardly thanks to the language of the original 'Contes Indiens'.

Thus when Mallarmé undertakes translation in both traditional and idealistic manner he limits the possibilities for his own discovery of language. The translation of Poe's poetry is an exercise which demands a faithful rendering. In his attempt both to re-create the atmosphere of the original and to do justice to his own admiration of Poe, Mallarmé almost entirely loses sight of the more interesting possibilities of translation. The constriction of the exercise is only alleviated to the extent that Mallarmé is translating poetry into prose. In the 'Contes Indiens' on the other hand, there is no such constriction, and Mallarmé is able to give a rendering that is faithful – and more than faithful – to the atmosphere rather than to the language.

The two sets of translations thus reveal an important fact about the circumstance of writing. When writing in admiration of Poe, Mallarmé was compelled by the strength of his admiration to use correspondingly powerful language. But when translating Poe, that very admiration restricts Mallarmé to a faithful rendering and hence to a lesser achievement in language. The same is true of the translations of Whistler's 'Ten o'clock', and of the pieces by Swinburne and Tennyson. Texts that are clearly literary may be a challenge to the translator, but they also compel his respect for the level of literature that has been reached. One should add that the gift of translating does not always go hand in hand with the gift of creativity. Also, translation is in many ways as unique and personal as creative writing: a translator might succeed in retaining the timbre and intention of one work, and fail completely with another. In the light of his success with the 'Contes Indiens', Mallarmé might best be described as an 'adaptor' rather than a translator.

Cervantes, in *Don Quixote*, offers the admirable image of translations as language that resembles the back of the tapestry, less richly coloured than the front, and obviously secondary to the original.[1] One revelation

---

[1] Cervantes, *Don Quixote*, trans. J. M. Cohen (Penguin, 1970), p. 887.

of Mallarmé's work is that a translation can appear to be a completely new tapestry, but without the blatancy that generally characterizes a novelty, since the basic pattern or story is the same. This would seem to apply best to the translations of poetry into prose, yet our expectations are reversed. The translations of Poe do resemble the back of the tapestry; whereas the 'Contes Indiens' are indubitably Mallarmé's creation. The lesson there, as in the 'Médaillons et Portraits', is that works which are lesser in Mallarmé's strictly literary estimation, provide better *material*, since a partial achievement in the language to be translated leaves far more scope for the translator.

The translation of Poe's poetry was undertaken in the manner of a tribute to one whose writings Mallarmé believed to be of supreme value. He is thus concerned to effect 'la juste revendication d'une existence de Poète par tous interdite' (226), and the tone of the 'Scolies' placed after the translations is largely uncritical, largely reverential. For example:

> Extérieurement du moins et par l'hommage matériel, ce livre, achevant après un laps très long la traduction de l'œuvre d'histoires et de vers laissé, par Edgar Poe, peut passer pour un monument du goût français au génie qui, à l'égal de nos maîtres les plus chers ou vénérés, chez nous exerça une influence. (223)

Mallarmé is clearly intent upon filling a gap – 'l'hommage matériel, ce livre' – than upon offering a challenge to Baudelaire's judgement that:

> Une traduction de poésies aussi voulues, aussi concentrées, peut être un rêve caressant, mais ne peut être qu'un rêve. (228–9)[1]

Mallarmé is characteristically apologetic about his translations:

> A défaut d'autre valeur ou de celle d'impressions puissamment maniées par le génie égal, voici un calque se hasarder sans prétention que rendre quelques-uns des effets de sonorité extra-ordinaire de la musique originelle, et ici et là peut-être, le sentiment même. (229)

Poe's poetry is of such a clearly identifiable nature that Mallarmé's modesty is in many ways unjustified. Its 'sentiment même' is not hard to recognize, and not hard to reproduce in another language, even allowing for the loss in certain alliterative effects. Mallarmé's reaction to the most

---

[1] Baudelaire was probably a better translator than Mallarmé in that he recognized the limits of what he could do and was never blinded by too great a reverence.

obvious traits of Poe's poetry is often curious. He writes of the poem 'The Bells' that it is:

> Une œuvre si nette et si sonnante regorgeant d'effets purement imitatifs mais toujours dotés de poésie première. (240)

The phrase 'poésie première' is ambiguous. In the context of Mallarmé's admiration it certainly suggests a high degree of praise, but there are also undertones of a reaction to a basic, and not necessarily great poetic achievement.

It is this 'poésie première' which remains the chief characteristic of original and translation alike. Of the poem 'Eulalie', Mallarmé says:

> Qui peut lire l'anglais devra, les yeux sur le texte, laisser comme chanter en lui ce petit poème de la musique la plus suave; et s'arrêter à des effets allitératifs étranges, tel le vers:
> And the yellow-haired young Eulalie became my... (233)

Not only does Mallarmé generally show restraint in the use of alliteration, but also there is evidence that he regarded its use with great circumspection:

> L'art suprême... dissimuler les jeux allitératifs, que trop de saisissable extériorité trahirait jusqu'au procédé, pour que le miracle du vers demeure un instant, inexplicable.[1]

The quality of alliteration is seen here as an over-obvious characteristic of language, denying in part its mysteriousness by showing too well where at least some of its effect comes from.[2] However, there is in Poe's poetry a considerable sense of mystery in the subjects or settings, so that it matters less that language should lose some of its expressive mystery by excessive use of crude literary effects. As a translator, Mallarmé might be more concerned with the sense of the words than with their atmosphere, especially since the lyrical qualities of the English language cannot be rendered adequately in French. Even if, as Mallarmé believed, 'cette impalpable richesse ne se perd pas tout entière au passage d'une langue à l'autre' (240), there is no doubt that a more powerful atmosphere is obtained in the French version by simple faithfulness to the sense of the text, rather than by an attempt to

---

[1] Mallarmé, *Correspondance*, vol. III, 1886–9 (Paris, Gallimard, 1969), p. 111.
[2] Since, however, much of Mallarmé's poetry is very alliterative, one should perhaps add that he was less disapproving of alliteration than of its mishandling or over-use. His own heavy use of it in, for example, 'Ses purs ongles' contributes to a subtle language game rather than appeals directly to the emotions.

reproduce the effects of Poe's language. Consider, for example, the first stanza of 'la Dormeuse':

> A minuit, au mois de juin, je suis sous la lune mystique: une vapeur opiacée, obscure, humide, s'exhale hors de son contour d'or et, doucement se distillant, goutte à goutte, sur le tranquille sommet de la montagne, glisse, avec assoupissement et musique, parmi l'universelle vallée. Le romarin salue la tombe, le lis flotte sur le vague; enveloppant de brume son sein, la ruine se tasse dans le repos: comparable au Léthé, voyez! le lac semble goûter un sommeil conscient et, pour le monde, ne s'éveillerait. Toute beauté dort: et repose, sa croisée ouverte au ciel, Irène avec ses Destinées. (202–3)

This is highly descriptive writing, descriptive of a realm of the imagination rather than of the real world, and its atmosphere is maintained by the use of words such as: 'mystique, obscure, vague, brume, sommeil'. It is a kind of writing which demonstrates the converse of many of Mallarmé's notions concerning what language can and cannot do. In an early letter (1864) Mallarmé wrote to Henri Cazalis:

> L'art suprême, ici, consiste à laisser voir, par une possession impeccable de toutes les facultés, qu'on est en extase, sans avoir montré comment on s'élevait vers ces cimes.[1]

One of the most obvious characteristics of Poe's writing is that he *does* show every step of the way, even to the extent of writing an account – not entirely serious – of the way in which 'The Raven' might have been conceived and written. But if Poe is not a subtle writer, he is consistently 'poetic'. His perceptions of the natural world are often not unlike those of Mallarmé, even if Poe states rather than evokes those perceptions. When Mallarmé is able to write of 'un étrange et fatidique climat qui gît, sublime, hors de l'Espace, hors du Temps' (206), or of 'une histoire obscurément rappelée des vieux temps ensevelis' (194), it is obvious that he is in the right kind of climate, that around the ever-present Subject of Poe's writing there is at least an assurance of poetry.

The 'Contes Indiens'

The translation of Poe could scarcely be said to constitute an experiment in Mallarmé's language, and the measure of success they have must be attributed to the strength of Poe's language rather than

[1] Mallarmé, *Correspondance*, vol. i, p. 116.

that of Mallarmé. However, the space that stands out as Mallarmé's own in the language of the 'Contes Indiens' is considerable. The circumstances in which the translation was undertaken are also very different here; indeed the proposal was that Mallarmé should re-write, rather than simply translate the stories. It is interesting that these translations should be far more successful than the two others of similar type that Mallarmé undertook: 'Les Dieux Antiques' and 'L'Etoile des Fées'. The translation of 'Les Dieux Antiques' is obviously a fairly literal one, and shows no more than Mallarmé's interest in the realm of legend and fairy tale. The charm of legends lies largely in the combination of simplicity and fantasy in the narration. The degree of unreality is such that no elaborate language is needed; indeed a very simple style of narration befits the nature of stories that are spoken rather than written in origin. For example:

> Hermès, fils de Zeus, et de Maïa, naquit de grand matin, dans une caverne de la colline Cyllénienne, et sommeilla paisiblement dans son berceau pendant deux ou trois heures. Sortant de la caverne, il trouva une tortue, la tua et de son écaille se fit une lyre, se fixant transversalement les cordes prises aux entrailles d'un mouton. (1207)

The unreality of the sequence of action is sufficient to produce an involvement on the part of the reader; while a more banal action, set in the real world, needs a stronger effect of style to involve the reader in what would otherwise be an uninteresting report. An interesting distinction between legend and fairy tale can be seen by comparing the extract above with a piece from 'L'Etoile des Fées':

> Bien, maintenant; elle était prête, équipée, pour son voyage d'exploration, et ne manquait plus que d'ailes pour s'envoler. A peine avait-elle proféré ce dernier souhait que, sentant quelque chose lui battre aux talons, en non moins de temps elle fut enlevée dans les airs. (1313–14)

Although the narrative style here is as simple and straightforward as in the piece from 'Les Dieux Antiques', the content of the narrative appears to be no more than a magical transformation of the real world, not an autonomous other world where 'anything can happen'. The human touch of being ready 'except that she had no wings on which to fly away' quite destroys the magical idea of being able to fly. The main idea of the text is in no way matched by the style of narration, and it is neither useful nor revealing to say that this is merely a bad translation (for in fact it is a better, in the sense of a more literal translation, than that of the 'Contes Indiens'). What it does show is that where the simplicity of legend is deserted in favour of what is obviously a magical replacement for human life, the translator is no longer in the presence of a sympathetic virtual language of event, and can only reproduce that which has already been transformed, if crudely, out of real life.

In the 'Contes Indiens', Mallarmé is given a framework of such suitable timbre and dimension that the opportunity of translation is almost a luxury. His imagination is asked to give only the cream of itself, without the need to play artisan and reason out shape and plot. He only has to 'aerate' the structure, to turn a smooth but infinitely suggestible substance of plot into a compatible movement of his own language. He has to work from a minimal and extremely attractive framework, and the reader is conscious, in Mallarmé's language, of the impact that framework made on him. He expands the original, but in a manner that complements rather than complicates, so that we are not conscious of reading both a story and a reaction to it.

All the 'Contes Indiens' are framed by a presence of the magical and the royal. Disguise always serves to reveal, ultimately, both royalty and beauty, and because the royal status of the characters is never in question, the reader is not concerned to ensure that heroes and heroines are as they appear to be. Language is thus free to deploy its full strength in suggesting the fluctuations of their status. Mallarmé does not simply tell us why it fluctuates, but allows his depiction of each new stage to carry the emphasis. Consider, for example, the description of the place of rendezvous between Soundari and Oupahara in 'Le Portrait En-chanté':

> Le berceau d'asôkas, terme de sa course; enfin il l'aborde, y séjourne, écartant doucement les tiges artificielles fleuries d'odorantes lanternes, qui s'abaissent sur un lit brodé de soie, mais vide. Complices de l'amour ou de ses serviteurs vigilants, attendent autour d'une ombrelle épanouie, un éventail aux oiseaux immobiles; une aiguière étincelante de gouttes mystéri-euses, diamants ou senteurs. (592)

The empty silken bed, the shadowy but glittering surrounds, all prefigure the atmosphere of the meeting, and to such an extent that the atmosphere becomes far more important than the inevitable meeting itself. The royal and magical status of heroes and heroines and the pattern their lives follow is perfectly compatible with the 'hierarchiza-tion' of poets, culminating in 'le Poète' or 'le Maître'. In the 'Contes

Indiens' there is no question of personality, only of an idealized structure within an autonomous setting. We are less involved with the thoughts of the heroine than with their reflection in her situation. For example:

> dans ce bijou, ce que, pour elle, résume, déjà de scintillements et de feu, sa rêverie à l'amant qu'elle ignore. (589)

or:

> elle tenait, la tête penchée, le tableau, comme pour y mirer son désir. (589)

Material objects are so transformed as to appear to contain the imminent event, just as the world of fashion appears already to contain the fashionable event. The atmosphere evoked by Mallarmé in the scene where Fleur-de-Lotus, in 'La Fausse Vieille' bathes in the lotus pond, clearly prefigures the happy ending of the story:

> Elle est sortie du bain, assise sur une marche basse de l'escalier de l'étang, pendant que s'évapore chaque goutte, diamants sur elle épars: ce suprême voile flotte aux contours, hésite et disparait comme un nuage idéal, la laissant plus que nue. (603)

This is by no means the language of folklore. The heroine, covered in sparkling drops of water that, far from clothing her, evaporate, leaving her 'plus que nue', is a Mallarméan portrait that typifies all the 'Contes Indiens'. Their archetypal narrative patterns give an impact of startling bareness that resembles the basic dynamism of Mallarmé's creative writing. What looks like ornamentation – here, of diamond droplets; in Mallarmé's writing, of complex syntax – is in fact the 'éclat' of a central simplicity or force.

The story of 'La Fausse Vieille' ends with the lines:

> certes, après tant d'aventures, elles avaient mérité le bonheur, qui est muet. (605)

The eventual presence of happiness may be wordless, but its possibility is both describable and sensuously present in the images used earlier. The possibility of the happy ending, veiled then only by sparkling drops of water, offers a rich moment to Mallarmé's language, further enhanced by the predictability of the plot. Mallarmé only needs to give indirect reminders of the outcome; the atmosphere of language will resolve any remaining doubts.

It is because the plots of these stories are both simple and predictable, that it is possible for details of landscape and situation to set off reverberations that never actually leave substantiality to become ideal, but nevertheless suggest a movement which is not unlike that of Mallarmé's 'transposition du fait à l'idéal'. The language of the 'Contes Indiens' illuminates that abstract notion, for both characters and objects are situated between reality and the lofty, distant implications of their magical status. This is effected largely by a concentration on the qualities of objects that are transformed by Mallarmé's perception rather than by any intrinsic magic. The end of 'Le Portrait Enchanté' is a good example of the way in which Mallarmé makes the setting carry the weight of the narrative:

> Le treillis d'or des lucarnes coupait par endroits le rayon matinal de lune; tandis que l'agonie stellaire d'une lampe, aux plafonds suspendue, animait un reflet d'invisibles danses. Il voletait aussi, dans les hauteurs, de grands éventails blancs qui, de leur aile, dispersaient à tous les recoins les parfums de délire et d'oubli, montant des cassolettes mal éteintes. Le bain comme un grand regard, veillant au jour qui vient, nappe limpide, attendait les dormeuses, plongées encore dans la transparence de leurs seuls songes. (596)

This protracted and delicate still-life could have found its elements in Mallarmé's later sonnets. It is no more than a still-life, supported, now invisibly, by the movement of the story that has passed, while its atmosphere contains, without events being any longer necessary, the end of the story. The happy ending traditionally associated with such stories offers every reason for indulgence of language, though usually it is with the sense of deliberately slowing the end, so that the reader may relish the triumph. Mallarmé's language here, with its atmosphere of calm and expectation, transforms the culminating emotional events by transferring the impact to the near transcendent quality of the material situation, as if that in itself were sufficient to tell of the action. It is not, of course, the action that Mallarmé is concerned to tell, but the way in which language is able to abide by a simple story-pattern and let it be known, exclusively through the quality of the language used, and not through statement alone, that 'they lived happily ever after'.

The plots of the stories may be simple, but they provide an extremely attractive basis for the language of Mallarmé's translation. The Rajah in 'Le Mort Vivant' has a brief span of life, contained in darkness, always subject to the will of the invisible and unpredictable Péri. He inhabits 'un cyprès...où quelqu'un d'absent paraît inviter l'intrus, qui monte, s'élancerait vers le ciel' (607), and later 'referma, sur ses paroles, un mystère, comme sa tombe connu de lui seul' (609). Within the tale and its unlikely happenings, this is really so, but the meaning of the words for Mallarmé the translator does not only lie in the events, but also in the sequence of images – death, closed, mystery, tomb, alone – and their capacity to leave the story to create a sequence that belongs to an equally mythical tradition of the poet's world. That sequence only holds to the function of narration by the slender threads of Mallarmé's syntax and the predictability of the story. The resolution of the pattern of events is unemphatic in all but its atmosphere:

> Voletant, glissant, bondissant. Une main candide s'érige et veut saisir un objet, sans doute, scintillant et amicalement balancé, dans l'air: mille grains, comme une pluie, tombent à terre, c'est le collier. (614)

Here it is the suspense which Mallarmé *collects* in its sparkling form; at the end of 'La Fausse Vieille' it is the narrative which is scattered in the pearls of the necklace; while the end of the Péri in 'Le Mort Vivant' is made manifest in 'un miroitement de joyaux au sein vertigineux des bayadères, arrêtées soudain renversées, ainsi que le reflet d'un vol circulaire supérieur de pierrerie ou d'âme' (615). Images of flying, sparkling, of innocence and jewels, do not merely decorate the narrative, they contain it, and form at the same time the implicit narrative of Mallarmé's sensibility as it moves along the substance of the plot.

The setting carries the narrative to such an extent that we are less concerned with the progression of characters than with the progression of qualities. It may seem paradoxical that these qualities, always so eminently magical and distinctive, are not the direct result of the semi-divine status of heroes and heroines, but are made evident in the physical setting. In 'Nala et Damayanti', significantly, it is not the gods but the humans that are godlike:

> Légère, comme des nuées flottant après une pluie d'automne, la vierge royale ondule sur l'argent et la soie d'un duvet de cygne. (618)[1]

It is the language rather than the action which lifts the story to its legendary status, making the heroine rather than the gods take on this quality of floating. Even more importantly, the quality of floating is

---

[1] Cf. the concluding pages of J.-P. Richard, *L'Univers Imaginaire de Mallarmé* (Paris, Editions du Seuil, 1961), p. 605, for a discussion of Mallarmé's predilection for the magical qualities of the physical rather than those of the godlike.

such that it takes precedence over the presence of the heroine herself. The aspirations traditionally associated with poetry (and usually uncomfortably found there, since they seem to postulate a world in which these miracles could actually happen) are allowed to 'live' in the manifestations of flying horses and magical transformations, messages carried by swans, dancers that evaporate, even kings who lose their kingdoms on a throw of the dice. All these actually perform in a borrowed universe, yet remain impossible and over-fanciful outside it, and outside the qualities of Mallarmé's language that give a support at once idealized and rooted in the perception of the material world. Mallarmé is thus able to *write* the transposition 'du fait à l'idéal' in a framework that allows for it. He is also able to experiment with the kinds of language that will express such a transposition without succumbing to the temptation of creating a universe in which these things virtually happen, instead of keeping the transformations and the magic within the qualities of language itself.

The striking qualities of Mallarmé's language in the 'Contes Indiens' arise out of the combination of legendary framework and imaginatively perceived setting; and the autonomy of language arises out of its transformation, rather than its depiction of the stories' action. One of the lessons of these translations is the usefulness, even the necessity, of a situation and action compatible with the qualities of language. By writing the pattern of events Mallarmé is able to evoke the qualities and atmosphere of that pattern, to create in his own language the emanation from the gratuitous virtual language of event. To take a simple example: a figure coming down the stairs makes in fact a rather jerky movement, but the general sense of the movement is that of descent. If the writer offers not only the three-dimensional action of the feet and the zig-zag of the stairs, but also, in the quality of his writing, the idea of coming down, then he is supplying the double need of poet and narrator, and suggesting at the same time the area in which the poet alone would work. Where the poet does not appear (as in the 'Etoile des Fées'), we see merely an example of that literature 'que les Anglais appellent la Fiction';[1] while the 'Contes Indiens' form an echo of 'La Fable inscrite à la page des Cieux et dont l'Histoire même n'est que l'interprétation' (545). A narrative of a simple legendary nature leaves Mallarmé ample space for a language which is in a sense superfluous to the narrative, yet forms a parallel language of atmosphere that contributes simultaneously to the needs of the story and to the instinct of the poet.

[1] Mallarmé, *Correspondance*, vol. II, p. 107.

'Les Mots Anglais'

Mallarmé described 'Les Mots Anglais' (along with 'Les Dieux Antiques') as 'des besognes propres et voilà tout' (663), and, on the surface,
it is not hard to see why: the opportunity of writing a language text-
book seems no more than an extension of the schoolmaster's chores. Yet
in the hands of Mallarmé it becomes something other than an exploration of the origins and characteristics of the English language; it is also
an exploration of what language can express before it is put to literary
use, or, in other words, of its fundamental expressive characteristics.
'Les Mots Anglais' may be a mere 'besogne', but it also forms part of a
larger scheme. As Mallarmé says:

> J'ai toujours rêvé et tenté autre chose, avec une patience d'alchi-
> miste, prêt à y sacrifier toute vanité et toute satisfaction, comme
> on brûlait jadis son mobilier et les poutres de son toit, pour
> alimenter le fourneau du Grand Œuvre. (662)

Within the context of Mallarmé's own 'Grand Œuvre' or exploration of
literary language it is certainly relevant to consider the very basis of
language. Indeed the image of the alchemist burning furniture and roof
beams is an apt analogy. What appears to be a banal contribution to the
'Grand Œuvre' is in fact a necessary one, not merely 'keeping the fire
burning', but having an effect also on the final result.

In a work of this kind, language itself is given all the weight that
Mallarmé asks for literature, but in a context where normally the weight
would tend towards historical explanation or analysis. However, as in
Mallarmé's other apparently less important prose work, it is always
possible to sense the confrontation between the creative mind and the
raw material of his creativity: language. Considering language as a
historical and scientific whole has unexpected advantages: the reader's
attention is focused expressly on language, on individual words even,
within a unified framework. Thus we see language both as an intricate
apparatus and as an identifiable whole.

The text opens with an emphatic reminder of the breadth of the task:

> Qu'est-ce que l'Anglais? Sérieuse et haute question: la trancher dans le sens où elle est faite ici, c'est-à-dire absolument, on ne le pourra qu'à la dernière de ces pages et tout analysé. (899)

Mallarmé is dealing with a question that cannot really be resolved, even on the last page of such a work, unless the exploration itself contributes to the sense of a resolution. However, Mallarmé does not so much aim to resolve problems as to gain full benefit from this opportunity of giving what he sees to be a proper emphasis to language. When he does reach the last page of 'Les Mots Anglais', he says:

> Par sa Grammaire (dont il n'est question que dans l'autre tome de ce Traité) marche vers quelque point futur du Langage et se replonge aussi dans le passé, même très ancien et mêle aux débuts sacrés du Langage, l'Anglais: Langue Contemporaine peut-être par excellence, elle qui accuse le double caractère de l'époque, rétrospectif et avancé. (1053)

Mallarmé indicates that his volume is not definitive, since other aspects are to be considered in a later volume, but more importantly because English demonstrates the instability of language, thus defying the presumption that its nature can be discussed once and for all. It can only be discussed, as language can only be used, idiosyncratically. That language is often unpredictable, that individual words break rules as often as they follow them, and that there is always a considerable displacement between the sense and the appearance of words, all allow for an active interest on Mallarmé's part. Indeed the enjoyment he obviously derives from his study of the rules and eccentricities of the English language sets the tone for the profound pleasure evident throughout the prose works. Enjoyment in itself would be little more than an unexpected bonus in the apparently minor works of a writer, but in the case of Mallarmé it points to the intrinsic life and power of language. Instead of setting up language in some sort of conflict with reality, Mallarmé presents it as a friendly tournament where neither is an outright winner. The splendour of the confrontation, however, aided by an appreciative audience, needs none of the usual judgement.

The English language is particularly suited to a study of this kind, since it is more unstable than French, and derives from so many root languages. Evidence of transformation within the language is thus easy to see:

> notre Science s'aperçoit que, loin de naître spontanément, ils ne

sont qu'une transformation, corrompue ou élégante, de parlers
antérieurs. Rien de spontané. (901)

Language operates in the same way as literature, since the progress of
literature also operates by means of a series of supersessions. Mallarmé's
reaction to Rimbaud showed that he saw literature as no chance or
meteoric eruption. The development of language (and literature) may
not adhere strictly to any rules, but it does have a perceptible and partly
ordered 'déroulement'. From his critic's vantage point in the 'Médaillons
et Portraits' Mallarmé was able to see this progression. His situation in
'Les Mots Anglais' is similar in that he is again looking at forms of
language from a distance, in this case the distance from foreign to
mother tongue:

> Etudier simplement du Français l'Anglais, car il faut se tenir
> quelque part d'où jeter les yeux au-delà; mais néanmoins
> vérifier auparavant si ce site d'observation est bon. Les rapports
> pouvant se rencontrer entre ces deux parlers, ou les différences,
> détermineront la justesse d'une telle étude; or, c'est une fois le
> *point de vue* (qui s'affirme au cours de ces pages) éprouvé. (902)

Mallarmé constantly considers how language appears when seen from
different situations, and as he says himself:

> On ne voit presque jamais si sûrement un mot que du dehors, où
> nous sommes: c'est-à-dire, de l'étranger. (975)

In almost all his prose he sees literature 'de l'étranger', and with
valuable results; in the same way here he turns his attention to individual words. It is said that the most efficient way to forge a signature is
to copy it upside down, since in this way you will only see it as a pattern
and not as a series of familiar symbols. In the same way it is, imaginatively, an advantage to look at the nature of words from the starting
point of another language, where you do not see words as clear elements
of a communicative code, but rather as varyingly strange transformations of a known language. Thus the discrepancies between the appearance and the sense of a word stand out much more readily.

Another important aspect of 'Les Mots Anglais' is the quality of
reading that it demands. The close attention we have to give to such a
work does not look at first like that which we give to creative writing.
Yet, strangely enough, we do look at words as historical or near-scientific entities with just the sort of fundamental and precise attentiveness we should give to creative writing. Nor is it out of place for
Mallarmé to remind us of this:

Lecteur, vous avez sous les yeux ceci, un écrit; dont l'enseigne-
ment est limité aux caractères propres à l'écrit, soit l'*orthographe*
et le *sens*...Qu'y a-t-il? des *mots*, tout d'abord reconnaissables
eux-mêmes aux *lettres* qui les composent, ils s'enchaînent et voici
des *phrases*. Un courant d'intelligence comme un souffle, l'esprit,
met en mouvement ces mots, pour qu'à plusieurs d'entre eux ils
expriment un sens avec des nuances. (902–3)

The situation in which Mallarmé is writing allows for an otherwise over-
obvious explanation. His remarks suggest that the reader does not
simply assimilate language. He does not convert it into a detachable
sense, but, by the application of 'un courant d'intelligence comme un
souffle', he discovers the life of the language, and reveals 'un sens avec
des nuances'. One can see more readily the life of language in a study
that does not appear to allow for it. This is shown by the experience of
reading of some of Mallarmé's lists of words in 'Les Mots Anglais'.

The effect of reading lists of words united only by their etymology is
not only one of heightened attentiveness to the evolution of meaning.
The reader also notices more clearly how the simple proximity of words
can generate a quality that is largely lost in sentences which progress in
order to convey a discursive sense. As Mallarmé says, characteristically,
in the middle of a discussion of the origins of English verbs:

De belles lignées de Vocables, tout entières, ne m'apparaissent
point à dédaigner. (1027)[1]

When words are set out in lists they have a considerable and unexpected
effect, not unlike that of reading the 'grimoire' to which Mallarmé so
often refers. The simplicity and repetition of the words is countered by
a strong sensation of mysterious progression, arising not so much from
the meaning of the words, as from the changes in meaning from word to
word. The 'souffle d'intelligence' seems to have been transferred from
the reader to the words themselves. It is interesting to compare a list
from a real 'grimoire' with one from 'Les Mots Anglais':

Mystery of Hellebore, Matter of Dew, Extract of Tin, Crocus of
Mars, Flower of Crude Jupiter, Dust of the fifth metal, Spirit of
Saturn, Juice of Amethyst, Liquor of Granates, Composition of
Gems.[2]

[1] One should see such wry comments in the light of the warmth and humour
of, say, Laurence Sterne's appreciation of language in *Tristram Shandy*. Or,
to take a later example, one is reminded of the way in which Samuel Beckett's
characters relish the few words upon which their existence seems to depend.
[2] Paracelsus, *The Hermetic and Alchemical Writings*, trans. Arthur Edward
Waite, vol. II (New York, University Books Inc., 1967), p. 193.

Déviations, curieuses à des titres divers, en le sens de mots passés du Français à l'Anglais: ACTUAL, veut dire *réel*, pas ACTUEL; CARPET, *tapis*, c'est notre CHARPIE; CHAPTER, avant d'être un CHAPITRE, fut une *guirlande* ou une couronne. (996)

Aux noms propres seuls appartient une transposition absolue et complète: le BELLEROPHON, vaisseau, sera pour ses matelots, BILLY RUFFIAN ou *ce sac à corde de Guillot*; et le *Chat Fidèle*, sur l'enseigne antique des auberges de la Conquête, accepte du populaire un *violon* dont il joue avec des mots: THE CAT AND THE FIDDLE. Mythologie, autant que Philologie, ceci: car c'est par un procédé analogue que, dans le cours des siècles, se sont amassées et propagées partout les Légendes. (997)

The quotation from Paracelsus shows how a list can operate a sense of gradual change – from Matter to Extract – without explaining the change. The words in the list are both explanation and example, and thus although language is basically at its most objective it also offers a different kind of meaning. Significance in a list of this kind lies in the way one stage seems to modify the next and the one before. Such a means of significance shows a parallel, however over-simplified, with Mallarmé's notion of the literary sense evoked by 'un mirage interne des mots mêmes'.[1] This seems to 'prove' that the qualities of mystery or mirage do not exist because they are magically conferred by poetry, but are inherent in language itself.

It is impossible not to be reminded here of Mallarmé's many comments on the essential and ephemeral subject of writing, or, as he describes it: 'le motif général qu'on appelle à tort sujet'.[2] The guiding line of etymology is a combination of the meaning and the form of words. In the lists of words the 'subject' appears and is distilled out of the process of reading. It appears in the discrepancies between one word and another, and in the simple process of change. The close concordance between this situation and that of literary language is clearly shown in 'Un Coup de Dés', where single words set up vibrations of sense which are expressed in subsidiary groups of words, not in order to form a narrative, but in order to convey the full strength of life and allusion that one word has. The possibility of a work like 'Un Coup de Dés' can be sensed obliquely across the investigations of 'Les Mots Anglais', 'aux limites de ce Sujet; là où s'égare un peu tout savoir', (1049) though the latter, dating from 1877, was written twenty years before 'Un Coup de Dés'.

---

[1] Mallarmé, *Propos*, p. 83.   [2] Mallarmé, *Correspondance*, vol. III, p. 95.

Perhaps the greatest importance of 'Les Mots Anglais' for Mallarmé lies in the possibility it offers of discussing the expressiveness of words without any need to consider them in the framework of phrase and sentence.[1] Mallarmé is able to consider those characteristics of language of which the writer in general and the poet in particular makes intuitive use. The writer adapts his language, largely unconsciously, to the similarity between 'wrinkled' and 'wrought', between 'deep' and 'dark'. In an etymological survey of words, the reader is at that level which is 'before meaning', although taking note of meaning, and this apparently 'lower' level is, to Mallarmé, a major one. It enables him to demonstrate how certain elements in language contribute to the often mysterious effects of poetry. For example:

> peut-on par exemple, dire que 'wr' authentiquement, désigne la torsion (932)

or:

> G a son importance, signifiant d'abord une aspiration simple, vers un point où va l'esprit. (938)

Similarly, the link that Mallarmé makes between 'step' and 'stamp' is in fact alliterative rather than strictly etymological, while:

> H traduit, quoique avec quelque vague, un mouvement direct et simple comme le geste de tenir avec la main, hâtivement même. (955)

Such comments may appear fanciful and inexact, but they are both precise and valuable in the context of the writer's interest in his own creative language. Two kinds of words that are familiar to the 'littérateur' are the onomatopoeic and the alliterative:

> Ces mots [sc.: les onomatopées] admirables et tout d'une venue, se trouvent, relativement aux autres de la langue (exceptons ceux comme 'to WRITE', écrire, imité du bruissement de la plume dès le Gothique 'WRITH', dans un état d'infériorité. (920)

It is characteristic of Mallarmé to choose the illustration of the verb 'to write', as if to remind the reader of the ultimate significance of the investigation, and it is even more clear, in the piece about alliteration, that Mallarmé is making the best possible literary use of this 'exercise'.

---

[1] Mallarmé's enjoyment of 'Les Mots Anglais' can be compared with that which is evident in Ivor Brown's 'personal dictionaries'. 'Words are my personal ploy', he says in A Word in Your Ear (Jonathan Cape, 1942), a sentence that could well stand behind Mallarmé's work too.

Mallarmé considers the gift of alliteration to be 'inhérent au génie septentrional' (921) (reminding the reader above all of the tributes to Poe), and takes it as the basis of an important notion concerning language:

> Pareil effort magistral de l'Imagination désireuse, non seulement de se satisfaire par le symbole éclatant dans les spectacles du monde, mais d'établir un lien entre ceux-ci et la parole chargée de les exprimer. (921)

The quality of Mallarmé's musing at this point suggests the desirability, at least notionally, of a language which could express, as alliterative words do to a certain extent, the *quality* of 'les spectacles du monde'. But he continues:

> et qu'il sera prudent d'analyser seulement le jour où la Science, possédant le vaste répertoire des idiomes jamais parlés sur la terre, écrira l'histoire des lettres de l'alphabet à travers tous les âges et quelle était presque leur absolue signification, tantôt devinée, tantôt méconnue par les hommes, créateurs des mots: mais il n'y aura plus, dans ce temps, ni Science pour résumer cela, ni personne pour le dire. Chimère, contentons-nous, à présent, des lueurs que jettent à ce sujet des écrivains magnifiques. (921)

It is only at this notional level that Mallarmé senses the desirability of a language that would truly express the quality of things, as well as identify them. He is obviously more interested in 'des lueurs que jettent à ce sujet des écrivains magnifiques', that is, in a progressive and deepening possibility of the 'chimère'. Complete knowledge on such a subject would scarcely be interesting to Mallarmé since it allows for no further development, and equally for no further mystery of language.

On the one hand then, Mallarmé is attracted by the notion of a fully expressive language, while on the other hand, much of the 'Mots Anglais' is taken up with consideration of the unpredictable 'rapport qui existe entre le sens des mots que je vais croire inconnu de vous, et leur configuration extérieure' (918). For it is because this 'rapport' is irregular that it is possible to judge one kind of writing literary and another 'reportage'. The expressiveness of language stems from the writer's varying success in overcoming the inadequacies of language. For example, despite its sounding very much like the word 'heavy', it is possible to write about 'heaven' and make the general effect a celestial one. It is far more valuable to the act of writing, as opposed to musing about its ultimate possibilities, that language should be imperfect, for if 'sens' did always correspond closely to 'configuration extérieure', then everyone (and no one) would be a poet. On the other hand one might say that if it were not possible sometimes to overcome what look like insurmountable and fundamental limitations of language, there would be no such thing as literature. A philology handbook, 'ayant trait aux mots en eux' (962) is able, unexpectedly, to demonstrate both the weakness of language as an expressive instrument, and the overcoming of that weakness. In fact 'Les Mots Anglais' almost amounts to a message to the aspiring writer, telling him not to despair of literary achievement in what seems to be an eccentric and intractable language:

> car il ne faut point oublier que tel fait anormal, où s'indigne le linguiste, cause la joie souvent du littérateur, voué à un travail de mosaïque point rectiligne. (1026)

There is no doubt that the English language is particularly rich in eccentricities, and it appears even more so when set beside French, which is, as Mallarmé points out, 'la langue neutre par excellence' (1033). Thus the interaction between the two languages provides Mallarmé with an interesting situation:

> La greffe seule peut offrir une image qui représente la phénomène nouveau; oui, du Français s'est enté sur de l'Anglais: et les deux plantes ont, toute hésitation passée, produit sur une même tige une fraternelle et magnifique végétation. (915)

The growth of the English language out of Anglo-Saxon and Romance roots showed Mallarmé a remarkable instance of the complexity, and thence expressiveness of language. It indicated too the impossibility of ever accounting for, or fully understanding its permutations. Language then appears, in both literature and philology, a maze which one should appreciate and develop rather than elucidate, and any study, or poem is merely an initiation into its possibilities:

> L'étude véritable d'un idiome étranger, ébauchée petit, doit être continuée par vous, grand, ou grandissant. Tout un dictionnaire s'offre, immense, effrayant: le posséder, voilà la tentative, la lecture des livres aidant et une fois sus les rudiments de la grammaire. (900)

Mallarmé may not succeed in convincing the merely dutiful student that 'learning languages can have hidden depths', but he himself obviously needs no convincing. His own study, 'ébauchée petit', generates an interest, even an excitement scarcely hidden between the lines. The syntactical resemblance of 'le posséder, voilà la tentative' to 'le suggérer, voilà le rêve' (869) is too strong to be overlooked. In both cases Mallarmé makes a statement of intention, if distantly – then modifies, removes it even, to a state of possibility only. However, the modification does not have the effect of deadening the statement; on the contrary, it opens a movement of great suggestive power. Furthermore, this appears less a whim of the author than a natural effect of considering language at a fundamental level. In a study of philology one learns certain facts about language, then finds that they move on to a greater significance when considered either against the historical evolution of language, or else against the movement of a creative use of language.

Hence it appears neither exaggeration nor mere self-justification in the poet to assert that:

> le Langage, chargé d'exprimer tous les phénomènes de la Vie, emprunte quelque chose; il vit...Les mots, dans le dictionnaire, gisent, pareils ou de dates diverses, comme des stratifications: vite je parlerai de couches. (901)

The geological metaphor Mallarmé uses here is an apt one, for it calls to mind not only a slow process, but also one which leaves miraculously clear evidence of its mysterious workings. Geological strata give information about past lives, and, as a whole, seem to present a new one, just as the English language, put together in what looks like an arbitrary way, forms the basis of an endless renewal in the hands of the 'littérateur'. In a discussion of the roots of language, Mallarmé shows again his fascination with the mysterious coherence of what looks like a vast apparatus:

> Qu'est-ce qu'une *racine*? Un assemblage de lettres...réduit à leurs os et à leurs tendons, soustraits à leur vie ordinaire, afin qu'on reconnaisse entre eux une parenté secrète; plus succincte et plus évanoui encore, on a un *thème*. (962)

And what Mallarmé says of the evolution of language could often equally well apply to the evolution of a piece of creative writing. For it is not only the structure of language that appears alive; each word too, is an intricate embryo:

> A toute la nature apparenté et se rapprochant ainsi de l'organisme dépositaire de la vie, le Mot présente, dans ses voyelles et ses diphtongues, comme une chair; et dans ses consonnes, comme une ossature délicate à disséquer. (901)

Mallarmé's sense of the process which leads words to their current significance is broad and imaginative enough to account also for the often mysterious thread that binds together the words of a poem:

> Un pareil fouillis de vocables rangé dans les colonnes d'un lexique, sera-t-il appelé là arbitrairement et par quelque hasard malin: point; chacun de ces termes arrive de loin, à travers les contrées ou les siècles, à sa place exacte, isolé celui-ci et cet autre mêlé à toute une compagnie. (900)

No believer in the hazards of what is traditionally known as inspiration, Mallarmé finds delightful confirmation of his belief that literature does not happen 'by chance'. However, the abolition of arbitrary inspiration does not bring with it a vanishing of all sense of mystery. It is indeed because language as both a historical and a literary entity arrives at its various points of significance in such an unpredictable yet precise manner that it has its particular, and often mysterious quality. Words that take their places in a process of evolution or in a poem seem deliberate and precise. That they should be the definitive result of unseen, perhaps unknowable processes, makes them far more mysterious than that which is merely veiled or obscure. So, as Mallarmé says in his introduction to the etymological tables of words:

> Ce qu'on nomme du *jeu*, il en faut, dans une mesure raisonnable, pour réussir quelque chose comme ce travail complexe et simple: trop de rigueur aboutissant à transgresser, plutôt que des lois, mille intentions certaines et mystérieuses du langage. (919)

The student of etymology has to be like the reader of poetry, apparently confronting only a piece or example of language, but actually confronting the whole of it in microcosm. It is at once 'complexe et simple'; it has 'mille intentions certaines' rather than laws. A study of etymology can reveal qualities as well as facts if the reader, with the help of 'ce qu'on nomme du *jeu*', is able to see language as a living organism.

Any student of the English language soon finds the meaning of, and necessity for 'ce qu'on nomme du *jeu*'. It is extremely hard to lay down laws in English philology. But Mallarmé sees this as no disadvantage in his aside – 'tant la loi (la meilleure) offre partout d'échappées' (989). However, there is another much simpler aspect of language structure which applies to most languages and which Mallarmé discusses a little, even though it does not, strictly, have a place in a study of philology. This is the structure created by different parts of speech, and by the varying degrees of use words have. Mallarmé sees a division between 'les mots purs, voire nuls, abstraits, immobiles, d'une part, et de l'autre en pratiques et en règles mises en usage par le discours' (965). One only has to think of the sonnet 'en yx' to see what Mallarmé means by words that are 'purs, voire nuls'. It actually appears a secret gesture of affiliation between language evolution and literary language use that there should even be such words in the dictionary. Yet such words are not crucial to the poet's task. Each word, of whatever length or familiarity, has its part to play, and achieves its impact or significance in the same way. Mallarmé's sensitivity to that impact extends even to this comment on the first consonant of a word:

> en elle gît la vertu radicale, quelque chose comme le sens fonda-
> mental du mot. (965)

It is this 'sens fondamental', as distinct from the meaning of words, that Mallarmé is able to discuss and reveal in 'Les Mots Anglais'. At that same level of first impact rather than meaning, we must look at his comments on the different parts of speech.

These comments almost adopt the manner of a guide book, treating word types and parts of speech as more or less impressive exhibits of language:

> Termes quotidiens et populaires et de souvenir touchant, il sied
> de leur rendre honneur: quoique vous ayez pu vous attendre à
> trouver à leur place des vocables d'un sens général et synthétique
> (ceux-ci, l'âme même du langage, perdus entre les Isolés). Re-
> marquer ce fait que les mots les moins usités servent souvent de
> conducteurs, inattendus et précieux, entre une double acception
> distante de deux termes considérables. (919)

The apparently light touch of 'il sied de leur rendre honneur' carries more weight than appears, for, as Mallarmé goes on to explain, less familiar words serve as guides to the attention of the reader, and they would not, of course, even appear strange if it were not for the presence of familiar and less often noticed words. Mallarmé's comment on the 'small' words – articles, pronouns and prepositions – is even more interesting:

> Par exemple, l'article, le pronom, la préposition employée isolé-
> ment (c'est-à-dire pas en affixe) la conjonction et la précieuse
> interjection, geste spontané de l'organisme vocal de la race, sont
> Gothiques: très bien, mais, de cela même que ces Mots servent
> d'articulation au parler ou de pivots, ils demeurent, d'autre part,

toujours plus ou moins cachés à l'esprit qui les sous-entend, ainsi que l'atteste jusqu'à leur brièveté. (1047)

There is evidence here of Mallarmé's perception that language has an instinct (973), in the 'geste spontané de l'organisme vocal de la race'. An even more striking contribution to the writer's 'travail de mosaïque point rectiligne' (1026) appears in the image of these 'lesser' words as means of articulation or pivot in the structure of the text. Such words tend to pass unnoticed not only because their sense is that of a link and never stands alone, but also because they are actually, physically, short words on the page. On the other hand, introducing the section on proper names, we find:

> Mêlés encore à la Langue, leur sens tient l'imagination en éveil; autrement, incompréhensibles ou anciens, c'est par leur aspect presque bizarre. (1041)

If words like articles and prepositions too often pass unnoticed, proper names, on the other hand, often stand out too much and dominate the text. It is interesting that Mallarmé has more to say about prepositions and about proper names than he does about straightforward nouns and verbs; of the latter he merely says: 'Les Verbes; qu'il y aurait à dire à ce sujet!' (1023) without developing it any further. One might infer, though, from Mallarmé's comparatively sparse use of verbs[1] that he saw their emphatic and active qualities as a 'false' movement, providing without effort what the reader could himself create. Words whose sense is static – such as nouns, pronouns, some conjunctions and preposi- tions – call for a greater skill on the part of the writer, and greater involvement on the part of the reader. If the writer's aim is to use language as creatively as possible, then he will have less need of the gratuitous 'life' or movement that verbs can contribute. In the 'Varia- tions' Mallarmé even goes so far as to use punctuation and layout as virtual and sparse parts of speech. Hence we should not be surprised by this comment in a letter of 1887:

> La vieille sentence avec un verbe, invariable, me fait l'effet d'un chimère et reste, pour les grandes synthèses compliquées de sentiment, l'orgueil d'un autre art.[2]

Mallarmé's discussion of parts of speech does not throw light upon the sentence form, but on the way in which language, in defiance of the

---

[1] For a discussion of Mallarmé's apparent dislike of verbs, see Norman Paxton, *Development of Mallarmé's Prose Style* (Geneva, Droz, 1968).
[2] Mallarmé, *Propos*, p. 135.

traditional sentence form, expresses its life and movement. The potential expressiveness of language is far greater than the 'chimère' of subject, verb and predicate.

Those aspects of 'Les Mots Anglais' that the reader can pick out easily as particular to Mallarmé rather than to philology in no way disrupt the work, nor appear to be untimely intrusions on the part of the 'littérateur' into the grounds of a scientific study. Indeed the value of 'Les Mots Anglais', as of 'La Dernière Mode' is that it is in carrying out the task with all the scrupulousness that it demands that Mallarmé is able to point to so many factors that play a part in his notion of literature. The popular saying that 'you only get out what you put in', is peculiarly relevant in the case of 'Les Mots Anglais' and 'La Dernière Mode', since in both cases it is only by taking the task seriously that Mallarmé is able to arrive at certain perceptions useful both to him and to his readers. These perceptions serve as both explanation and even 'proof' of notions seen elsewhere in the more openly creative writing. Also, the discovery or confirmation of important ideas in unexpected contexts convinces the reader that he is witnessing the making of a creative language. When we read that words 'move' by their 'mirage interne' or by 'la réciprocité des feux distantes par leur inégalité mobilisés', we may think Mallarmé fanciful or purposely obscure. But in 'Les Mots Anglais' the reader – and one might imagine Mallarmé too – sees that intuitive discoveries in language can be confirmed in unexpected places. And these perceptions only arise because a study like 'Les Mots Anglais' teaches us to notice, and more importantly to feel what we read, to consider words not just as vehicles of sense but as entities in their own right.

4

'La Dernière Mode'

Seemingly the most extraordinary of Mallarmé's prose works, 'La Dernière Mode' forms a perfect complement to the revelations of 'Les Mots Anglais'. In that book the various literary perceptions appeared only implicit in the philological study, and thus remained at a preliminary or notional stage. 'Les Mots Anglais' may have been undertaken simply as a duty, but it does show what possibilities there could be in a less dutiful experiment.[1] In 'La Dernière Mode' we see how an essentially non-literary – and non-scientific – situation can provide a testing ground, an opportunity to 'prove' that the findings of 'Les Mots Anglais' are valid. Language can, even in a situation of apparently limited breadth and depth, perform its sense. It can be used in such a way that its impressiveness or reality is equal to that of the world to which it refers.

Writing 'La Dernière Mode' is further enhanced for Mallarmé by the fact that it is possible to perform two tasks at once. The 'abonnée' will find all she needs in the descriptions and advice that Mallarmé gives, while Mallarmé himself is free to *enjoy*, in a way that is both serious and light-hearted, the transformations of the everyday world and those of the language needed to present them. The delight evident in the translations of the 'Contes Indiens' is heightened by the fact that the spectacle of 'La Dernière Mode' is basically not an unreal one. We are not, here, in the realm of legend and fantasy, but intricately involved in the atmosphere given by a series of real objects. After one description of a ball dress, Mallarmé writes:

> Fermant les yeux à d'adorables motifs dont me tente la description, je poursuis, stricte et brève. (799)

Mallarmé is here using an almost journalistic idiom, but he intends a

---

[1] Mallarmé wrote 'La Dernière Mode' in 1874, three years before 'Les Mots Anglais'. There is no question of one's having prompted the other. For the reader of today, chronology is less important then the relative position of the two experiments within the total work.

truth: his great enjoyment of the descriptive task *does* demand that he limit his rapture. And neither the rapture nor the 'abonnée' would gain from more lengthy descriptions. When writing about materials however, it is necessary to be more precise, and enjoyment too can be given freer rein:

> Satins, velours et toutes les étoffes du soir, prennent là un chatoiement ou une profondeur, qu'une autre nuance, employée comme fond, serait inhabile à y apporter. (844)

The two words 'chatoiement' and 'profondeur' suggest a virtually physical appreciation of the objects being considered. The materials basic to high fashion are so rich and subtle that they cannot remain static when described, as is usually the case, but emanate an atmosphere which must, if due justice is to be done, be sensed physically. In an article on perfumes, Mallarmé writes:

> Tout à fait à la mode et luxueux, ces aromates n'ont, si l'on veut, rien à faire avec le cabinet de toilette: remplissant dans le boudoir les flacons bizarres de l'étagère, saxe, venise, bohème, etc. Verreries rares et porcelaines d'où s'échappe une odeur précieuse, quel charmant cadeau d'étrennes: et une boîte de parfums ne renfermera-t-elle pas une volupté bien autre que n'est le contentement apporté par le sac de bonbons. Je m'arrête parce qu'il y aurait, à ce sujet, mille choses curieuses à dire! (834)

There are reminders here of Baudelaire's fascination with perfumes and their 'volupté', and reminders too, of Mallarmé's predilection for the 'still-life'. This taste may seem in direct contrast with his tactile apprehension of objects. But a still-life is an arrangement of objects and seems to come to life because it is so arranged. As 'un souffle d'intelligence' or the imagination can make lists of words move, so a rich perfume can bring to life the 'cabinet de toilette'. In much of 'La Dernière Mode' we see these two phenomena join forces: the words both bring to life and suffuse with richness the objects of fashion.

The imprint that Mallarmé makes upon 'La Dernière Mode' is not only evident in the language used; it can also be seen in the references that are made throughout to poetry, poets, and books in general. Although literature is only of peripheral interest in a fashion magazine, it does play a rôle there, and the very difference between that rôle and the rôle that it plays for Mallarmé is revealing. For example, a typical 'abonnée' of 'La Dernière Mode' would probably envisage the poet as a figure from romantic myth. In one of the 'Chroniques de Paris', à propos of a play by d'Hervilly, Mallarmé writes:

Qu'aucun éventail ne s'agite, effarouché: car ce gynécée tant que le tome qui l'emprisonne en ses stances demeure fermé sur votre étagère, va et vient, rit et babille aux climats divers, libre parmi les aiguilles de glace, les bananiers ou les obélisques roses. Par une loi supérieure à celle qui, chez les peuples barbares, enferme véritablement la femme entre des murs de cèdre ou de porcelaine, le Poëte (dont l'autorité en matière de vision n'est pas moindre que celle d'un prince absolu) dispose avec la pensée seule de toutes les dames terrestres. (803)

Mallarmé jokes a little at the expense of his more timorous readers, but what is perhaps a more serious insult to them would certainly have passed unnoticed. The figure of the poet here holds sway over 'les dames terrestres' regardless of whether his works are actually read or not. It was evident in the 'Médaillons et Portraits' how important the notion of the Poet, or 'Maître' was to Mallarmé, and it appears again here, bereft now of all practical problems. (For the reader of 'La Dernière Mode' it does not matter whether or not the poet merits the title of Poet; he only has to uphold the mythology. A good hostess will always introduce with due reverence and awe a guest who is a Poet.) The framework of 'La Dernière Mode' not only allows the romantic image of the poet to have full status, it actually encourages it.

It allows too, for an existence of literature which is not merely romantic. Mallarmé often refers to the fact that the 'abonnée' is not likely to read literature, that her books will usually lie unopened. So, relishing the rich setting in which 'La Dernière Mode' is likely to be read, he can also enjoy the idea that books only exist in this setting in a state of possibility, like an unopened bottle of perfume:

Seule une dame, dans son isolement de la Politique et des soins moroses, a le loisir nécessaire pour que s'en dégage, sa toilette achevée, un besoin de se parer aussi l'âme. Que tel volume demeure huit jours entr'ouvert, comme un flacon, sur les soieries ornées de chimères, des coussins . . . (716)

It remains unopened or 'entr'ouvert', but essentially unread, and it is left to Mallarmé to make the connection between the setting of the room and the content of the book, while the occupant of the boudoir will probably only remember the title, then isolated but redolent:

le titre d'un tome, s'inscrit à jamais dans notre mémoire, bref et *complet*. (716) (emphasis mine)

The 'abonnée', simply knowing the title, adds an aura of literature or

poetry to her surroundings; while Mallarmé, certainly more familiar with
the contents, needs only the title as a rich reminder that the content is
perfectly compatible with the setting in which it remains unread. It
pleases Mallarmé more that the book should lie unread in such a setting
than that it should be read as a mere vehicle of sense. The situation thus
fits Mallarmé's *notion* of the book as it is apprehended out of variously
imperfect circumstances. It could not happen that a 'femme du monde',
much concerned with the clothes she wears and settings in which she
wears them, would actually read the text as Mallarmé reads it. Thus the
evidence points again to the displacement of theory and practice: the
book cannot, practically, be read in the setting that befits its atmosphere
(and thus it is more aptly left open and unread in that setting); while a
reading in an imperfect setting – in 'real' life – stimulates the 'nuage
d'impressions' that is so suggestive of an idealized setting:

> Un livre est tôt fermé, fastidieux, et on laisse le regard se délasser
> dans ce nuage d'impressions qu'à volonté dégage, comme les
> anciens dieux, la personne moderne pour l'interposer entre les
> aventures banales et soi. (717)

One of the greatest delights for Mallarmé in writing 'La Dernière
Mode' was that his 'abonnées' would indeed be very likely to read in
this way, superficially, in dilettante and desultory fashion, and that it
should not, for once, even matter that they should be such cursory
readers. Their whole aspect and attraction was such that it appeared
perfectly compatible with the substance of that which they were
actually unable to appreciate. Thus in the context of 'La Dernière
Mode', the reader virtually becomes the book, and the book itself is but
an ornament in a world of ornaments.

Such a world is not by any means bereft of ordinary dimensions.
That of time plays an important rôle. Mallarmé either has to write
before the event or after it, never at it – that is the place of the gossip
columnist or impartial master of ceremonies. In writing before the
event he is forced into what might otherwise look like an indulgence in
detail. For example:

> une Toilette de visite en velours et satin ardoise avec garniture de
> plume ondulée, une autre en cachemire rose avec bandes de gaze
> blanche brodées en soie plate; puis une Robe de Bal en poult-de-
> soie bleu avec tulle illusion jais blanc et guirlande de volubilis
> roses. (776)

Two circumstances – simple visiting, and the more grandiose Occasion –

have to be covered here. Details crowd one another, and so give an impression not only of types of clothing, but also of a type of life, the social whirl to which the 'abonnée' might aspire. Such descriptions are only preparatory, intended both to inform and to add to the excitement of preparation; they do not constitute the Occasion, but announce its possibility or its imminence. The compatibility of this situation with that of Mallarmé's prose as a whole – preparing the spectacle but not yet constituting it – is extraordinarily clear, yet does not interfere with the practical function of the language. In fact, the more practical and descriptive the language, the more obvious the parallel. Meticulous explanation can, if taken far enough, give a foretaste of the event itself. Mallarmé has a clear picture of the task in hand:

> Suivre l'existence parisienne dans ses plaisirs et ses obligations, partout, cérémonieuse ou intime, voilà encore la visée que montre une lecture même inattentive du Journal. Les fêtes: pour les fêtes? Oui, et parce qu'elles sont le prétexte et l'occasion à s'habiller. (762)

Even a swift or superficial reading of such a journal should, Mallarmé believes, offer the 'abonnée' a taste of the 'fêtes' to which she may or may not go. Also, since many readers would not be Parisians it is all the more necessary to create an image of the capital as focus of the fashionable world. The dimension of time must expand here to accommodate those for whom the social event is never in preparation, but beyond all hope of realization.

Mallarmé thus has to beguile both the blasée and the naïve reader. The near-dramatic flourish of presentation will arrest the attention of the first, and dazzle the second:

> Tissus, nuances de ces tissus, etc., tout ce que déjà nous annonçâmes avec quelque mystère, nouveautés à l'état presque encore d'échantillon chez d'illustres faiseuses, est maintenant connu et su de toutes les femmes. (780)

Such secrecy surrounds new styles and materials that the journalist, although he only describes trends and does not create them, seems to assume great power. To add to it, he can also draw upon the impact of foreign names and distant times in his descriptions:

> Les Etoffes pour Costumes habillés: Lyon nous offre ses fayes et ses failles, ses poults-de-soie, ses satins, ses velours à nuls autres pareils, ses gazes et ses tulles, ses crêpes de Chine acclimatés par

88

une fabrication qui, un jour, les exportera au pays même du thé; enfin, les tissus lamés d'or et d'argent, goût somptueux, magnifique, ressuscité de jadis. (781)

One does not even need to know the difference between all these materials to be impressed by them. Mallarmé, like the modern advertiser, clearly sets out to dazzle his reader, not in order to 'sell his ideas', but because the situation offers a great opportunity to evoke the atmosphere of a 'fête' simply by enumerating the qualities or its component parts. Though banal in meaning, the words 'Lyon nous offre ses fayes et ses failles' launch the reader, almost invite her to the 'fête'. Even clearer in its invitation is this:

> Ces étoffes: qu'en faire? avant tout des chefs-d'œuvre. Quant à moi, sans avoir pareille visée, je vais, sollicitée simplement par le désir d'esquisser tout de suite une toilette faite en l'un de ces délicieux cachemires tendus de tout à l'heure, céder à ce désir. (781)

Mallarmé's well-known modesty accords perfectly with the switchback of feminine illusion and realism; finally he gives in only to the desire to make a sketch and not a masterpiece. As he says elsewhere:

> On n'a qu'à le vouloir, pour se figurer une longue jupe à traîne de reps, de soie du bleu le plus idéal, ce bleu si pâle à reflets d'opale, qui enguirlande quelquefois les nuages argentés. (783)

In some of the 'Chronique' sections of the magazine, Mallarmé has a different perspective: he has to report on those events which gave 'éclat' to the preceding fortnight. In this situation he sees that understatement works better than excessive detail. He must suggest something like: 'out of all the wonders of the past fortnight, how can I pick out any one moment?'

> Et c'est maintenant, hélas! qu'il nous faut arrêter, car non seulement la Chronique de ce Journal, mais le Journal tout entier, y passeraient, s'il s'agissait de dire les soirs de ces derniers jours, qui sont redevenus des soirées. Un Mois et plus encore était derrière nous, avec son vaste rien qu'il fallait raconter: car comment, sans faire cela d'abord et sans remettre enfin à la quinzaine future le tableau de ce qui poind aujourd'hui et brillera alors d'un éclat très-vif, rattacher nos paroles de maintenant à l'écho d'une causerie lointaine, en même temps qu'à celles de bientôt; et, pour la première fois, prendre date? (734)

The rich and dazzling world that makes a 'soir' into a 'soirée' defies full graphic description; the writer must choose, arrange, and so create in words what is essential to the 'vaste rien'.[1] It matters neither to the 'femme du monde' nor to Mallarmé that one 'soirée' very much resembles another, or that, for reasons other than those Mallarmé gives here, it should be genuinely impossible to 'prendre date'. Such 'problems' are resolved in 'La Dernière Mode' by highlighting various aspects apparently inessential to the final effect, and so focusing both past and future revelations.

The objects of fashion

In 'La Dernière Mode' Mallarmé has to write of clothes, objects and settings that are all more elaborate, more rarefied than the normal. Thus a simple transcription of the difference between these and the ones that would merely serve some purpose unnoticed, can be made without any obvious peculiarity or effort of language. The accumulation of such differences constitutes the bread and butter of fashion. In another public situation, that of reporting on the 'Exposition de Londres' of 1872, Mallarmé shows how it is possible for descriptions of certain kinds of objects to give off an almost literary 'éclat'.

Some years after the Letters from the 'Exposition de Londres', Mallarmé wrote:

> Pavoisements, lueurs, c'était, cet été, celui de l'Exposition inoubliable pour beaucoup d'ici, à deux pas de l'ébat, et de l'engouement et du bruit: je songeais, devant tant d'abandon, à d'éternelles choses, et depuis j'ai continué, avec la reprise mondaine de la saison. (499)

We see here Mallarmé's fascination with the fashionable world and the hold it has upon time and upon the imagination. With its ephemeral 'pavoisements' and 'lueurs' it prompts thoughts of 'éternelles choses' which, for Mallarmé, can only be literary. Mallarmé's reports from the exhibition are written in unexceptionable public style, and the very simplicity of the largely graphic descriptions only serves to indicate that the interest for Mallarmé was that in such a situation language did not have to create any literary effect since reality, one might say, had done it instead. However, it was not that Mallarmé had the opportunity in

---

[1] The quality of the 'rien' in 'La Dernière Mode' can be compared with the first line of Mallarmé's poem 'Salut' (27): 'Rien, cette écume, vierge vers'. Although each 'rien' refers to something quite different, they are not different in tone and emphasis.

these Letters, of writing about works of art. The voluptuousness, often the vulgarity of the exhibits makes that clear from the start. One must consider, then, why the florid and the vulgar should constitute, in writing, an interesting point of departure.

The question is answered by the *level* at which each object is seen. For example:

> Des tendances moins rétrospectives sont indiquées par une somptueuse table de métal et de pierre, cuivres dorés et rouges, marbres bleus et rouges, ornementation d'amour et de guirlandes de M. *Christofle*. (667)

The reader does not simply envisage a table, but is given the features which distinguish this table and its rich ornamentation. We see it as a certain density of decoration rather than as a table. The only point at which the hand of Mallarmé might be sensed is in the last phrase – 'ornementation d'amour et de guirlandes', a slight ellipsis more reminiscent of the poet than of the reporter. Of another decorative element, flowers, we read:

> Quant aux fleurs, courtes et de couleurs tranchées, ce sont, n'est-ce pas? des imitations, artificielles, et faites pour jouer la mosaïque. (681)

Not only are the flowers artificial, but also they are seen as part of a pattern rather than as flowers. Thus transformed, they belong to a realm between reality and art. The clock, on the other hand, offers different possibilities:

> leur irrémédiable malheur demeure précisément que le sujet – un sujet pour un meuble chargé de nous avertir de l'heure! – accuse une facture magistrale. (668)

Mallarmé cannot see the clock as an object whose decoration only serves to heighten the effect of telling the time. Time needs no decoration, or, according to a romantic view of the world, time is all decoration. In either case, the sheer discrepancy of uniting time and decoration is overlaid by the simple possibility of pointing to both in the same context.

This situation demands a presentation which, although straight-forward, moves towards the partial obscuring of the original object in favour of a greater emphasis on the effect it creates. The parallel with one of the main objectives of Mallarmé's poetry could hardly be closer, and the poet's delight shows through the reporter's formality at the end of the second Letter:

Je suis heureux, Monsieur le Rédacteur en chef, que vous m'ayez donné, à l'intention de vos lectrices, l'occasion de répandre, sur ce luxe de soieries et de dentelles déployées, l'écrin de nos bijoux exposés. (673)

The reader feels that this is not merely an expression of politeness, that there is a genuine sense of gratitude for the opportunity to write about the Exposition. One revelation of Mallarmé's writing here is that the vulgar, when more or less adequately described in language is no longer necessarily seen as vulgar. Mallarmé's descriptions do not show the *extent* of the decorativeness (the mark of vulgarity, perhaps) but show the object as it appears through and is transformed by decoration. An attempt to reproduce in language the actual extent and effect of the excessive decoration would distort the reader's vision of the object, and be tedious to the writer.

It is evident from the Letters from the 'Exposition de Londres' that Mallarmé does not exclude objective reality, even of the most banal kind, from the possibilities of language. Sensitive perception of that reality not only allows for subtle effects of language, but actually appears, in the wide scope of 'La Dernière Mode', to create an expressive power as great as that of poetry. The only possible predicament of the poet confronted by the spectacle of the fashionable world is this:

Quelle réunion de richesses! Nous n'avons que deux choses à faire: ou songer une demi-journée devant chaque œuvre exquise, ou promener un de ces regards ravis et sagaces qui contiennent toute la somme de vision dont notre œil est capable pendant un instant, pour ne conserver, ensuite, que quelques notions exactes et générales. (683)

In 'La Dernière Mode' we see both the 'regards ravis et sagaces' and the 'quelques notions exactes et générales'. In practice the great gamut of splendour poses no problems for language; it is even useful that the writer should have to select, arrange and refine his material, for he is thus forced to follow the process of perception itself. To see how important that process is, one should look at a piece of writing where it is not evident at all: *Igitur*.

In *Igitur* Mallarmé explicitly sets out to 'solve the problem' of creative writing:

C'est un conte, par lequel je veux terrasser le vieux monstre de l'Impuissance, son sujet, du reste, afin de me cloîtrer dans mon grand labeur déjà réétudié. S'il est fait, je suis guéri. (1580)

92

The sense of powerlessness that the writer experiences 'devant l'Azur' or 'L'Idéal' is one which the writing of *Igitur* does not succeed in conquering.[1] Its weakness stems largely from Mallarmé's attempt to create a story out of his intuition of literary and imaginative processes. The basis of the story lies in 'l'esprit humain' moving towards its absolute; the real world is only present as an instrument of narrative. It is the direct concern with an ultimate condition of language which has a limiting effect on the language itself. It is not possible to 'faire le présent absolu des choses' by saying so, and in writing the phrase, Mallarmé succumbs to the temptation that he himself criticizes, that of believing that by listing precious stones one thereby creates them (870). If Mallarmé seems constantly to delay writing his 'Œuvre' by considering language from a series of largely non-literary vantage-points, his tactics are in a way justified by the composition of *Igitur*, where it is evident that he has not found an idiom which unites form and content. Since this 'conte' is an isolated moment in Mallarmé's work, it is reasonable to assume that he found the story form unsuccessful or at least less compelling than his other experiments.

If one compares the clock described in the Letters from the Exposition with the one that appears in *Igitur*, the reserve and lack of conviction of the latter is obvious:

> J'ai toujours vécu mon âme fixée sur l'horloge. Certes, j'ai tout fait pour que le temps qu'elle sonna *restât* présent dans la chambre, et devînt pour moi la pâture et la vie. (439)

It is here not the clock as object but the idea of time that preoccupies Mallarmé. His almost desperate expectation – that time's presence should remain fixed in the room – makes a demand on the reader's attention such that language cannot have the impact it had in the far more frivolous description of the clock at the Exhibition. Frivolous in reality, it offered possibilities to Mallarmé's language. The clock in *Igitur* is of greater philosophical importance, but its physical presence is hardly felt, and the language used to evoke it is proportionately weak.

A preliminary conclusion can be reached here concerning the relation of Mallarmé's language to real objects and settings. It appears that where language attempts to create an autonomous world distinct from the real world but related to it in structure, it has less effect *as* language,

---

[1] Writing like that of 'La Dernière Mode' seems to suggest that language which sets out to try and overcome deficiencies or defy them is doomed to failure as creative expression. If this is not true of all writers, it appears to be the case with Mallarmé.

perhaps because much of its strength must be directed towards sustaining its own autonomy.[1] On the other hand, when language merely *borrows* an aspect of reality it is proportionately freer to create its own effect, in the knowledge that circumstance – be it legend or the fashionable world – exists both as safeguard and as a 'point de départ' with which the reader will be familiar.

No 'point de départ' could be safer or more generous than that of 'La Dernière Mode'. Mallarmé does not only have to write about fashionable clothes; he must concern himself with the whole range of the 'abonnée's' interests. As 'Marliani-Tapissier-Décorateur' he talks about décor. The ceiling, for example:

> Blanc comme une feuille de papier sans poème et plus vaste, ou voilé de nuage sur un azur à tant le mètre, tel est le *ciel* offert au regard de l'hôte, les yeux levés et enfoui dans son fauteuil. (770)

The 'Cabinet et Bibliothèque' receives an elegy even more reminiscent of Mallarmé's poems and remarks about the place in which books can be read and written:

> avec des livres nombreux à dos de basane marqué de titres d'or, le Site, éclairé par un lustre hollandais, est (grâce au peu d'élévation de nos logis) simple, beau, enfermé et solitaire: un peu comme une chambre luxueuse de navire. (771)

The description moves between the mature and specific 'Site' and the boyish vision of a study that resembles a ship's cabin. The rows of richly bound books link these two extremes: merely decorative to the 'abonnée', they are essential to Mallarmé.

The objects of which he writes are not in any way 'objets d'art', but simply objects transformed by a literary imagination and by a regard for design or decoration. 'Le beau ordinaire' in no way challenges language (as it might be a challenge to write about a work of art[2]) yet it does demand more than simple 'reportage'. Hence there is a valuable balance between the reality of objects and their transformation by decoration here, or, elsewhere, language. 'La Décoration! tout est dans ce mot' (712). Mallarmé is emphatic, and it is not hard to see why. It is the decorative element in objects which contributes to the spectacular or impressive whole. If an object were more than decorative, if it were a work of art, then its dominance would detract from the evocative

---

[1] Such autonomy is traditionally granted to poetry, but not to prose.
[2] Compare the situation in which Mallarmé does write of a work of art: the pieces in the 'Médaillonsits' et Portra on the Impressionist painters.

qualities of the merely decorative or ornamental. The work of art is perhaps the object completely, or as far as possible, transformed by the medium of art; while the decorative object is only partially transformed. In the world of fashion, reality is transformed so far as to be decoration, not so far as to be art. The basic alphabet of objects necessary to fashion to a considerable degree lose their fundamental functions in order to bring out the presence of the decorative.

However, if objects appear so transformed as to lose their original functions, it is only through having so elaborately and distinctly fulfilled them. In order to play a part in a decorative spectacle, it is necessary first to have rehearsed it. Thus distinctions must be made between one kind of dress and another:

> avec tel autre Costume vous pouvez garder la maison, abritée contre la longueur des heures par cette soie ou ces dentelles, ravie et à moitié nouvelle pour vous-même. (762)

The 'femme du monde' admiring a new self in the mirror at home is also preparing for a different situation and different clothes:

> 'Une robe, traînante et collante, en dentelle noire, semée bizarrement d'acier bleu à reflets d'épée: puis dans les cheveux relevés en diadème, quatre rangs d'énormes diamants mêlés à leur ombre, perdus dans la noire splendeur.'
> Quelle vision miraculeuse, tableau à y songer plus encore qu'à le peindre: car sa beauté suggère certaines impressions analogues à celles du poète, profondes ou fugitives. (832-3)

Although Mallarmé says that such a vision should be dreamed rather than described, it is only by close attention to the detail that the state of dreaming can actually be reached. Similarly, the poet observes the banality of language and of reality, and creates out of that, rather than out of any dream, his poetry. Mallarmé must describe the detail and even the function of fashion in order to evoke the 'éclat' it has. That detail is such that a short step transforms the real situation into a situation of literature. If fashion journalism constitutes a foretaste, a credible prediction, of the effect of fashion, it can also offer a taste of the effect that literary language can have.

The image of fashion

Mallarmé does not, as another might, use the image of fashion. He cannot, in writing a fashion journal, follow this advice of Rodenbach:

Est-ce que les mots ne sont pas fanés comme des visages? Mettons les mots en un tel éclairage qu'ils aient l'air fardé; et nous créons ainsi l'apparence d'une nouvelle langue, qui sera maquillée, faisandée, une vraie langue de décadence, conforme aux temps où nous sommes.[1]

Rodenbach's advice ignores the notion that it is only meticulous observation of the real world which can operate the transformation of language. The idea that it is possible to 'maquiller' language and so transform its expressiveness, is equivalent to the illusion that by disguise or dressing up one is changing the reality of the world. Mallarmé does not set out to embellish language or to use only the most brilliant words. Neither does he, by a wise and constant distancing from the task in hand, make fashion an intricate metaphor for language. Thomas Carlyle, in *Sartor Resartus* does just this. He never fails to make his intentions clear, and the book is a virtuoso performance of metaphor:

> Language is the Garment of Thought: however, it should rather be, Language is the Flesh-Garment, the Body, of Thought. I said that Imagination wove this Flesh-Garment; and does not she? Metaphors are her stuff. . . still fluid and florid, or now solid grown and colourless? If those same primitive elements are the osseous fixtures in the Flesh-Garment, Language – then are Metaphors its muscles and tissues and living integuments.[2]

This straightforward symbolism entirely avoids the process of transformation which for Mallarmé is the basis of the diverse literary events in which he involves himself. Although the effect of Carlyle's writing is clearly entertaining, it is not because of the qualities of either language or clothes, but because of the direct parallel drawn between the two. The reader merely understands Carlyle's words, smiles perhaps, and passes on. There can be no question of those varying patterns of trust and involvement which distinguish response to literature. From the beginning it is clear that the words are only a primary stage inviting participation in a quite different reality:

> The beginning of all Wisdom is to look fixedly on Clothes, or even with armed eyesight, till they become transparent.[3]

Language exists here at an almost gleeful level of enigma, in order to take the reader on to a sphere already posited as 'more significant':

[1] Georges Rodenbach, *L'Elite* (Paris, Bibliothèque Charpentier, 1899), p. 49.
[2] Thomas Carlyle, *Sartor Resartus* (Chapman and Hall, 1885–8), p. 49.
[3] *Ibid.* p. 45.

In a Symbol there is concealment and yet revelation: here therefore, by Silence and by Speech acting together, comes a double
significance.[1]

Mallarmé's writing in 'La Dernière Mode' does not posit a 'third man'
so clearly; indeed to do so would be to deny participation in language
as a means of communication, in favour of a reality suggested behind it.
Carlyle's writing is based on theoretical, if humorous ground; whereas
Mallarmé's is based on practical ground, not within the event but in
preparation for it, at a stage where involvement with details is all-
important. It would clearly be impossible for Mallarmé's language to
follow the details of fashion and its attendant world and at the same
time perform a symbolic task. But from time to time Mallarmé does
make explicit his delight with the possible parallels between the world
of fashion and the world of language. The very difference between the
way he expresses his delight, and the way Carlyle expressed his is itself
revealing. For example:

> M. Worth, seul, a su créer une toilette aussi fugitive que nos
> pensées. (783)

or:

> Une robe, étudiée et composée selon les principes appelés à
> régner un hiver, est moins vite inutile et défraîchie qu'une
> Chronique même de quinzaine: avoir la durée de tulle illusion ou
> des roses artificielles imitant les roses et la clématite, voilà
> vraiment le rêve que fait chaque phrase employée à écrire, au
> lieu d'un conte ou d'un sonnet, les nouvelles de l'heure.[2] (784-5)

In Carlyle, language, like clothes, appears to cover some more fundamental significance; in Mallarmé, the parallel between the two is quite
different. Mallarmé is interested in the way that the style of a dress can
resemble the ephemeral quality of thoughts, or the way in which its
spectacular impressiveness stems largely from its artificiality. The considerable and protracted artifice of the fashionable world has an
'éclat' not because it is entirely unreal, but because it is a transformation of an ordinary world of clothes and people. As Mallarmé shows,
language is not concerned with being as real as the rose it describes,
nor is it so artificial as to disown the rose. It re-produces those qualities
of the rose which have the durability of 'tulle illusion ou des roses

[1] *Ibid.* p. 151.
[2] Once again, the phrase 'voilà vraiment le rêve' reminds us of the famous
comment: 'le suggérer, voilà le rêve'. (869)

97

artificielles'. The fashionable world thus appears to be situated at a point in relation both to reality and to total artifice which is compatible with the needs of Mallarmé's notion of literary language. We are not concerned with a symbolic or even a metaphorical situation, as in Carlyle's writing, but with a compatibility of level.

What guarantees the real and unreal splendour of both literature and fashion is a reversibility of language and object. The language of fashion clothes a pantomime which would not exist without that language, just as 'a poet's words are of things that do not exist without the words'.[1] Fashion depends upon superfluities of decoration, and literature upon a measure of distinctiveness and sometimes apparent obscurity, that give each a certain 'finish' separating them from normality. Though precarious and possibly ridiculous, the transformation of the real into the unreal, of the necessary into the unnecessary, is as compelling as the process which turns method into dream. The process accords object with effect so subtly and so minutely that there can be no question of saying: 'on the one hand there is spectacle and on the other hand there is a spectacular thing'. Nor can one say: 'here is a language of literature, and over there is literature'.

In the tribute to Villiers we saw how Mallarmé was fascinated – both seriously and delightedly – by the phenomenon of distillation or nobility. The world of fashion demonstrates just such a process; it is constantly seen to ride the surf rather than swim in the sea, and yet does so with the naïveté of a child following a magician's act. In order to follow the world of fashion through its act, Mallarmé is obliged to put language through a series of statuesque poses, each involving a high point of decorativeness. It is necessary to go through extremely precise operations of descriptions which, without the analogue between fashion and literature, would appear only to be exceptionally cautious descriptions meant to create the clearest possible representation. The world of fashion makes the further illuminating point that all the care and precision do not go towards the creation of something that is seen for its precision; they contribute to an impression only, an impression of splendour or grandeur, of Spectacle. Similarly, the almost mathematical care that goes into certain kinds of writing is not ultimately seen as care or precision. Reading is an operation that reciprocates the precision of manufacture, and culminates in an impression or experience at a level not unlike that of the social occasion.

There is, too, evidence of the complicity between fashion and language in the discriminations Mallarmé has to make in order to dis-

[1] Wallace Stevens, *The Necessary Angel* (Faber, 1960), p. 32.

tinguish one fashion from another. Fashion is not novelty (despite designers' claims), but variation of existing themes. In one ensemble it is the 'façon seule de la jupe' which is distinctive. In another:

> Si les tissus classiques du bal se plaisent à nous envelopper comme d'une brume envolée et faite de toutes les blancheurs, la robe elle-même, au contraire, corsage et jupe, moule plus que jamais la personne: opposition savante entre le vague et ce qui doit s'accuser. (797)

The ball-dress, and, indeed, the description of it, serves to

> rendre légère, vaporeuse, aérienne pour cette façon supérieure de marcher qui s'appelle danser, la divinité apparue en leur nuage. (797)

The movement of the writing is not a simple one that proceeds from description to function; it indicates the relation of that movement to the nature of the reality concerned. A ball-dress cannot be described without some indication that it is a dress for dancing in, and not for morning wear. Similarly, creative writing in some measure indicates by its form the nature of its contents. The apparently commonplace and insignificant in the realm of literature can be given life and validity by the illustration of a completely different though compatible realm. Description gives 'rien que de parfait, d'exact et d'absolu' (831); while the movement of that description is more explicit and offers:

> une opposition délicieuse et savante entre le vague et ce qui doit s'accuser. (797)

All aspects of 'La Dernière Mode' offer Mallarmé the opportunity of writing with the effect of expressing the qualities of language as well as the varieties of fashion. The secondary articles – on interior decoration, 'haute cuisine', city events – all reflect a world which, evoked by the most graphic description, recalls the quality or 'éclat' of literature. However, Mallarmé does not postulate each moment of writing about fashion as a symbol or even metaphor for parallel moments in writing (about) literature. He is not trying to make the significance of fashion 'reach' the significance of language, and in this sense his writing is not in the simple sense 'précieux'.[1] There is no measure of obscurity in the connection between fashion and language. The parallel does not imply a symbolism operating a subordination of means to end. 'Préciosité'

[1] Cf. the perceptions of René Bray in *La Préciosité et les Précieux* (Paris, Editions Albin Michel, 1948), part IV, chapter I.

suggests not only obscurity but also an element of tension caused by metaphor that attempts to capture as it were 'more than reality'. The reader does not sense that quality which Bray sees as basic to 'préciosité':

> Elle [la préciosité] naît d'un effort qui n'atteint pas son but, d'une tension excessive; elle est inadéquation entre la poésie rêvée et la poésie exprimée.[1]

This quality is sometimes evident in the writing of the 'Variations', but in 'La Dernière Mode' the parallel between fashion and language is so extended and so constant (the reader feels that there is little question of one aspect's being any more 'significant' than any other) that the 'abonnée' would certainly not notice it. While to the reader who is only concerned with the element that is Mallarmé's, any possible tension in the parallel is relieved by Mallarmé's evident enjoyment of the situation, an enjoyment which is manifest sometimes in explicit parallels between fashion and literature, and sometimes in the simplicity of carrying out a public task. There is no question of succeeding or failing to 'keep up' the parallel, or of over-working its possibilities. Mallarmé obviously undertook the task because he sensed its possible wealth as an exploration of language. Thus one might say that there is 'préciosité' in his basic attitude, but that the situation mostly prevents its becoming explicit. Where it does become explicit we find usually something like: 'une toilette aussi fugitive que nos pensées' (783), a simile that is merely a throw-away to the 'abonnée'. As a fashion journalist Mallarmé is fully allowed these stylistic devices; they are even expected in such a situation.

Other devices are also expected. Mallarmé can admit the simple pleasure of describing certain objects. In so doing he will appear to address the reader with a tacit comment of the kind: 'this is so beautiful that it gives me pleasure to write about it'. While his private pleasure is that the description, the saying of the object *is* genuinely as impressive to him as the seeing:

> Collier de chien. Qu'est-ce? Je le dis simplement pour le dire: un petit ruban en velours noir qui, derrière le cou dont il fait le tour, s'attache par une boucle carrée, dans laquelle il passe et tombe. Mille lettres en diamants étincellent avec l'éclat captivant d'un secret qui se montre et ne se livre pas: prénoms et noms entrelacés de celle qui porte le collier et de celui qui a fait don. (746)

The operative words, for the reader of Mallarmé, are 'je le dis pour le

---

[1] *Ibid.* p. 319.

dire'. It is a confession of enjoyment that a straightforward graphic description should create such effects. Fashion can be, as Mallarmé says elsewhere 'perle à perle raconté' (714) without excuse or explanation. The initials on a necklace are even half-concealed by the splendour of the diamonds in which they are spelled out. Mallarmé does not point explicitly to any parallels here. Yet in writing this description his language must appear mannered or euphuistic, as the language of poetry also can. What is more important than the similarity between this writing and poetry, is the relation of each to reality. Mallarmé's joy in writing about the 'collier de chien' is that he is inventing nothing; that his words reflect as truly as possible what he sees. This is also true of his creative writing, though in a less obvious way. There too language transcribes what the writer sees, and what he sees is considerably affected by his understanding of the nature of language. Hence, where creative language can sometimes be described in a general way as 'précieux', that of fashion journalism appears to deserve the epithet in two ways. First it is bound, of its nature, to appear mannered and un-real; second, the often-glimpsed parallel between literature and fashion in the writing of 'La Dernière Mode', makes Mallarmé's form of journa-lism even more susceptible to the epithet.

It is neither a relevant accusation nor a just compliment to say that the writing of 'La Dernière Mode' is 'précieux'. In one general sense it was bound to be, and only occasionally does Mallarmé give more speci-fic evidence. In general his writing is deft and deliberate enough to prevent our noticing, or even thinking of the work as a precarious private enterprise. It is only when our attention is turned away from the writing itself that we are able to impose rationally the 'précieux' parallel between fashion and language. It is not noticeable in reading because Mallarmé keeps our attention focused upon numbers of appa-rently minute details in the quality and variation of objects. A poem may be made up of similar details, yet the result there is often obscure or at least enigmatic. In the context of 'La Dernière Mode' much can be left out without confusing the reader. Furthermore, whereas in poetry the enigmatic presentation of reality usually seems to suggest an un-reality or ideal only partially reached, in the world of fashion all that is demanded is an aspect of each object. The ideal only partially reached is here the cumulative effect of such objects, and Mallarmé can satisfy his readers with only a foretaste of that. Without making any mention of poetry, he is able to restore some equilibrium there too.

The objects of fashion are compatible with those of poetry since they clearly exist at a level between the banal and the ideal. Never banal, that is the first commandment of fashion, yet only ideal in the degree to which they contribute to an accumulation of splendour, while retaining elements that unite them indisputably to normal objects. The butterfly, for example, as a fashionable decoration, does not have to look exactly like a real butterfly, nor does it have to appear in a setting natural to it:

> Courrier presque exceptionnel que le présent: car voué d'abord aux fêtes, il n'a trait enfin qu'à des solennités ou à des plaisirs véritablement très-rares. Quoique réel et très-réel, son rôle, dans l'ensemble de ceux de la saison est de porter le cachet véritable de la Fantaisie. Ce cachet, il lui sera donné surtout par une nouvelle complétant les informations qui précèdent: c'est, quoi? l'annonce d'un emblématique Papillon qui, vaste, superbe, taillé dans les tissus légers et délicieux, élèvera son vol immobile à hauteur, Mesdames, de l'une ou de l'autre de vos joues. (764)

The butterfly as a decoration is not so much a transformed object as a transformatory one; its presence alters, for example, a hair style:

> Vos frisures feront tomber leurs anneaux dans l'intervalle des deux ailes. (764)

We are not concerned with whether the butterfly looks real, only with the effect it has on the ensemble, and the way in which it contributes to the transformation of the ensemble.

The fan is another case in point still more interesting because it also appears in Mallarmé's poetry. In the world of 'La Dernière Mode' the fan is a purely decorative piece of modesty, its practical purpose inconsiderable, it constitutes, visually, the only object between the 'femme du monde' and her setting. Its movement is one of fluttering, a movement that is highly evocative of the physical and emotional situation in which it exists, and it is the movement, rather than the shape of the fan, heightened by its decorations or jewels, which is most obvious. Hence it is not the substance and shape of the fan which are important, but only the impression its movement gives.[1] Similarly:

> la garniture dominante pour robe, qui sera la plume; rien de joli et de chatoyant à l'œil n'est-ce pas? comme cet ornement, que la barbe en soit frisée, qu'elle soit luisante et lisse. (729)

It is the texture of the feather that is important; it is situated at a level between the simple physical basis and the inapprehensible (the 'je ne

---

[1] See also Mallarmé's delicate image of the fan in 'Quant au Livre', p. 374.

sais quoi' of effect or atmosphere in any spectacle). Most of the objects which Mallarmé describes in 'La Dernière Mode' are rich in atmosphere and suggestion. In one of the 'Eventail' poems, on the other hand, we see what can happen when the sensibility of the poet develops the possibilities offered by the objective world:

> Avec comme pour langage
> Rien qu'un battement aux cieux
> Le futur vers se dégage
> Du logis très précieux. (57)

The poem provides the language that the form of the fan suggests, and while its expressiveness is great, there enters an element of ingenuity – 'that the movement of a fan should actually suggest this' – which is genuine, if highly accomplished 'préciosité'. It is highly accomplished since the impact of the language actually takes precedence over the possible strangeness or strain of the relation between fan and language.

In 'La Dernière Mode', on the other hand, the question of strain does not even arise, since the reader sees only the possibility offered by the qualities of certain objects. Despite the splendid effects, language is still firmly attached to the presentation of objective reality. The point is not that the 'exercise' of writing about fans and feathers appears valuable, but that the existence of such objects suggests the possibility of writing, as far as possible, the sensation they offer. The 'Eventail' poems offer a virtual 'language of the fan' which may turn out to be a silent one:

> Vertige! voici que frissonne
> L'espace comme un grand baiser
> Qui, fou de naître pour personne,
> Ne peut jaillir ni s'apaiser. (58)

But the objects of 'La Dernière Mode' have, so to speak, no language other than themselves; they are seen as partial transformations of past models, and so invite further transformation: for the 'femme du monde' at the next social event, and for Mallarmé, in the processes of language.

Perhaps the most compelling feature of such a transformation is that we are only conscious of the origin (the objects) and not of the end of the process (as in the fairy story where we actually see the frog turn into the prince). The reader can discover how language and fashion are related, in a situation where there is none of the strain that is detectable in the 'Eventail' poems. These last challenge the perceptions made in 'Les Mots Anglais' concerning the possible correlation of language and reality; while the language of 'La Dernière Mode' shows us the kind of perception the poet must have in order to be able even to consider the creation of a written 'Eventail'. He must see:

> Qu'il glisse, ce châle, des épaules avec ses plis orientaux et enveloppe d'autres merveilles: tout le délicieux écrin que nous avons, pierre à pierre ou perle à perle, raconté. (714)

His descriptions must suggest not only the charm of the present object, but also its quality of precursor of 'the real spectacle'. The whole of the writing about fashion is of course concerned with preparation for fashionable events; and this situation is itself compatible with the effects of language made in the descriptions. The writer is always moving 'perle à perle', while the invitation 'qu'il glisse, ce châle', suggests not only a sensuous reality, but also the imaginative reality of the movement which pre-figures revelation. The sentence itself moves imperceptibly from one world to another, from rich material gliding smoothly from the shoulders, to the sensation of describing the richness of that material. Mallarmé endows all the materials he describes with a splendour befitting their eventual use rather than their present state:

> Le génie qui métamorphosa des tissus en papillons et en fleurs le cède encore devant la splendeur pure et simple des tissus eux-mêmes, tulle blanc lamé d'argent à côté de bandes de satin blanc, ou poudré d'or ainsi que de la poussière de gemmes multicolores. Pas d'ornementation inutile dans ce cas, ni de surcharges vaines, autres que les mille complications tirées de la *façon* seule de la jupe, volants, bouillonnés, placés comme ceci, comme cela, hauts, bas: rien de plus que de prestige éparpillé et lumineux. (799)

The last phrase of this passage can be taken as a summing up of the 'abonnée's' sense and anticipation of splendour, and yet it is also a just comment by Mallarmé as well, on his own terms. Such an accumulation – where materials, aided by 'la *façon* seule de la jupe', provide the richness – constitutes 'ce prestige éparpille et lumineux'. At the same time the virtuosity of language needed to bring out the details that establish its brilliance resembles a different, but parallel inventory of language tones.

The effect of sustained involvement in such a preparation is almost hypnotic. The reader is led through a series of colours, tones and styles whose impact is such that language is as noticeable as the images of fashion it presents. Poetry, on the other hand, is concerned with keeping up a delicate balance between language and perceived or felt reality. The prose of 'La Dernière Mode', by remaining scrupulously close to observed reality, creates a powerful effect of the *potential* expressiveness of language. Northrop Frye makes the observation that:

> Just as extreme realism of 'trompe l'œil' in painting seems to acquire, when pursued far enough, the unnatural glittering of hallucination, so it is prose, the rhythm of ordinary conscious-ness, which provides the corresponding quality in literature.[1]

The quality of hallucination may not be the chief effect at which literature aims, but the fact that it is evident, and outside poetry, suggests that Mallarmé had seen certain fundamental expressive quali-ties in language. Part of his discovery was that such expressiveness does not have to belong to the realm of unreality traditionally associated with poetry. A faithful observation and transcription of certain aspects of reality can create it as readily, if not more easily. The poem's hallucina-tory or enchanted qualities arise from the fact that we cannot see why it is so. The prose of 'La Dernière Mode' can show us that such qualities are not lost when we know both the details and the general effect of the reality concerned. The description of a dress – as advertisers well know – may be far more compelling than the real thing. Reduced to such everyday terms, Mallarmé's fascination with 'La Dernière Mode' be-comes more understandable, and it is not hard to see why, on re-considering the enterprise, he should say:

> un journal, La Dernière Mode, dont les huit ou dix numéros parus servent encore quand je les dévêts de leur poussière, à me faire longtemps rêver. (1625)

'La Femme': the subject of fashion

It is perhaps because Mallarmé does not set out to propose, in 'La Dernière Mode', an autonomous realm of language, that he very nearly succeeds in doing so. He achieves this by what looks like in-essential perception of surfaces, not depths. Some of Oscar Wilde's aphorisms are close in spirit to Mallarmé's enterprise. For example:

> The aim of art is simply to create a mood.[2]

or

> In matters of grave importance, style, not sincerity is the vital thing.[3]

---

[1] Northrop Frye, *The Well-Tempered Critic* (Bloomington Indiana U.P., 1963), p. 91.
[2] Oscar Wilde, *Complete Works* (Collins, 1948), p. 981.
[3] *Ibid.* p. 359.

Such attitudes seem to deny all possibility of depth and focal point. The fashionable world certainly has more style than sincerity; equally certainly it creates a mood. Yet decorative or stylish surface has a value beyond that of frivolous embellishment. A strong consciousness of surfaces, apparently denying any reality of 'subject', actually permits a clearer virtual view, or intuition, of the reality beneath, much as the symbol tends to give a clearer view of the thing symbolized. However, where symbolism isolates the object, consciousness of surface unites surface and object in an obvious rhythm or movement which, paradoxically, allows the reality beneath a greater presence and expressiveness. The realities with which literature, and especially poetry, are concerned, are such that they are better expressed by a rhythm of surface than by a stationary precision of depth. Thus, in Mallarmé's poetry and in much of his prose, the reader does not so much see the subject or focal point as feel the impact of its discrete but positive presence.

It is interesting to see how Mallarmé deals with the question of the basic 'subject' of 'La Dernière Mode':

> Somme toute, jamais ne régnèrent plus superbement les tissus opulents et même lourds, le velours et presque les brocarts d'argent et d'or, non moins que, léger, moelleux, clair, le nouveau cachemire qui se porte le soir; mais parmi cette enveloppe, somptueuse ou simple, plus qu'à aucune époque, va transparaître la Femme, visible, dessinée, elle-même, avec la grâce entière, de son contour ou les principales lignes de sa personne (alors que, par derrière, la magnificence vaste de la traîne attire tous les plis et l'ampleur massive de l'étoffe). (833)

Out of the accumulated splendour of surface and setting 'va transparaître la Femme', or the essence of 'La Dernière Mode'. It is no real shock to see the 'heroine' here; Mallarmé is not altering his own rôle in order to bring her into view. Yet the way in which he introduces her is remarkable for its emphasis. Throughout 'La Dernière Mode' we have in effect seen 'les principales lignes'; we have seen, from various tangents, the space into which she is to step. It thus seemed scarcely necessary that she should appear. Even the feminine minuteness of the perceptions always guaranteed her existence. For example:

> Toutefois, la mode ne se répète pas et, si une pareille ornementation, nette, dure et déjà connue, va alterner avec la plume floue, molle et toute nouvelle, insistons, certes sur un point, c'est

que, les costumes donnés, il reste véritablement si peu de soie à
découvert, que cette garniture presque ancienne nécessite la
trouvaille de dessins et d'un mode tout autres de l'appliquer.
(729)

Such minute, even over-scrupulous attention to detail results in the
effect described in the earlier quotation. Clothes neither hide nor disguise a woman, but allow her to appear, and to a certain extent prefigure the kind of appearance she is going to make.

Taking up once again the parallel between the fashionable world and
language, it is not hard to read the appearance of 'La Femme' as an indication also of the 'Idée même et suave' (368), or that which is essential to literature. The essential appears as a reflection at the centre of
varied, colourful, *in*essential projections. It is not necessary, in the
framework of 'La Dernière Mode', to mention the centre of it all, 'la
Femme', except in the manner of a journalist who wants to make an
ancient truth into a gimmick (for example that 'femininity will be the
theme of the Spring collection'); and the fact that it is not necessary
is highly compatible with Mallarmé's view of the 'subject' of writing.
Mallarmé frequently refers to his notion that the subject of literature
appears by writing the effect rather than the 'chose':

> Tout le mystère est là: établir les identités secrètes par un deux
> à deux qui ronge et use les objets, au nom d'une centrale pureté.[1]

The fashionable world is also dependent upon the balance and rhythm
of effect, even if apparently lacking the 'centrale pureté' of language.
It encounters, too, the same problems about the placing of what appears
to dominate. In a situation whose effect depends upon consistency of
'éclat' and not upon isolated examples of brilliance, it is not easy to
accommodate that which demands the status of focal point.

The jewel is, of course, the pinnacle of decoration in dress; it is intended to be the focal point, the highlight of the display. If 'La Femme'
is basic to the world of 'La Dernière Mode', the jewel is its apex. The
effect of clothes and wearer is that of an apparition; whereas the jewel
seems to constitute a definitive presence. In the first issue of 'La
Dernière Mode', Mallarmé discusses the nature of the jewel:

> Aujourd'hui, n'ayant pas même, par le fait, sous la main les
> éléments nécessaires pour commencer une toilette, nous voulons
> entretenir nos lectrices d'objets utiles à l'achever: les Bijoux.
> Paradoxe? non: n'y a-t-il pas, dans les bijoux, quelque chose de

[1] Mallarmé, *Propos*, p. 148.

107

permanent, et dont il sied de parler dans un courrier de Modes, destiné à attendre les modes de juillet à septembre.

Cherchons le Bijou, isolé, en lui-même. Où? partout: c'est-à-dire *un peu* sur la surface du globe, et *beaucoup* à Paris: car Paris fournit le monde de bijoux. (711)

The invitation 'Cherchons le Bijou, isolé, en lui-même' is not taken up immediately. Mallarmé discusses different types and fashions in jewellery before returning to the quality of the 'bijou isolé'. He sees the necessity – and the charm – of telling the reader of the extended and concentrated collection that Paris offers. When he does come back to the art of wearing jewellery, he writes:

> et je conseillerais à une dame, hésitant à qui conférer les dessins d'un bijou désiré, de la demander, ce dessin, à l'Architecte qui lui construit son hôtel, plutôt qu'à la faiseuse illustre qui lui apporte sa robe de gala. Tel, en un mot, l'art du Bijou. (712)

If the reader can answer the question 'why an architect?', he is well on the way to understanding Mallarmé's notion of the Subject, or focal point of a piece of writing. The point which arises in connection with the jewel as high point of the display is: how is the centrepiece to stand out as such, and not as mere component part? Or: how, out of the dazzling display of objects in either the world of fashion or the world of poetry, is it possible to distinguish a Subject? What Mallarmé shows us is that the subject is not the topmost diamond on the tiara, nor is it the fan that gives the title to the poem; it is that which emanates from the whole arrangement.

Mallarmé often refers to the necessity of structuring, and indeed his failure to appreciate Rimbaud's work certainly stemmed in part from his reaction against the spontaneous appearance of the writing. In a letter to René Ghil, Mallarmé says:

> Vous peut-être, c'est la tentative de poser dès le début de la vie la première assise d'un travail dont l'architecture est comme dès aujourd'hui de vous; et de point produire (fût-ce des merveilles) au hasard.[1]

The comments on 'le bijou' in 'La Dernière Mode' seem to support this. If the jewel appears as the culmination of a spectacle comprising dress, décor, and so on, if it is an ineffable moment in the spectacle, then its shape and position should not be declared by a mere grammarian who

---

[1] Mallarmé, *Propos*, p. 120.

can parse the folds and complications of one part of the ensemble – the clothes – but by one who has a sense of the whole. Similarly, the poet is not one who can state something like 'Beauty is Truth, Truth Beauty', but one who can show by the whole of his writing that it is so. For Mallarmé, an architect is not merely someone who designs buildings. We have seen how the structure of a dress, although appearing amidst 'brouillards d'or et de pierreries' (797), is essential to the effect of general splendour, and how only a precise series of descriptions can lead to an effect of hallucination or enchantment. The notion is reminiscent of the observations in 'Les Mots Anglais' concerning the way in which an investigation of rules in language can actually show the expressiveness of language. The sense of placing that gives full effect to a jewel in its setting would seem to be part of the 'architectural' task, since a chance placing of it is generally not adequate. But an important reservation must be made, namely, that abiding by rules and sense of architecture does not rely for its effects upon a straightforward symmetry, but rather creates a sense of symmetry out of that which, in real life and measurement, is not actually symmetrical.[1] The principle is an extension of the Greek technique of making pillars slightly curved in order that they should appear straight. Out of the discussion of jewels there appears a riddle, diverting enough for the world of fashion, but central to Mallarmé's notion of the expressiveness of language: when is a jewel not a jewel? When it is in the middle. Without making an explicit parallel between words and jewels, Mallarmé shows here, as an implicit culmination of ideas hinted at elsewhere, that the notion of a jewel in language – the 'mot juste', the so-called perfection of arrangement in language that characterizes poetry – can be illustrated by an explanation of the use of jewels.

In a description of a fan, Mallarmé points out: 'Le Sujet se place de côté et non au milieu.' (714) The 'Sujet', with its capital 'S', is a clear reminder that Mallarmé is not merely writing about fashionable decoration, though of course the smooth context is not 'marred' by any explicit suggestion of another relevance. The exact reason why 'le Sujet se place de côté et non au milieu' will be made clear in the writing of the 'Variations'. It has to do with the inadequacy of language as seen in 'Les Mots Anglais', with the notion that the meaning of the word is not found precisely within the word, but as an accumulation, or refraction from the situation that words form. Language, like the world of fashion, creates the effect of a halo or aftertaste stemming from the

---

[1] Cf. the comments of Joseph Joubert, *Carnets*, vols. I and II (Paris, Gallimard, 1938), 'Laisser quelquefois le lecteur achever la symétrie entre les mots et ne faire que la tracer' (vol. II, p. 706).

presence of its objects, but not attributable to any one point. The 'halo' of the fashionable world, the 'aftertaste' of literature, both constitute an apparent moving away from the centre or meaning, and thus they can be said to be compatible in much the same way as two people, very different in character and ambition, might be said to get on very well. However, the 'subject' of each world is not thereby entirely denied. It is unobtrusive – it is scarcely necessary to mention 'La Femme' in connection with 'La Dernière Mode'; and similarly the title of a poem does not need to play any strong rôle. It is also blatantly seen in the general atmosphere. Beauty, for example, is not inherent in the use of that word, but in the individual perception of it in a particular form of expression. Thus the real jewel, if it is placed in the centre of the arrangement, can overpower the 'architecture' in which the spectator anticipates and virtually provides the 'subject' or apex. The intuition of architect and dress designer alike, often expressed in the banal phrase 'it looks just right there', is not unlike the writer's intuition of the 'mot juste'. The strength and authenticity of the 'mot juste' is rarely sensed outside conversation, since it is only the spoken word which commands full attention to its rhythm. In conversation the word does seem to create a 'space' which awaits the 'mot juste' of appropriate strength and imaginative size.[1] The complicated interplay of words and personalities can, in conversation, create an almost three-dimensional space in which a flash of verbal genius seems to fit indisputably, followed either by laughter or silent acknowledgement of the feat.

In written language, words must create the rhythm to which tone, facial expression and tempo contribute in conversation, and, in this situation, the notion of the 'mot juste' alters. In poetry all or most words could be described as 'mots justes'; whereas in prose we either imitate the rhythms of conversation, or suggest that there is a virtual 'mot juste', unsaid, existing only to the extent that the other words, forming the setting, choose to reflect it. If we substitute the word 'jewel' for 'mot juste', this can be said: a jewel in the centre permits only one quality of the jewel to count, its most obvious brilliance; it does not suggest a world that it has transformed, of which it is the apex, but delineates a single entity which can only signal a world now to come (an explanation, or 'chant de joie'). The quality of the jewel is that it is, as the high point of a transformation, rich in suggestion of the world of which it might be a part. In order to realize the full potential in words of the 'realm

---

1 Cf. Mallarmé's notes on pages 851–3, especially: 'C'est donc puisque la Conversation nous permet une abstraction de notre objet, le Langage, en même temps que, site du Langage, elle nous permet d'offrir son moment à la Science, dans la conversation que nous étudierons le Langage.'

within a jewel', the setting must be graded, architecturally, in such a way as to make the progression mainly unperceived by the spectator/ reader (much as the lights at the end of road tunnels are graded to lessen the difference between artificial and natural light) so that although one point, in fact, could be said to have more brilliance or significance, it is actually distributed over the attentive presence of the surrounding areas.

The spectacle of language and fashion

In 'La Dernière Mode', Mallarmé gives indirect expression to certain notions concerning the nature and possibilities of language, and his success effectively denies the necessity of 'a language to describe language'. The descriptions of fashion show us how reality and our perception of it can demonstrate, not just adequately but emphatically and distinctly, that literature is not an isolated 'other' world, but a transformation, operated by language, of this one. Mallarmé obviously looks at the world of fashion with the eyes of a 'littérateur'; he reveals those qualities of the world which are, so to speak, susceptible to the qualities of language. So aptly and convincingly does language capture the series of dazzling tucks and folds 'plissés de tulle noir à l'intérieur' (710), that the reader, though *knowing* that this is an aspect of the real world, finds it touched with a measure of the unreality associated with literature.

> Les robes de ces solennités mondaines, c'est la fantaisie même, aventurée parfois, hardie et presque future, qui se fait jour à travers des habitudes anciennes. Qui regarde, y voit, mêlés au satin, des symptômes dont se révèle déjà le secret, sous la gaze, sous le tulle ou sous les dentelles. (797)

Fashion can appear to give intimations of a secret (the secret of future fashions) in much the same way as literature, and especially poetry, does. Thus it appears charged with a degree of unreality, together with a degree of possibility, reminiscent of some of Mallarmé's perceptions concerning the work of other writers. Also, if the 'secret' of fashion lies partly in its anticipation of future styles, it concerns too the transformation of the present. In any description of the objects of fashion there is room for apparent secrecy and obvious transformation.

Mallarmé's observations and descriptions of the clothes and objects of the fashionable world show that he had an intuitive understanding of the relation between words and objects at least equal to that of more recent literary critics. For example, Roland Barthes is well-versed in

111

conceptual explorations of areas which Mallarmé intuitively understood, and it might seem that Mallarmé was perceptive almost 'in spite of' his lack of real, in the sense of conceptual, knowledge. But any coincidence of ideas in the writings of Mallarmé and Barthes only points once again to the richness of language that each recognizes. It is interesting to compare a piece by Barthes about the unreality of literature, with the writing of 'La Dernière Mode'. For example:

> Autrement dit, par rapport aux objets eux-mêmes, la littérature est fondamentalement, constitutivement irréaliste; la littérature, c'est l'irréel même; ou plus exactement, bien loin d'être une copie analogique du réel, *la littérature est au contraire la conscience même de l'irréel du langage*: la littérature la plus 'vraie', c'est celle qui se sait la plus irréelle, dans le mesure où elle se sait essentiellement langage, c'est cette recherche d'un état intermédiaire aux choses et aux mots, c'est cette tension d'une conscience qui est à la fois portée et limitée par les mots, qui dispose à travers eux d'un pouvoir à la fois absolu et improbable.[1]

Barthes evidently *knows* about the existence and the importance of unreality in self-conscious or literary language. Yet if the reader senses that Barthes has assimilated exploration and proof in this conceptual conclusion, he can find in Mallarmé, and especially in 'La Dernière Mode', evidence of the proof in action. Barthes's analysis performs in a completely different mode the task that Mallarmé's fashion writing (and also that of the 'Variations') performs by a greater concordance of language with that which it is expressing. The tension of which Barthes writes, although nowhere more evident than in poetry, is obviously sensed by Mallarmé when he attempts to capture the quality of certain natural and artificial phenomena:

> or à quelles tentures demanderons-nous ce monde aquatique, monstrueux, frêle, riche, obscur, et diaphane d'herbages et de poissons, si décoratifs! Tout tableau, peint ou brodé, a comme un voile d'immobilité jeté sur la vie mystérieuse de ces paysages fluviaux ou marins: comment, ce fond de mer ou de fleuve le posséder véritable? (821)

Written language, no less than pictures, has its own 'voile d'immobilité', its own manifestation of the tensions that belong to performance, to great expressiveness. The predicament of the designer, no less than the

---

[1] Roland Barthes, *Essais Critiques* (Paris, Editions du Seuil, 1964), p. 164.

writer, is that of maintaining that degree of unreality which poises art between banality and dream.

Similarly, to take up Barthes's contention that 'la littérature est au contraire la conscience même de l'irréel du language', it is interesting to compare Mallarmé's intuitions of the compatibility between the spectacle or 'irréel' of fashion, and that of language. Fashion appears as a spectacle because it is formed out of a preoccupation with tones, colours, styles, variations, none of which are in any way necessary to the functioning of the objective world, but which are not, on the other hand, actually detached from it. Thus, in describing fashion, Mallarmé does not have to see to it that language transforms its objects, for they are transformed already. J.-P. Richard makes the observation:

> Mieux encore: l'objet privilégié, ce sera peut-être dès lors l'objet sans importance, celui qui nous suggérera le mieux la notion de sa gratuité, de sa légèreté ontologiques, celui qui manifestera le plus positivement son vide intérieur: le *bibelot*. Et ce bibelot devra être, en outre, tout près de s'abolir... Il ne cherchera pas à nous cacher son insignifiance, ni sa fragilité, il les affichera bien au contraire, il en fera sa définition même. Dans un monde absurde, l'exil ainsi n'a pas de signification. Autant vaut nous plonger alors dans l'*ici* et dans le *maintenant*, pour en goûter sans illusion toute l'exquise saveur superficielle. 'Fuir ce monde? On en est...'[1]

Although I think there should be more emphasis here on the spectacle rather than on the insignificance of such objects, the last phrases, followed by a quotation from Mallarmé, are just and important. It is also interesting that Richard points to the connection between the objects of 'La Dernière Mode' and those of Mallarmé's poems. In both cases, Mallarmé is not attempting in any way to escape from the immanence of the material world, but is intent on capturing its qualities in language. It is clear, however, that he did not believe the powers of language to be in any way miraculous, since he only tries out its expressiveness on those aspects of the real world which seem most suggestible (fashion in 'La Dernière Mode', landscape in some of the 'Variations', theatre in 'Crayonné au Théâtre, for example). Thus he does not define the relation between words and things, but demonstrates how it works in certain circumstances.

If the objects of 'La Dernière Mode' appear present, embedded 'dans l'*ici* et dans le *maintenant*', it is not because the reader sees each one in its entirety, but because he sees it according to the distinctiveness

[1] Richard, *L'Univers Imaginaire de Mallarmé*, p. 298.

113

which makes it part of a spectacle. Language which evokes or describes a physical spectacle is obliged, in the very process that distinguishes a day dress from a ball dress, to take on at least some measure of that spectacle. For example, when describing a very minor aspect, the artificial flowers made for a hat, Mallarmé writes:

> On pourrait dire de ces dames qu'elles ont les doigts de roses du matin, mais d'un matin artificiel, faisant éclore des calices et des pistils d'étoffes. (800)

The obvious and mannered artifice of the metaphor 'qu'elles ont les doigts de roses du matin' perfectly fits the unreality of the flowers themselves. Although it is certainly not necessary for Mallarmé to describe the flowers in this way, his doing so performs the dual function of persuading the 'abonnée' of the flowers' qualities, and of showing that language too can take on the splendid artifice that distinguishes these flowers from real ones. The writing of 'La Dernière Mode' offers Mallarmé a constant flow of such opportunities. The accumulation of metaphor and rich language is largely thrown away on the frivolous reader who scarcely reads, in Mallarmé's sense of the word, but as far as possible lives the pages of the journal. Mallarmé, on the other hand, is left with precisely that element which his poetry suggests, but can only suggest. There is no gratuitousness in poetry, and the sparseness of language that results leaves the poet open to accusations of obscurity. In fashion writing there is no obscurity, and, to the 'abonnée', no poetry either. In writing that is clearly 'de circonstance', there is no sense of anything being hidden (a measure of obscurity is even 'expected' in poetry); the words say and are what they are saying. But, in 'La Dernière Mode', the writing has a secret (in the rich order of events that the poet and not the 'femme du monde' perceives) when it appears to have none; while in purely creative writing there appears to be a vast secret (the traditional mysteriousness of poetry) when in fact there is none, for the words, in this circumstance too, are saying and are what they are saying. Thus we have the paradox that, in language, honesty has the appearance of a lie, and vice versa; and the paradox is only clarified by remembering that we are concerned with a medium, a means of communication, and that the medium is itself an appearance that the writer has created.

Few would dispute that the language of poetry has a strength of distinctive appearance that constantly draws attention to itself. 'La Dernière Mode' shows that prose can have the same qualities, for here, spectacle is never far away, and the language which describes or evokes it is under a certain obligation to pay tribute to its splendour. The 'armature mystérieuse' of such writing is probably the present splendour of the words and the future splendour of the real spectacle, rather than the detail of advice and description. There is no other framework, and no story to be told. If there is any story in the writing of spectacle, it is only reminiscent of the impossible, eternal story, whose narrative detail is relatively unchanging and whose atmosphere is unmistakable. Many fashion magazines do indeed include such stories, where sentiment never seeps but pours, where there is no aim other than the inevitable end, no hidden hand of subtle and secret reaction to excuse the obvious. We have seen that Mallarmé believed Wagner's works, with their grandeur of spectacle, to belie Wagner's theories. In writing 'La Dernière Mode', Mallarmé is satisfying the demand for story (or practice), while the telling of the story provides, in its very nature, the theory too.

In some of the 'Chroniques de Paris' Mallarmé takes the opportunity to imagine himself present at some social function. For example, in one issue we find him imagining the reactions of the audience at the opera to a new décor:

> Eloge point banal, le plus juste et le plus neuf, décerné par les femmes à un faiseur de plafonds qui, quoique de l'école, a su, au modèle général et presque abstrait de la Beauté traditionnelle, substituer les Types que nous voyons à tout instant surgir d'une loge ou d'une voiture ainsi que la perfection variée ou se pencher au bal sur une épaule, mais toujours projeter très-loin ce regard qui rêve, à quoi? à la perpétuité dans quelque ciel supérieur et idéal : vœu qu'a, cette fois, accompli l'Art, par le talent d'un artiste audacieux jusqu'à ne pas hésiter devant l'apothéose du visage contemporain. C'est, pour toutes les femmes, la fête authentique de la Saison. (735)

Mallarmé does not merely describe the décor, but strengthens its mythical dimension by imagining the thoughts of those who are there and fitting them to the quality of the setting. If the artist who provides the décor for 'la fête authentique de la Saison' knows how to fit his work to the circumstance, Mallarmé is no less aware of the possibilities that arise in writing about the same circumstance. Indeed the opera house is well suited to dreams of 'la perpétuité dans quelque ciel supérieur et idéal'. Nineteenth-century opera was a prodigious spectacle and social occasion. Its conventions were fairly strict, thus operating a clear hold upon time, upon the whole tradition of telling stylized stories

115

with music, in an age when the 'genre' was clearly defined, without lapses or concessions to personality, or any stepping out of the acknowledged framework to wag an admonishing moral finger. Perhaps it is the lack of constraint from the real world which makes Mallarmé's writing in 'La Dernière Mode' so much of a piece with operatic convention. There is a containedness of spectacle, to the very last trailing of the harp or veil, a complete accomplishment within a frame that seems defined by the contents (which are in fact the medium used to create it) and not by any outside event or observer. This is an accomplishment that appears so complete that there can be no question of things within the frame suggesting anything that is not. If opera or the spectacle of fashion appear complete and autonomous, it is precisely because they are inadequate transcriptions of reality, because the medium they employ overcomes the partial nature of their original version of the world. Out of the situation of dominating medium and partial reality, appears a spectacle that provides the intuition that its 'subject' is none other than the means used to create it.

It is because one cannot say directly, nor explain 'what spectacle is', that it is necessary for Mallarmé's language to *perform* in such a situation, in much the same way as it must 'perform' poetry in order to show 'what poetry is'. A sense of spectacle can hardly appear out of investigation or explanation; one can only explain by following the spectacle. Investigation of the nature of opera, would involve comparing it, separating it into component parts, removing the audience, extinguishing the chandeliers, real and imagined, and this very process would progressively deny the presence of spectacle which is fundamental to opera. The particuliarity of spectacle is not communicated by a parallel particuliarity of language, rather by a relatively low level of language which then suggests, by its intricate perceptions, a performance that it is then itself secretly creating.

Any manifestation of the imagination is, in a sense, a performance. The degree of tension in figurative language (stretched to a high degree in 'précieux' writing) certainly suggests a performance made possible by long rehearsal. Mallarmé's position in writing 'La Dernière Mode' was such that he was stationed within the trappings and splendour of a real live performance. He was thus able to show that it is not simply imagery that makes language into a performance, but that scrupulous observation of reality can have the same effect. Few people go to the opera to witness a drama, or even to listen to music; equally few go to a fashionable event for anything other than involvement in a spectacle to which they themselves, by their appearance, have contributed. The theatre is a clear figuration of such an Occasion; the setting is imprinted upon the clothes, the jewels that reflect, echo, trace tacit conversations across the painted dome, with cherub lights in pizzicato to the chandelier:

> Un sourire! mais il circule déjà, à peine formé, dans les salles aux lourdes portières, attendu, détesté, béni, remercié, jalousé; extasiant, crispant ou apaisant les âmes; et c'est en vain que l'éventail, qui crut d'abord le cacher, éperdu maintenant, tente de le ressaisir ou de dissiper son vol. (719)

There is a unique concordance of audience and setting, in itself sufficient to be called a spectacle. In the vast suggestion of grandeur amongst the theatre audience, the spectacle on the stage fits the mould without effort, fits even the tilt of the chin towards the stage; while the music comes from a source semi-obscured in the pit, not hidden because there is no need to create the whole illusion – half is there in the audience, and half is on the stage:

> La voix de l'un, allant retrouver au balcon, aux loges, au plafond et parmi le lustre, l'or partout prodigué, pour lequel elle est faite la voix des ténors. (734)

The metaphorical golden voice finds an ephemeral realization amongst the gilt of theatre balconies and ceilings.

The delicate image, quoted above, of the fan that tries to hide or contain a smile, is an apt reminder of the quality of spectacle endlessly 'nous échappant'. Mallarmé's projection of the dreams of the 'femme du monde' that move 'vers l'idéal' are admirably paralleled by the constant movement of fashion, always altering style and ornament, never more exciting than when it is about to be seen for the first time. The fashion journalist must 'résumer vite le résultat définitif de la métamorphose dans le Costume', (833), in full knowledge of the ephemeral nature of any apparent 'résultat définitif', and knowing too, that each fashion will be, for the brief moment of its apparition, the most adequate possible gesture 'vers l'Idéal'. In the world where there are 'pas de souliers que ceux des bals futurs' (727), where we read a 'Chronique: mais sans passé? car nous arrivons avec notre seul avenir, inconnu' (716) it is obviously difficult to 'prendre date'. In fact it only appears possible to capture the present in the 'éclat' of its intimations of the future and its reminders of the past.[1] The development of fashion thus follows the

---

[1] Cf. George Steiner's thought-provoking comments on the relation of language to past and future: 'Is poetry, in some fundamental sense, always

same patterns as the development of literature, even to the extent that, at certain moments, traditional form is revered for the contrast of its degree of permanence. A wedding dress, for example, is treated as a design which should not be radically altered. Mallarmé shows reverence for a traditional form which befits a traditional human state, much as the sonnet form befits the love poem:

> la coutume antique de vêtement féminin par excellence, blanc et vaporeux, tel qu'il se porte au Mariage... Cela ne crie pas, une Toilette de Mariée: on la remarque, telle qu'elle apparaît, mystérieuse, suivant la mode et pas, ne hasardant le goût du jour que tempéré par des réminiscences vagues et éternelles, avec des détails très-neufs enveloppés de généralité comme par le voile. (763)

If the timelessness of the wedding dress is best felt in traditional or near-traditional styles, the general tenor of the time-scale in the world of fashion is probably better indicated by this passage:

> Aussi bien, maintenant, les yeux éblouis par des irisations, des opalisations, ou des scintillements, ne pourrions-nous regarder, sans peine, quelque chose d'aussi vague que l'Avenir. (715)

Mallarmé is not concerned with the actual shape and material of future fashions; he is concerned simply with the fact that the future can be guessed from 'irisations' and 'opalisations', much as future literature is intuited out of like sensations, perhaps uncertainly or imperfectly offered by existing 'fashions' or literary 'genres'. A writer like Mallarmé who is as interested in elucidating what constitutes a language of literature as in creating 'an example of literature', discerns and collects the 'irisations' of both the physical world and the literary world, so that his language expresses the quality rather than the content of each. The fickle brilliance of fashion gives at least two valuable clues: that such a language and such a quality will have the character of a spectacle, and that such a language must be learned through a process of variation and distillation, rather than evaluation, if it is to accommodate, ultimately, the highest distillation of which language is capable: poetry.

part remembrance and part prophecy – the very reality of past and future being wholly a convention of language?', *Extraterritorial* (Faber, 1972), p. 149.

5

The language of theatre

The degree of delight and assurance that showed Mallarmé to be, in every sense, master of ceremonies in 'La Dernière Mode', bowing to the public nature of the task, intuiting its possible private significance, and creating something which took account of both, is curiously answered by the writing of 'Crayonné au Théâtre'. Not only do we lose sight almost completely of the enjoyment manifest in Mallarmé's discussions of spectacle in 'La Dernière Mode'; it is also apparent that the theatrical notions found elsewhere in his writing (in his appreciation of Villiers, for example) are by no means fulfilled by his experience of conventional theatre. The very fact that the language of 'Crayonné au Théâtre' is considerably more difficult, and more strained, than that of 'La Dernière Mode', suggests that Mallarmé was no more at ease confronting the reality of the theatre of his time than he was when, in 'Igitur', he confronted the reality of composing a story. This is not to say that the writing of 'Crayonné au Théâtre' is without value or untypical of Mallarmé; but it is apparent that mixed feelings about contemporary theatre, set against a well-established predilection for all that the notion of theatre involves, create a difficult task both for Mallarmé's tact, and for the preservation of his real feelings on the subject. The reader too is taxed far more, and must extract with care Mallarmé's often obscure comments on the relation between theatre and language. He must also take into account the fact that, because Mallarmé is now discussing more than performing (though paradoxically in the realm of theatre), his language will naturally appear to be set at a greater distance. An obvious exception to such problems is Mallarmé's writing on dance. Here we find that the distance between theory and practice is effortlessly crossed, and language 'performs' its sense.

The different editions of the 'Chroniques de Paris' in 'La Dernière Mode' give comparatively little detail about the plays being performed at the time. This is not simply because Mallarmé was again bowing to the needs of his 'abonnées' – more interested in the fact of a 'première'

119

than in the quality of a play – but also because the influence that the theatre had on his writing did not have much to do with the theatre as it then was. The phrase describing the reopening of 'Héloise et Abelard': 'rappelés par des mains prêtes d'avance à applaudir' (824) seems to reflect his attitude towards most of the plays of the time, and it is essentially the atmosphere of theatre that we find in the 'Chroniques', and which we might expect to find elaborated in the writing of 'Crayonné au Théâtre'. The very first of the 'Chroniques' is essentially an invitation to the theatre, not an invitation to see any particular play:

> Quelle inévitable traîtrise, au contraire, dans le fait d'une soirée de notre existence perdue en cet antre du carton et de la toile peinte, ou du génie: Un Théâtre! si rien ne vaut que nous y prenions intérêt. Pas de nues dont l'on puisse s'environner, sous la lumière réelle du gaz, autres que la robe de tissus vaporeux, froissés dans l'impatience. Vaines, splendides, incompréhensibles, de vivantes marionnettes devant nous proclament à haute voix leur sottise, sur un fond d'ennui intense et exaspéré; et qui fait d'elles comme les acteurs d'un cauchemar spécial, très-rare, heureusement. (717)

Mallarmé's fascination with the theatre is certainly manifest in 'La Dernière Mode', but the emphases placed on its different aspects are often unexpected, often apparently perverse, as for example in the comment:

> La vraie représentation est, dans cette nuit de gala, non ce qu'éclaire la rampe, mais le lustre. (717–18)

To say that the performance was only in the chandelier appears highly 'précieux', yet in 'Crayonné au Théâtre' the notion appears again somewhat more specifically:

> 'La chose qu'ils voulaient faire?' ne prit-elle pas le soin de prolonger vis-à-vis d'une feinte curiosité 'je ne sais pas, ou si...' réprimant, la pire torture ne pouvoir que trouver très bien et pas même abominer ce au-devant de quoi l'on vint et se fourvoya! un baîllement, qui est la suprême, presque ingénue et la plus solitaire protestation ou dont le lustre aux mille cris suspend comme un écho l'horreur radieuse et visible. (293)

In both cases, the chandelier is seen as a culminating representation of the atmosphere provided by the theatre.[1] In the first case the chandelier

---

[1] Cf. Jacques Schérer, *Le Livre de Mallarmé* (Paris, Gallimard, 1957), 'Il

was the figuration of splendour; in the second case the figuration, in what are now its crystal tears, of boredom, incomprehension, and vain, splendidly manifested, fashionable 'ennui'.

The deflection of attention from theatrical performance to the constant, if inessential, presence of the chandelier is so arresting in the first essay, entitled 'Crayonné au Théâtre', and also so subtle in its suggestion, that it is evident that Mallarmé is by no means simply a dissatisfied theatre-goer. He is concerned to distill, much as the chandelier seems to distill, or 'résume' the atmosphere of the theatre, and so formulate not a series of recommendations as to which play should be performed where, and why, but an understanding, simply, of the form of its impressiveness to the 'littérateur'. The chandelier is a perfect reservoir of the theatre's atmosphere, appearing to change much as the colour of a weather indicator changes, but retaining certain fundamental qualities:

> Seul principe! et ainsi que resplendit le lustre, c'est-à-dire lui-même, l'exhibition prompte, sous toutes les facettes, de quoi que ce soit et notre vue adamantine, une œuvre dramatique montre la succession des extériorités de l'acte sans qu'aucun moment garde de réalité et qu'il se passe, en fin de compte, rien.
>
> Le vieux Mélodrame occupant la scène, conjointement à la Danse et sous la régie aussi du poète, satisfait à cette loi. Apitoyé, le perpétuel suspens d'une larme qui ne peut jamais toute se former ni choir (encore le lustre) scintille en mille regards. (296)

For all its glitter, its splendour, for all its definitive summing up of the event that is the theatre, the chandelier actually shows that 'il se passe, en fin de compte, rien',[1] that its magnificence is empty, and theatre a splendid artifice which has at least one invaluable quality, also apparent in the chandelier, that of being 'le perpétuel suspens d'une larme qui ne peut jamais toute se former ni choir'. The theatre is not only, in the fashionable sense, an empty artifice, but also, as we shall see in much of Mallarmé's writing, pitifully abused by playwrights and producers. It is none the less a place where, first, there is enormous scope for players, writers and producers, and second, a rich moment for the sensitive

suffit pour satisfaire notre esprit – de l'équivalence de lumière que contient un *lustre*. Le lustre assure le Th. qui suffit à l'esprit' (feuillet 86).

[1] The word 'rien' has here its ordinary meaning, rather than the richer Mallarmean sense (as in 'Rien cette écume . . .'). This is an indication of Mallarmé's disappointment and disillusionment with contemporary theatre, and an intimation of what, ideally, the chandelier could offer.

'littérateur' who can enrich his understanding from the example of the theatre. Mallarmé's image of the brilliant but precariously suspended chandelier is apt in many ways, not merely as pointing the contrast between the possibilities and the actuality of theatre, but also as a summary of Mallarmé's involvement with the theatre. He senses the potential for both spectator and creator of theatre, yet finds that the excitement inherent in such notions can only dangerously confront reality. Hence in 'Crayonné au Théâtre' the reader finds a constant and sometimes bewildering shift of tone: on the one hand excited, and having the character of observations essential to Mallarmé, and on the other critical, even to the point of acerbity, of the state of theatre at the time. The writing moves between the single-line paragraph, the assured assertion that: 'Le Théâtre est d'essence supérieure' (312), and the despairing and also crushing show of interest shown in:

> Aussi me suis-je intéressé à la rumeur d'autre chose qu'une anecdote mise debout avec des airs insupportables de vraisemblance. (337)

Mallarmé and contemporary theatre

Nothing is clearer in 'Crayonné au Théâtre' than Mallarmé's impatience with the theatre of his time. That his reaction should be so decided itself indicates how important the theatre was to him:

> Mais où point, je l'exhibe avec dandysme, mon incompétence, sur autre chose que l'absolu, c'est le doute qui d'abord abominer, un intrus, apportant sa marchandise différente de l'extase et du faste ou le prêtre vain qui endosse un néant d'insignes pour, cependant, officier.
>
> Avec l'impudence de faits divers en trompe-l'œil emplir le théâtre et exclure la Poésie, ses jeux sublimités (espoir toujours chez un spectateur) ne me semble besogne pire que la montrer en tant que je ne sais quoi de spécial au bâillement; ou instaurer cette déité dans tel appareil balourd et vulgaire est peut-être méritoire à l'égal de l'omettre. (330–1)

The reign of insensitive theatre – 'emplir le théâtre et exclure la Poésie' – meant that Mallarmé was forced to consider all the more carefully what it was that constituted the theatrical, and to what extent it could be thought and experienced outside the theatre. Much of the essay 'Crayonné au Théâtre', most of 'Le Genre ou des Modernes', and also parts of the 'Notes sur le Théâtre' deal a substantial blow to both playwrights and audiences of the time. Such criticisms both suggest the supremacy of the book as an atmospheric and essential form, and also point to the sensitivity that Mallarmé brought to the theatre. For example:

> Et... et – je parle d'après quelque perception d'atmosphère chez un poète transposé dans le monde – répondez si demeure un rapport satisfaisant, ici, entre la façon de paraître ou de dire forcément soulignée des comédiens en exercice et le caractère tout insaisissable finesse de la vie. Conventions! et vous vous implanterez, au théâtre, avec plus de vraisemblance les paradis, qu'un salon. (318–19)

It is certainly the 'tout insaisissable finesse de la vie' that Mallarmé captures in his writing, and that he would expect also of the theatre. It may be difficult to present a 'salon vraisemblable' on the stage, but practical difficulties are no guarantee of art. That Mallarmé is not merely and dogmatically opposed to realistic theatre is evident elsewhere:

> Loin que j'incrimine le moraliste demandant à la rampe la mise en lumière d'un principe, erroné ou juste, par des personnages contemporains de s'être servi en véritable homme du métier, simplement et loyalement d'un moyen authentique de théâtre, comme qui dirait un tour ou une jonglerie (tout l'Art en est là!) lequel consiste à feindre son avis prouvé par un fait demeuré hypothétique, le plus de temps que la disposition des spectateurs le permet, pour suggérer cependant à l'esprit des conclusions qui seraient exactes en supposant que le fait sur quoi tout repose fût vrai. Quoi de plus conforme à la loi de Fiction: c'est, par son emploi judicieux, créer de beaux ou salutaires sentiments avec rien dans la main, leur gagnant le temps de prendre possession de vous; mais pourvu que ce néant ne s'avère pas, avec prestesse dissimulé à l'instant fatal! (341)

The mention of 'jonglerie' is interesting in that it seems to lower the tone of what one might imagine as Mallarmé's extremely lofty notion of theatre, stemming from comments such as: 'Le Théâtre est d'essence supérieure.' But it merely shows that Mallarmé's concern is with the theatricality of theatre. Even if a play sets out to demonstrate a moral or set of morals, it does not necessarily deny its theatricality; the show of juggling morals or conventions can form a pattern no less spectacular, no less theatrical, than that of juggling wooden bottles.[1] Another

---

[1] As Mallarmé reminds us in his tribute to Maupassant and his modern 'Mille et Une Nuits'.

important point is referred to here, that of the essential Fiction of the theatre, that of making a performance with 'rien dans la main'.[1] If it is only the isolated moment of a Shakespeare that can create in theatre both the 'finesse de la vie' and the theatricality of theatre, it is perhaps more common, and certainly entertaining, to encounter the second part. The theatricality of theatre was seen both implicitly and explicitly in 'La Dernière Mode'; it also appears in any appreciation of the 'vieil enchantement redoré d'une salle' (343).

When Mallarmé does write favourably of playwrights or productions, it is always with a view to bringing out the qualities of theatre in general, rather than proposing one play or another as masterly in itself. Dujardin, Maeterlinck, and Banville's dramatic poem 'Le Forgeron' receive what is probably the highest praise Mallarmé ever gave to the actuality of theatre as opposed to the notion of it. Although Mallarmé clearly does not see Dujardin's work as the complete fulfilment of the possibilities of theatre, he is obviously impressed by his manœuvring of characters:

> Je ne saurais dire mieux des personnages sinon qu'ils dessinent les uns relativement aux autres, à leur insu, en une sorte de danse, le pas où se compose la marche de l'œuvre. Très mélodiquement, en toute suavité; mus par l'orchestre intime de leur diction. (326)

This comes after a short summary of the plot of the play, put in inverted commas, as if Mallarmé wanted to suggest that the summary was not really part of his enterprise, but a convention demanded of him by his rôle as drama critic, that what he was really interested in was the effect of the interplay between the characters, the innate drama of this (quite apart from what happens) and its likeness in quality to the drama of words alone. Earlier in the same piece, Mallarmé comments on what might be the spectator's expectations:

> le spectateur n'allait-il pas reconnaître comme une musicale célébration et figuration aussi de la vie, confiant le mystère au langage seul et à l'évolution mimique? (326)

In most drama, Mallarmé believes, such a spectator is likely to be disappointed. Although Mallarmé praises the interplay between the characters, on the other hand he remarks:

---

[1] As Beckett certainly does in his plays. Cf. also the comment, reported by George Moore, concerning a play Mallarmé proposed to write, in which the only two characters were to be 'moi et le vent', cit. in Haskell M. Block, *Mallarmé and the Symbolist Drama* (Wayne State University Press, Detroit, 1963), p. 46.

L'attrait majeur qu'exerce sur moi la tentative de M. Dujardin vient incontestablement de son vers. (327)

He also devoted a paragraph to criticism of Dujardin, reproaching his over-direct manner in the finale:

A quoi bon le décor s'il ne maintient l'image: le traducteur humain n'a, poétiquement, qu'à subir et à rendre cette hantise. (327)

Mallarmé obviously thinks it necessary that the playwright, in order to create the 'hantise' of theatre should first have appreciated its full strength. Despite the attractive literary qualities of Dujardin's work, it is clearly not, for Mallarmé, a complete success so far as recognition of the qualities of theatre is concerned.

Maeterlinck, on the other hand, provides a different kind of experience:

Autre, l'art de M. Maeterlinck qui, aussi, inséra le théâtre au livre! (329)

Where the poet can install 'une source de drame latente qui reflue à travers le poème' (as Mallarmé writes of Régnier's work, 329), the dramatist has a much more explicit 'source de drame'. Maeterlinck, however, largely avoids the usual problems of the dramatist by making the most salient quality of his plays their atmosphere:

Pelléas et Mélisande sur une scène exhale, de feuillets, le délice. Préciser? Ces tableaux, brefs, suprêmes: quoi que ce soit a été rejeté de préparatoire et machinal, en vue que paraisse, extrait, ce qui chez un spectateur se dégage de la représentation, l'essentiel. Il semble que soit jouée une variation supérieure sur l'admirable vieux mélodrame. Silencieusement presque et abstraitement au point que dans cet art, où tout devient musique dans le sens propre, la partie d'un instrument même pensif, violon, nuirait, par inutilité. (330)

The quality of Maeterlinck's drama appears to Mallarmé to be an unreal avoidance of the theatrical, in which characters and events combine to form an expressive silence more than an impressive drama. Although the strong atmosphere of Maeterlinck's plays seems to Mallarmé to have the effect of a superior form of melodrama, constantly assuring (or over-assuring) us of a sense of theatre, it is also an avoidance of its other aspects. The veil of fiction, of the theatrical spell, is so consistent that the language, both actual and virtual, of the characters is almost without importance.

> Lear, Hamlet lui-même et Cordélie, Ophélie, je cite des héros reculés très avant dans la légende ou leur lointain spécial, agissent en toute vie, tangibles, intenses: lus, ils froissent la page, pour surgir, corporels. Différente j'envisageai la *Princesse Maleine*, une après-midi de lecture restée l'ingénue et étrange que je sache; où domina l'abandon, au contraire, d'un milieu à quoi, pour une cause, rien de simplement humain ne convenait. (329)

One would expect Mallarmé to give higher praise to a play whose characters were less human and more ethereal, but it appears that to Mallarmé the highest form of drama is that which involves the human being as he is transformed by the theatre, so that, even when read rather than seen 'ils froissent la page, pour surgir, corporels'. Theatre is not, to Mallarmé, the presentation of different worlds and different human beings, but of worlds and human beings transformed by the presence of the theatre, just as situation and object are transformed by being written. Hence, while appreciating fully the qualities of Maeterlinck's achievement, Mallarmé's enthusiasm is, although whetted, certainly qualified.

Mallarmé wrote about Maeterlinck from reading the plays rather than seeing them performed, and many of the articles in 'Crayonné au Théâtre' are written from a standpoint outside the theatre. He often refers to his position as 'armchair critic'. If the term is now a derogatory one, it is less so in the case of Mallarmé, since it leads him to consider the nature of theatre, and its connection with the book, none of which might have come to mind had he spent many evenings confronting works that arouse a reaction such as this one:

> Vu *le Crocodile*.
>
> M. Sardou à qui l'on sait une dextérité grande, est l'homme qui souvent me paraît, plus qu'aucun, offusquer de l'opacité vaine de ses fantoches la lumière éparse comme une frémissante pensée à l'ascension du rideau. (337)

It is not necessary to go often to the theatre in order to write thus of the moment when the curtain goes up; and if it goes up on 'l'opacité vaine de ses fantoches', then the armchair critic is probably present at the most valuable spectacle. In another of the 'Notes sur le Théâtre', Mallarmé writes:

> Autrement! je le sais, les ressorts ou pièces de serrurerie dramati-

que sont les mêmes en ce temps-ci que jamais. Un jeu de statisti-
que littéraire aisé consiste à les compter. (338)

It is not ingenuity of plot which guarantees theatricality, and indeed
there is little doubt that to Mallarmé, ingenuity of plot, with its parallel
ingenuity of 'life-like' characters, denies the theatre the qualities proper
to its existence –

> comment s'y intéresserait-on autrement! ajoutait la docte in-
> compétence oublieuse que le moyen de familiariser des specta-
> teurs avec un personnage doit en art tenir du miracle et non
> imiter l'expédient usité dans l'existence qui consiste à l'avoir
> fréquemment recontré et d'être imbu de ses affaires, jusqu'à
> l'ennui. (339)

Theatre does not gain by borrowing from life. This is made clear later
in the same passage:

> A savoir que les rôles féminins, comme ici d'une rêche et folâtre
> demoiselle malaisée à marier, ou de gaillardes et ceux de vieilles
> surtout, gagnent à paradoxalement être joués par l'homme: ils
> écartent ainsi l'irrévérence puis prêtent à un cas trop rare où
> persiste chez nous l'impression d'étrangeté et de certain malaise
> qui ne doit jamais, quant à une esthétique primitive et saine,
> cesser tout à fait devant le déguisement, indice du théâtre, ou
> Masque. (339)

The reader might expect a man like Mallarmé, with his 'fireside' view of
theatre combined with his highly 'difficult' and intellectualized writing,
to disdain the more fundamental aspects of theatre; but it is the basic
qualities of theatre which especially attract him. The sense of 'malaise'
or mysteriousness evident in any childish or unsophisticated reaction to
theatre (and to any of its 'poor relations': circuses and Punch and Judy
shows) is fundamental to theatre. It is this quality that assures us
that we are in the presence of a spectacle, and demonstrates the
essential difference between the things of art and the things of life.
Mallarmé writes of this in a passage about the adaptation of novels into
plays:

> L'adaptation, par le romancier, d'un tome de son œuvre, cause,
> sur qui prend place très désintéressé, un effet de pièce succédant
> à celles fournies par le théâtre dit de genre, sauf la splendeur à
> tout coup de qualités élargies jusqu'à valoir un point de vue:
> affinant la curiosité en intuition qu'existe de cela aux choses

quotidiennement jouées et pas d'aspect autres, une différence –
Absolue...

Ce voile conventionnel qui, ton, concept, etc., erre dans toute
salle, accrochant aux cristaux, perspicaces eux-mêmes son tissu de
fausseté et ne découvre que banale la scène, il a comme flambé
au gaz! et ingénus, morbides, sournois, brutaux, avec une nudité
d'allure bien dans la franchise classique, se montrent des caractères. (321)

The paragraphing here shows Mallarmé's desire to emphasize. Behind
the 'tissu de fausseté' of the theatre itself 'se montrent des caractères'
who have not walked straight from real life, but are creatures of the
theatre. Similarly one might say of literary subjects or 'characters' that
they are defined by being creatures of language.

It was not merely the playwrights of the time who were guilty, in
Mallarmé's eyes, of denying theatre its basic qualities. Hypothesizing
the reactions to Wagner's work, Mallarmé writes:

Il surgit au temps d'un théâtre, le seul qu'on peut appeler caduc,
tant la Fiction en est fabriquée d'un élément grossier: puisqu'elle
s'impose à même et tout d'un coup, commandant de croire à
l'existence du personnage et de l'aventure – de croire, simplement, rien de plus. Comme si cette foi exigée du spectateur ne
devait pas être précisément la résultante par lui tirée du concours
de tous les arts suscitant le miracle, autrement inerte et nul, de la
scène! Vous avez à subir un sortilège, pour l'accomplissement de
quoi ce n'est trop d'aucun moyen d'enchantement impliqué par
la magie musicale, afin de violenter votre raison aux prises avec
un simulacre, et d'emblée on proclame: 'Supposez que cela a eu
lieu véritablement et que vous y êtes!' (542)

If there were aspects of Wagner's work that Mallarmé certainly could
not deny, they were probably those that had to do with the necessity of
submitting to the spell of the presentations, and the fact that Wagner's
so clearly made a spectacular impact on 'le miracle, autrement inerte et
nul, de la scène'. Despite the impressiveness of this, Mallarmé obviously
believed that the audiences of the time were so unresponsive that they
would fail to submit to the spell, and would demand a 'simulacre' of
life. In 'Le Genre ou des Modernes' we see Mallarmé at his most acerbic,
writing of contemporary audiences, and it is curious to remember how
he wrote of the same audiences in 'La Dernière Mode', uncritical then,
and relishing only the brilliant inanity of fashionable gatherings. But

when he is considering theatre as a notion that is valid in itself, and also crucial to his notion of the book and of writing, his attitude changes abruptly:

> Que firent les Messieurs et les Dames issus à leur façon pour assister, en l'absence de tout fonctionnement de majesté et d'extase selon leur unanime désir précis, à une pièce de théâtre; il leur fallait s'amuser nonobstant; ils auraient pu, tandis que riait en train de sourdre la Musique, y accorder quelque pas monotone de salons. Le jaloux orchestre ne se prête à rien d'autre que significances idéales exprimées par la scénique sylphide. Conscients d'être là pour regarder, sinon le prodige de Soi ou la Fête! du moins eux-mêmes ainsi qu'ils se connaissent dans la rue ou à la maison, voilà, au piteux lever d'aurorale toile peinte, qu'ils envahirent, les plus impatients, le proscénium, agréant de s'y comporter ainsi que quotidiennement et partout: ils salue-raient, causeraient à voix superficielle de riens dont avec pré-caution est faite leur existence . . . (314–15)

Such near-acidity of tone in one famed for his tact and politeness can only mean that Mallarmé was so horrified by the contemporary theatre that he preferred to keep his criticisms at a journalistic and impersonal level, and to remain as far as possible detached from any judgement on it. Furthermore, it would be quite in keeping with his notion of an autonomous literary language to write of theatre as a notional rather than a real entity. The reader's image of theatre is, then, one that language as much as reality seems to have created.

The presence of theatre

Whatever the inadequacies of the actual theatre, it is always possible for Mallarmé to have recourse to the presence that the theatre has, even *is*. He admits that he rarely goes to the theatre, and asks himself:

> Alors pourquoi. . .
>
> Pourquoi! autrement qu'à l'instigation du pas réductible démon de la Perversité que je résume ainsi 'faire ce qu'il ne faut, sans avantage à tirer, que la gêne vis-à-vis de produits (à quoi l'on est, par nature, étranger) en feignant y porter un jugement: alors qu'un joint quant à l'appréciation échappe ou que s'oppose une pudeur à l'exposition, sous un jour faux, de suprêmes et intempes-tifs principes'. (297)

In any theatrical experience 'de suprêmes et intempestifs principes' are at stake. Individual plays may show no consciousness of this, but for Mallarmé any experience at the theatre, or just the memory of it, can by simple strength of presence summon to mind essential thoughts. The mystery and suspense that often figures in the plots of the plays themselves – and perhaps especially in the bad ones – is also evident in the setting of the theatre, and is often referred to. For example, in a passage about the nature of French melodrama, we find:

> Les axiomes s'y lisent, inscrits par personne; un avant tous les autres! que chaque situation insoluble, comme elle le resterait, en supposant que le drame fût autre chose que semblant ou piège à notre irréflexion, refoule, dissimule, et toujours contient le rire sacré qui le dénouera. La funèbre draperie de leur imagination, aux Bouchardy, ne s'obscurcit jamais d'ignorance – que l'énigme derrière ce rideau n'existe sinon grâce à une hypothèse tournante peu à peu résolue ici et là par notre lucidité: plus, que le sursaut du gaz ou de l'électricité, la gradue l'accompagnement instrumental, dispensateur du Mystère. (297)

The make-up of the theatre itself, the divisive curtain, the elaborate décors, the magical lighting, (the dim and probably, in Mallarmé's time, flickering light of gas or electricity, made an admirable contrast to the massive and brilliant chandeliers that usually formed the centrepiece of the ceiling) all contribute a sense of mystery. We see a series of more or less veiled gestures towards that which 'notre lucidité' can resolve, alongside the constantly sighted 'hypothèse tournante', or uncertainty inherent in our perception of theatre and audience, fiction and drama. The impressiveness of that uncertainty is such that it seems for Mallarmé to outweigh both the limitations of plays and the unresponsiveness of audiences. Thus, in a way, it is of little importance to Mallarmé's real response to theatre that his actual experiences of it should be so far from ideal. Confronted by a realm and a form of communication which have much to do with a sense of mystery, suspense and uncertainty, it is perhaps easier to elucidate the causes and the interest of such phenomena when the play is neither gripping as reality nor convincing as theatre. Then, of course, any contact with a play that *does* fulfil some or all of Mallarmé's vision of theatre (*Hamlet* is the supreme example) is both overwhelming and invaluable. In 'Crayonné au Théâtre' the situation is not unlike that of the 'Médaillons et Portraits', where Mallarmé was forced to consider works which in no way (for the most part) came close to his own idea of literature. But there

Mallarmé was concerned with literature. In 'Crayonné au Théâtre', in the presence of a different, if highly suggestive idiom, it is to be expected that he should create, in his writing, a less perfect blend of the actual and the notional than the one that arose out of writing about the literature of others.

And where in the 'Médaillons et Portraits' Mallarmé was able, in his own writing, to supplement and even supersede the writing of others, in the theatre there is no question of superseding nor even of supplementing, though there is evidence of Mallarmé's own desire to contribute to the theatre of his day.[1] However, the difference between the idiom of theatre and the idiom of language is not such that Mallarmé can with impunity consider the one without reference to the other. It is because of the very strong concordance that he sensed between the notion of theatre and the expressiveness of language, that his invectives against the inadequacy of contemporary theatre are so strong; that the theatre is so often discussed as an abstract entity, and that the tone of his theatre criticism is so uneven. It is because the possibilities of theatre touch Mallarmé so deeply that he is led to such opposite poles of invective and abstraction. There is no cover, as there was in the writing of 'La Dernière Mode', no refuge in a consistent, if consistently superficial, convention of expression. If refuge there is, it lies in the series of remarks on the essential nature of theatre. The most insistent of these, the short note 'Sur Le Théâtre', leaves no doubt as to Mallarmé's reasons for wanting to write about the theatre:

> Je crois que la Littérature, reprise à sa source qui est l'Art et la Science, nous fournira un Théâtre, dont les représentations seront le vrai culte moderne; un Livre, explication de l'homme, suffisante à nos plus beaux rêves. Je crois tout cela écrit dans la nature de façon à ne laisser fermer les yeux qu'aux intéressés à ne rien voir. Cette œuvre existe, tout le monde l'a tentée sans le savoir; il n'est pas un génie ou un pitre, qui n'en ait retrouvé un trait sans le savoir. Montrer cela et soulever un coin du voile de ce que peut être pareil poème, est dans un isolement mon plaisir et ma torture. (875–6)

Significantly the 'Théâtre' of the beginning of the piece has become a 'Poème' by the end. Even a rational connection between this solemn concept of theatre and the dramas one can go and see is sufficient to guarantee Mallarmé's fascination with the theatre. The relationship of this note to the projected content of the posthumously published

---

[1] See Block, *Mallarmé and the Symbolist Drama*, chapter I and *passim*.

131

'Livre' is obvious, yet this is not the limit of its interest. Mallarmé saw the notion of theatre to be inherent in the workings of book, mind, perception and nature, so the moment of writing about the theatre itself would be more challenging than any other. But if it is more challenging, is is also less feasible, since, granted the theatre inherent in 'un Livre, explication de l'homme', the very act of writing about the theatre would itself be theatrical. The attempt would be something like taking the bull by the horns, and the final sentence of the note above, with its standardized romantic combination of 'plaisir' and 'torture' is borne out by the styles and attitudes found in 'Crayonné au Théâtre'.

So obvious is Mallarmé's desire to capture in words the presence that theatre has, that he seems to use actual experience and traditional concepts to illuminate his own view. Thus it appears not tedious but necessary to cover the possibilities offered by an indifferent melodrama, by Maeterlinck, mime or ballet. Nor is it essential that so great a span should be united, rationally and intellectually, with the single title of 'theatre'. The elucidation of what theatre is, cannot concern itself with the unification of all examples of the form: its existence as a notion depends upon diversity, and upon a tacit understanding that, of all the roads that lead to Rome, no one resembles another. It is, then, Mallarmé the 'liseur à l'écart' (315), and not Mallarmé the traditional drama critic, who shows the importance of a notion of the theatre that can account for all its forms.

Its fundamental form is, to Mallarmé, the 'théâtre de l'esprit':

> Un théâtre, inhérent à l'esprit, quiconque d'un œil certain regarda la nature le porte avec soi, résumé de types et d'accords; ainsi que les confronte le volume ouvrant des pages parallèles. (328)

The 'theatre of the mind' is perhaps for Mallarmé only a susceptibility to the theatrical, but it is also undoubtedly connected with the dramatic whole that forms the notion of the book. This can only be built up in a series of varyingly imperfect glimpses; whereas the theatre, however elusive its underlying force and quality, creates a strong impact both in imagination and in actual presence. The possibilities of bringing the impact of theatre to the notion of the book are obvious:

> La jouissance vaine cherchée par feu le Rêveur-roi de Bavière dans une solitaire présence aux déploiements scéniques, la voici, à l'écart de la foule baroque moins que sa vacance aux gradins, atteinte par la moyen ou restaurer le texte, nu, du spectacle.

Avec deux pages et leurs vers, je supplée, puis l'accompagnement
de tout moi-même, au monde: ou j'y perçois, discret, le drame.
(328)

Such phrases suggest at first glance that Mallarmé the drama critic
needs to pay constant homage to the superior form of the book. However, as a 'littérateur' he needs also to see all aspects of human reality
and perception as contributing to the sense of the theatre. Despite the
overtones of spiritual grandeur or spiritual pretentiousness that writing
about theatre only escapes with difficulty, there is evidence enough
that Mallarmé was never so blinded by the impressiveness of the
parallel between book and theatre as to ignore the subtleties of the
relationship. Nor does he ignore its minor pleasures. The 'Dreamer-
king' of Bavaria, with his lavish and empty theatre, had only to turn to
the rich experience of the poem on the page to find the simple drama of
black on white, the creative spectacle of words.

In the piece entitled 'Solennité', Mallarmé writes about the parallel
in more detail, though with no less intensity:

Quelle représentation! le monde y tient; un livre, dans notre main,
s'il énonce quelque idée auguste, supplée à tous les théâtres, non
par l'oubli qu'il en cause mais les rappelant impérieusement, au
contraire. Le ciel métaphorique qui se propage à l'entour de la
foudre du vers, artifice par excellence au point de simuler peu
à peu et d'incarner les héros (juste dans ce qu'il faut apercevoir
pour n'être pas gêné de leur présence, un trait); ce spirituellement et magnifiquement illuminé fond d'extase, c'est bien le pur
de nous-mêmes par nous porté, toujours, prêt à jaillir à l'occasion
qui dans l'existence ou hors l'art fait toujours défaut. (334)

Although Mallarmé, as a 'littérateur', naturally tended to weight such a
parallel towards the supremacy of the book, it is always evident that
there is a balance, almost a mirage, between the notion of the book and
the notion of theatre. The whole phenomenon that is the theatre can be
seen as a virtual text; while the actual text of a book can, by its intensity of impact, appear to shed its literary qualities and become only
spectacle – 'ce spirituellement et magnifiquement illuminé fond
d'extase'. Mallarmé notes at the end of 'Planches et Feuillets', that the
Poet is 'l'ordonnateur de fêtes en chacun' (330), thus pinpointing what
was already implicit in 'La Dernière Mode', or the sense of spectacle
that Mallarmé sees as essential to the poet's vision of the world. It is a
spectacular and not an abstract form of expression which best suits the

intensity of 'le pur de nous-mêmes'. On the other hand, the sheer splendour of 'the theatrical' needs, to make the experience complete, the precision of idea and sensation that is only found in the greatest playwrights. This both suggests the difference between a good and a bad playwright, and indicates what are, to Mallarmé, the qualities essential to writing, qualities that forcibly deflect the reader from the common image of a writer of 'ivory tower' obscurity towards something far more tangible.

Writing about the theatre brings out with invaluable insistence the fact that contemplation of an abstract notion such as literature, actually needs, when it has reached a certain pitch of intensity, to be sensed physically. It seems to demand the support of an image such as theatre, with all its splendours of trappings and of performance. There is much in 'Variations sur un Sujet' concerning the physical sensation of writing, of the book, the page, and letters of the alphabet, all of which is clearly connected with Mallarmé's thoughts on the theatre. But at a simpler and more general level, it is apparent that the notion of theatre, however imprecisely worked out, contributes to Mallarmé's thought on literature a sensation of inapprehensible splendour, combined with the indefinable mystery or enchantment which lies at the basis of all performance, and also at the basis of Mallarmé's sensation of reality.

His appreciation of the three-dimensional book is interesting for its combination of the abstract and the simple enjoyment common to all bookish readers. The book is an ordinary coffer of extraordinary secrets:

> Oui, le Livre, ou cette monographie qu'il devient d'un type (superposition des pages comme un coffret, défendant contre le brutal espace une délicatesse reployée infinie et intime de l'être en soi-même) suffit avec maints procédés si neufs analogues en raréfaction à ce qu'a de subtil la vie. (318)

By considering the ordinary physical dimensions of the book, Mallarmé is led also to see its inner qualities. The delicate image of the book as a casket (doubtless containing treasure) composed of an infinite number of folded pages, suggests the relationship that language has with the world. The pages of the book, closed against 'le brutal espace' of potentially hostile readers or simply unfavourable occasions, seem to resemble the way we apprehend things. The analogue suggests experience as an accumulation of infinitely thin, even, transparent leaves that finally form the tone or colour to which we can give a name.

Some of Mallarmé's images and analogues may appear over-dramatic –

134

even in this theatrical context – but they are true to his conception of the critic's rôle:

> La Critique, en son intégrité, n'est, n'a de valeur ou n'égale presque la Poésie à qui apporter une noble opération complémentaire, que visant, directement et superbement, aussi les phénomènes ou l'univers. (294)

Mallarmé, little given in his maturity to declarations of such near-cosmic proportions, alters their impact in practice. It will be seen how, when he writes of the basic elements of theatre, and especially of those theatrical forms which seem to have most presence – ballet and mime – he deflects the attention of the reader subtly away from 'les phénomènes ou l'univers' and into the phenomenon of language, with the tacit reminder that it is only by sounding in depth the visible and apprehensible world that it is possible truly to write its qualities.

Elements of the theatre: myth, suspense and hero

Although theatre, with its inevitable suggestion of the relation of microcosm to macrocosm, is likely to arouse thoughts of universal rather than merely artistic implication, Mallarmé is sensitive to the fact that theatre is simply the 'type' of art. It is the form which, by 'le concours d'arts divers scellés par le poésie' (313), is most susceptible to that presence of myth or strangeness which appears to reveal something about the universe. The last of the 'Notes sur le Théâtre' ends with the observation:

> Tant on n'échappe pas, sitôt entré dans l'art, sous quelque de ses cieux qu'il plaise de s'établir, à l'inéluctable Mythe: aussi bien vaut-il peut-être commencer par savoir cela et y employer la merveille de trésors, qu'ils soient documentaires ou de pure divination. (345)

Mallarmé significantly advises that one should '*employer* la merveille de trésors', not just contemplate it. All that he says about the mythical or cosmic character of the theatre, and by extension the book, is characterized by great emphasis on the sensation it gives, as opposed to the spiritual significance it has. The 'Rêverie' on Richard Wagner contains much about the mythical side of theatre:

> Le Théâtre les [les Mythes] appelle, non: pas de fixes, ni de séculaires et de notoires, mais un, dégagé de personnalité, car il compose notre aspect multiple: que, de prestiges correspondant

135

au fonctionnement national, évoque l'Art, pour le mirer en nous.
(545)

On the one hand, the myth is singular, unified out of needs and expectations; on the other hand, its particular quality arises from the fact that:

> L'Homme, puis son authentique séjour terrestre, échangent une
> réciprocité de preuves.
> Ainsi le Mystère. (545)

The mystery and impact of myth are not, according to Mallarmé, the result of purely abstract or spiritual contemplation; it is felt as the culmination of our ordinary perceptions of the world. The 'réciprocité de preuves' between man and the world he experiences is, of course, doubly evident in the theatre. Here reality not only interacts with reality, but also with fiction, and the whole is contained magically within 'cet antre du carton est de la toile peinte, ou du génie: un Théâtre' (717), as Mallarmé calls it in a characteristic remark in 'La Dernière Mode'.

Even in the highly abstract fragments of 'Le Livre' there is evidence that, despite the spiritual connotations of the notion of theatre, or, more especially, of ceremony and performance, there is great emphasis on the physical basis. For example, one of a series of notes that appear in slightly altered form throughout the 'Livre':

> – le Héros – dégage – l'Hymne
> (maternel) qui le crée, et se
> restitue au Th. que c'était –
> du Mystère où cet hymne enfoui[1]

On the same page we find the comment:

> Dr. [ame] n'est insoluble que parce qu'inabordable,

a just testimony to the impressiveness of the theatre, and to the fact that its mysteriousness is not due entirely to the cosmic qualities it appears to convey, but to the fact that it is only out of an apprehension of the whole movement which constitutes theatre that it is possible to know its full weight.

> La scène est le foyer évident des plaisirs pris en commun, aussi
> et tout bien réfléchi, la majestueuse overture sur le mystère dont
> on est au monde pour envisager la grandeur. (314)

---

[1] *Le Livre*, feuillet 4 (A).

If theatre is but the overture to the 'mystère dont on est au monde pour envisager la grandeur', the reader can assume that the 'real' work is to be found elsewhere, much as Mallarmé's (and Proust's) remarks about the Book suggest that it is only glimpsed and never completed. We can also see here that the 'grandeur' is not to be found at any definitive point, but only along the progression. As Mallarmé says in a passage about ballet: 'un sacre s'effectue en tant que la preuve de nos trésors' (296) – 's'effectue' rather than simply 'is'.

In some of the 'Variations', the pieces under the heading 'Offices', it can be seen how Mallarmé reacted to the atmosphere of the church, and how his reaction complements admirably his appreciation of the theatre. Religion makes its mark at many points, but almost always from the point of view of its atmosphere. In fact the note with perhaps the most openly religious connotations appears near the beginning of the first essay of 'Crayonné au Théâtre':

> l'attirance du théâtre qui montre seulement une représentation, pour ceux n'ayant point à voir les choses à même! de la pièce écrite au folio du ciel et mimée avec le geste de ses passions par l'Homme. (294)

This may look like religious reverence, but it is also intensely theatrical. There is no direct evidence that Mallarmé is more interested in the imperfect mime, performed by man, of the 'pièce écrite au folio du ciel', than in the mystical (or Platonic) notion that there is basically one Play, of which all others are but a shadow. There are none of the metaphysical doubts and hesitations of the early writing, no taunt from the 'Azur', no anguish that the empty sheet of paper, or even that which has been inscribed, should not match the 'folio du ciel'. In fact the strength of 'mimée avec le geste de ses passions par l'Homme' is such that the unseen, divine model seems less interesting. Or that, as we read in 'Catholicisme':

> sommairement il s'agit, la Divinité, qui jamais n'est que Soi, où montèrent avec l'ignorance du secret précieuse pour en mesurer l'arc, des élans abattus de prières (391)

'Mesurer l'arc' appears more interesting than the fact of 'Divinité', not simply because it can be 'measured', but also because it allows for that progression which is essential to our knowledge that there is, as the case may be, a divinity or 'Idée'.

The last piece in 'Offices', entitled 'De Même', deals essentially with the atmosphere of religion in general and the church in particular.

Mallarmé makes it clear that he is not concerned to give opinions of any kind on the subject of religion:

> Néanmoins pénétrons en l'église, avec art: et si, le sait-on! la fulguration de chants antiques jaillis consumait l'ombre et illuminait telle divination longtemps voilée, lucide tout à coup et en rapport avec une joie à instaurer. (395)

The sombre shadow of the church is taken over by the illumination of music, much as the 'trou magnifique ou l'attente' (294) of the theatre is filled each night by the performance. The church, like the theatre, gives a very strong impression of 'event before the event', perhaps because, as Mallarmé remarks:

> Toujours que, dans le lieu, se donne un mystère: à quel degré reste-on spectateur, ou présume-t-on y avoir un rôle? (395)

Mallarmé answers his own question in the paragraphs that follow, evoking the way in which the atmosphere of, in this case, the church comes into being, gradually, through the interplay of voices – 'car voici le miracle de chanter, on se projette, haut comme va le cri!' (396) – the congregation, and the priest:

> Quoique le prêtre céans, n'ait qualité d'acteur, mais officie – désigne et recule la présence mythique avec qui on vient se confondre; loin de l'obstruer du même intermédiaire que le comédien, qui arrête la pensés à son encombrant personnage. (396)

The image of the priest manipulating the strings of a mythical presence, supported by music, and especially the organ – 'il exprime le dehors, un balbutiement de ténèbres énorme', (396) – must have appeared to Mallarmé in many ways the ultimate theatrical performance, all the more suggestive since the chief actor was not even present:[1]

> Telle, en l'authenticité de fragments distincts, la mise en scène de la religion d'état, par nul cadre encore dépassée et qui, selon une œuvre triple, invitation directe à l'essence du type (ici le Christ) puis l'invisibilité de celui-là, enfin élargissement du lieu par vibrations jusqu'à l'infini, satisfait étrangement un souhait moderne philosophique et d'art. Et, j'oubliais la tout aimable gratuité de l'entrée. (396)

The unorthodox bias of Mallarmé's writing about the church is further emphasized in the continuation of this passage; he discusses

---

[1] As in 'Le Nénuphar Blanc'.

the fact that the Palais du Trocadéro has borrowed from the church, each being an 'édifice voué aux fêtes' (397). The characteristics of such an edifice form an interesting pattern. The high point of the church 'performance' was the 'essence du type...puis l'invisibilité de celui-là', which is a static notion. Then, on the other hand, the celebration creates an 'élargissement du lieu par vibrations jusqu'à l'infini'. The implications of these two phenomena touch the idea of the book as well as the theatre. For the essence of the theatre, that which makes the theatre 'd'essence supérieure', and the governing 'Idée' or essence of the book, are not visible; they can only be apprehended out of a sensitive involvement in all aspects of the whole. If the essence or 'Idée' in either theatre or literature seems over-abstract or unconvincing, it is certainly justified by the evidence of transformation we find in performances of each. The multiple aspects of theatre, contrasting what was a bare stage, divided from the empty auditorium by a curtain – 'cette toile qui sépare du mystère' (351) – interact, and appear virtually to expand the area of vision, both actual and imaginative or spiritual.

It is interesting that the many figures or diagrams in the fragments of *Le Livre*, in their intricate shuffling of fundamentals – such as 'Héros', 'Hymne', 'Vie', 'Théâtre' – have the same mirific effect. It seems as if the fact that the writer has been caught, so to speak, in his shirt sleeves, merely musing, has given rise to just the same dazzling effect of apparently infinite expansion that can be felt in the theatre. Although it would degrade unnecessarily Mallarmé's intentions to suggest that he meant, in the notes for *Le Livre*, to create no more than a mirage of theatre, it is a tribute to his own conviction about the 'identité du Livre et de la Pièce'[1] that his words should have this effect. Also, since so many of the 'feuillets' contain diagrams which shift slightly the order of the components of the envisaged 'Livre', while very few deal with the 'content', it is likely that Mallarmé was fascinated by the mirific effect of the structure, and likely too, that he might consider for his own opus, as well as for the 'secret intime' of religion that:

> L'heure convient, avec le détachement nécessaire, d'y pratiquer les fouilles, pour exhumer d'anciennes et magnifiques intentions. (397)

One important characteristic of both theatre and church performances is the sense of communion. The 'enchantement redoré d'une salle' (319) that Mallarmé mentions is not merely a generous but superficial evocation of the theatre. It is obvious that Mallarmé himself was highly

---

[1] *Le Livre*, feuillet 129.

susceptible to the powers of the theatre, both to its fundamental structure, and to the character of its happenings. The box-like, or, better, globe-like qualities of the theatre, with the division between audience and stage, and often an orchestra pit as well as a curtain at the dividing point, are clearly the ideal setting for an autonomous evolution (within the globe) to which both actors and audience contribute, and in which both are so involved as to be largely unaware of the impact of their united enchantment. Hence it is not hard to see why Mallarmé should make so many references to the chandelier that is often found high in the middle of the theatre roof. Its position and splendour, the infinite reflection and refraction of its facets, seem, in practical terms, the only way of paying homage to the complexity of the interaction, and to the resultant, essential quality from which the spectator, especially of the Mallarméan 'coin du feu' kind, can sense the presence of theatre. Mallarmé is certainly not alone in noticing the importance of the audience in the appreciation of theatre, yet his emphasis is distinctive. He does not simply see the audience as the more or less appreciative recipient of the play, neither does he only see it as the spectacle of splendour equal to that of the play and the theatre, as was largely the case in 'La Dernière Mode'. But one aspect of the emphasis seen in 'La Dernière Mode' is continued in 'Crayonné au Théâtre' in a slightly different form. The audience is not merely as theatrical as the play, it is also as mysterious as the whole theatrical event, for:

en la foule ou amplification majestueuse de chacun gît abscons le rêve! (298)

Here is a reversal of expectations that Mallarmé obviously enjoyed. One might expect a play to have dream-like qualities distinguishing it from real life, but the reign of realism in the theatre effectively destroyed that charm. Yet no ineptitude or insensitivity can alter the dream-like qualities of a large, even an inattentive audience. The mysteriousness of the individual reaction to any given event is clearly fascinating to Mallarmé. And this is intensified when it is a question of considering a large mass of individuals, all reacting at the same time to the same thing, but silent, showing nothing of their reactions, and appearing to be no more than a vast blotting-paper soaking up the effect of the play. Yet their very silence, as well as their position, row upon row right up to the aptly named 'paradis', suggestive of the mass of those who are not in the theatre, is curiously compatible with the silence of theatrical effect – regardless of what is said or done – and compatible too with the suggestions of infinity that are so often a part of theatre, either in the

traditional stage setting of pillar rows that appear to stretch back for-
ever, or else in the fact that the audience may well identify with the
plot of the play, thus appearing to deny its fiction and its theatricality,
but in fact merely putting it in infinite abeyance. Hence it is not merely
the content of the play that provides a sense of suspense, of drama, and
consequently of theatricality. The audience, contained and arranged
within the globe, are also part of the dream. Mallarmé, as the omniscient
spectator (or 'le lustre') remarks:

> avec la proclamation de sentiments supérieurs, rien ne me captive
> tant que lire leur reflet en l'indéchiffrable visage nombreux
> formé par une assistance. (324)

His view of the theatre and its audiences has a ring to it that is almost
reminiscent of the complex distillation of the alchemists, with the
suitable epilogue which, to the alchemists, was the discovery of the
ultimate, pure and simple truth (or gold), and to Mallarmé was the
essence of theatre.

Another aspect of the audience that Mallarmé found attractive was
that not only could he see 'l'indéchiffrable visage', but also he could
sense that the possibilities in the apparent lack of reaction were extremely rich:

> La foule qui commence à tant nous surprendre comme élément
> vierge, ou nous-mêmes, remplit envers les sons, sa fonction par
> excellence de gardienne du mystère! Le sien! elle confronte son
> rich mutisme à l'orchestre, où gît la collective grandeur. (390)

Although this was written specifically about concert audiences, a concert is only an abstraction, and hence perhaps an intensification, of the
theatre experience in general. Mallarmé's 'reading' of the audience is
certainly more intense here. He sees the mysteriousness inherent in
the music virtually transferred, or converted into the silent currency
of the audience. One might say also that the special or strange
qualities of literary language seem to correspond to – or even create –
the human propensity towards myth and dream. The movement
between any spectacle and its spectators is always reciprocal, but in
the case of theatre it is magnified to an almost hallucinatory level.
The degree of attention which the sensitive reader can reach and
recognize in certain experiences of reading is further clarified by the
experience of the theatre, where it is often possible to feel the mass of
people united either in their suspense, their enjoyment, or simply their
appreciation. Their united feeling is an extraordinarily live backdrop or

accompaniment to the action on the stage, so alive that each step of the play is instantly conveyed and transformed into that mysterious life that is the attentiveness, the involvement of the audience. Something of this attentiveness is caught in Mallarmé's piece on 'La Fausse Entrée des Sorcières dans Macbeth':

> l'auditoire s'immobilisait dans une vacance au-delà, s'y figeait; un besoin naît détente ou du moment humain, extrême, qu'une sensation très aiguë se rompt et divise nos fibres autour de sa brisure. (347)

The atmosphere of suspense in an audience is perhaps the most powerful and also one of the most common. It is easily noticed, easily described (how many theatre critics have written for the newspaper: 'a thrill ran through the audience when...'); it is the perfect figuration of a reaction, and is a figuration too, of those moments in the appreciation of any art form, but especially music or poetry, when the attentiveness of the reader/audience is heightened by the feeling, even the fear, that its intensity of feeling cannot last. The theatre can teach the writer, and the reader, about the patterns of involvement, and, in its greatest works, can show how it attains a communication that is not merely dramatic in the superficial sense, but also in the sense that its effect on the audience is equal to, as it were, its effect on itself. (An effective moment in a play is only effective in relation to the rest of the play.) 'La Fausse Entrée des Sorcières dans Macbeth', the last of the pieces in 'Crayonné au Théâtre', and written only a year before Mallarmé's death, contains a particularly good example of Mallarmé's feeling for dramatic effect, and of the way in which his perception of detail reveals the consistent eye of the poet reading from the world his own version of the 'folio du ciel' (294).

Mallarmé's hesitation in beginning this piece itself prefigures the quality of the observations to come:

> Introduire le funeste Chœur, par quel moyen? je lis bien, sous le titre, après
> 'Un lieu vide, tonnerre et éclairs.' (Entrent les trois sorcières.) mais pure indication courante et peut-être apocryphe: les sœurs vieilles n'entrent pas, sont là, en tant que le destin qui pré-existe et si, en effet, leur apparition dans ce lieu, particulièrement, que traversera Macbeth, oh! elles accourent de près, elles ne vagabondent pas loin du tout, vives à tracer un circuit suprême, immédiatement le temps d'échanger du doigt, en secret, sur le parchemin de lèvres déjà muettes, le baiser d'un rendez-vous ultérieur. (349)

Mallarmé would like to dispute the stage direction relative to the witches' entrance, since their effect is such that it is unimaginable to him that they could ever have been anywhere but there on the stage, wrapped in the mystery traditional to them. They are there, 'en tant que le destin qui préexiste', holding not only the threads of Macbeth's life and fortunes, but also those of the theatre itself. It is fitting therefore, that in the stage directions regarding their leaving the stage, we find, not that they 'go out', but that they 'disappear':

> – il n'est pas inscrit sortent, comme elles sont *apparues* et non, d'après la teneur, *entrées*.
>
> Les présenter, insisté-je, comment? Au seuil et qu'elles y règnent; même en prologue participant de la pièce: extra-scéniquement. (349)

Mallarmé notes that this scene is never considered to be the first in the play; its strangeness makes it at once detached from the play, and also a veil whose atmosphere will stretch right across the play:

> Le prodige, antérieur – que de bizarres, artisanes tissent de leurs chuchotements le sort! plane et s'isole; n'eut lieu, du moins régulièrement ou quant à la pièce: on en fut témoin, tant pis, on le devait ignorer, comme primordiaux antécédents obscurs ne concernant personne. Vous assistez, sachez, par mégarde, à un complot – pas de sorcières relevant de la figuration ou des accessoires, mais dissipées si entrevues, authentiques donc, qui sait? réelles. (350)

Mallarmé gives the witches a highly theatrical status (indeed he remarks that 'le public apprécie une découverte par lui faite indûment' (350)), in suggesting that the curtain 'simplement s'est levé, une minute, trop tôt, trahissant des menées fatidiques' (351). But the implications are still more interesting. If it is possible to present on the stage an action or scene which does not appear to be part of the play, but which has a considerable influence on it, not unlike an unnoticed unwinding of the coil of mystery (and mist) in which the 'vieilles sœurs' first appear, and if such an action or scene appears to be something which has not been, so to speak, created for the occasion, but which was always there, and is thus a part of the theatre, then the resulting effect will be one in which the spectator can actually sense the form of theatre presenting, and receiving the play. The witches at the beginning of *Macbeth*, and in their subsequent appearances, imperceptibly forge our reactions to the play, in much the same way as an adjective modifies a noun. Just as the adjective is usually forgotten before the noun, so the witches will be forgotten before the violence of the rest of the play, and, as the subtlety of different forms of language indicates, if largely unnoticed, the expressiveness of language, so the apparition and disappearance of the witches in *Macbeth* indicate with a subtlety difficult to achieve by the use of figures on the stage, the condition that is the theatre.

Mallarmé's reading of this fragment of *Macbeth* shows how the substance of art can indicate the form of art, and how it is only this combination which guarantees for the spectator/reader the essential nature of the experience, the whole, or spectacle 'comportant je ne sais quoi de direct ou cette qualité de nous provenir à la façon d'une libre vision spirituelle' (343). It is important that, once the bounds of spectacle are accepted, the 'libre vision spirituelle' comes *from* us rather than, or as well as, *to* us. If theatre can only be sensed out of the operation of forces made visible, equally it is only the willing imagination of the spectator that can make the synthesis and hence see that his own powers ✓ of assimilation have brought about the 'vision'. Similarly, in the situation of the book and the reader, it is the imagination which compiles, in a virtually physical sense, the offerings of words and connotations to form each particular literary experience. The physical figuration of the component parts of theatre constitutes a lesson also in respect of reading, and, when he writes of the adaptation of novels into stage plays, Mallarmé notes this with obvious delight:

> Art qui inquiète et séduit comme ce que l'on perçoit vrai derrière son propre manque d'habitude: car s'établit une délicieuse ambiguité entre l'écrit et le joué, ni l'un tout à fait ni l'autre, qui verse, le volume presque à part, l'impression qu'on n'est pas tout à fait devant la rampe. (342–3)

This ambiguity can also be sensed in the act of reading. In an intense passage written about, or rather *from* the impact made by Banville's 'Le Forgeron', Mallarmé gives a highly dramatic account of the effect of language:

> Ainsi lancé de soi le principe qui n'est – que le Vers! attire non moins que dégage pour son épanouissement (l'instant qu'ils y brillent et meurent dans une fleur rapide, sur quelque transparence comme d'éther) les mille éléments de beauté pressés d'accourir et de s'ordonner dans leur valeur essentielle. Signe! au gouffre central d'une spirituelle impossibilité que rien soit exclusivement à tout, le numérateur divin de notre apothéose,

quelque suprême moule qui n'ayant pas lieu en tant que d'aucun objet qui existe: mais il emprunte, pour y aviver un sceau tous gisements épars, ignorés et flottants selon quelque richesse, et les forger. (333)

The extraordinary clarity and intensity with which the reader apprehends the 'Signe!', at once a still moment and co-ordinated multiple movement of 'les milles éléments de beauté', is certainly reminiscent of those passages in which Mallarmé evokes a different drama, that of ballet. For example:

Ainsi ce dégagement multiple autour d'une nudité, grand des contradictoires vols où celle-ci l'ordonne, orageux, planant l'y magnifie jusqu'à dissoudre: centrale, car tout obéit à une impulsion fugace en tourbillons, elle résume, par le vouloir aux extrémités éperdu de chaque aile et darde sa statuette, stricte, debout – morte de l'effort à condenser hors d'une libération presque d'elle des sursautements attardés décoratifs de cieux, de mer, de soirs, de parfum, et d'écume. (309)

Mallarmé writes in a very similar way about two different phenomena, and, in so doing, evokes a strong sense of movement. That this should be so in the piece about ballet is hardly surprising, since the only way to pay any kind of homage to the phenomenon of the dance is to evoke, as far as possible, the impression given by its movement. Yet that it should also apply to language indicates how deeply Mallarmé felt the expressiveness of dance, and gives the mark of truth to a statement that might otherwise appear to be over-facile, that ballet is 'la forme théâtrale de poésie par excellence' (308). Ballet seems to express in the same way as language expresses, with the additional point that the essence of ballet is also the *way* in which it expresses, not *what* it expresses.

The word 'Signe!' is thus strategically placed in the middle of the passage above, suggesting that it is neither the introduction nor the culmination, but a fundamental element whose quality is such that it stands abruptly, almost suspenseful 'au gouffre central', slightly detached from the whole by Mallarmé's characteristically forceful punctuation, yet fulfilled by the dramatic fluctuations between movement and the intensity of the still point. Both passages are remarkable for this effect, which represents a positive demonstration of the 'mirage interne des mots mêmes.'[1] In the passage about Banville there is a mirage of movement out of what is actually the stillness of words, while the

[1] *Propos*, p. 83.

145

passage about dance demonstrates a precarious but sure sense of the stillness apprehended out of the complex movements of the dance. In the first passage, the beginning is static, but infinitely auspicious: '. . .le principe qui n'est – que le Vers!'; that which is static in the sense of the words is modified by the slight suspension, or catching of the breath, provided by the punctuation. The intensity, and delight, of that combination is then relieved to a certain extent, and given a degree of sensuous expansion and calm in the 'épanouissement (l'instant qu'ils brillent et meurent dans une fleur rapide sur quelque transparence comme d'éther)', if surreptitiously retaining a degree of precariousness in the qualities of appearing and disappearing 'dans une fleur rapide'. The movement is taken up again by the insistence of 'mille éléments de beauté pressés d'accourir et de s'ordonner dans leur valeur essentielle', only to halt again, to pause at what can then be the only possible culmination of the combined movement and suspense – 'Signe!'. If the 'signe' were the dancer, it would be clear that she would no longer be perceived as a human being, though not with intent to transport her into another realm, only to indicate that, by the intensity and strength of her evocatory movements, she must be 'jamais qu'emblème point quelqu'un' (304). Thus the sign, or symbol, appears to be only an emotional necessity, appearing at the point where the pattern of events has reached such a height that it is no longer relevant to talk in terms of the visible, yet still mistakenly reverent to remove entirely to the realm of the invisible. The precarious situation between the visible and the invisible, between the real and the unreal, is, it is obvious in these two passages, brought about by the presence and apprehension of dramatic movement. We sense 'ce dégagement multiple autour d'une nudité' created by the dancer (or by language) yet 'planant l'y magnifie jusqu'à la dissoudre'. The movement of the dancer seems to deny the presence of the dancer, just as the movement of language can appear to deny the presence of language in favour of sensation alone, when in fact it is this apparent disappearance of either language or dancer that assures us of the adequacy, of the supremacy, of their presence. The strength of Mallarmé's writing here lies largely in the recognition that it is only in the absence of 'quelque suprême moule'[1] that language can fulfil itself and demonstrate its qualities, not by rivalling reality, but by borrowing, adapting, 'pour y aviver un sceau', recognizing the 'gisements épars', and finally 'les forger'. The dancer seems to provide a very intense image of this process, because the complication of her movements suggests, to the persistently iconic mind of the spectator, that

---

[1] Cf. Mallarmé's comments in 'Les Mots Anglais', pp. 918, 921.

the dance must 'mean something', while in fact the dancer 'morte de l'effort à condenser hors d'une libération presque d'elle des sursaute-ments attardés décoratifs de cieux, de mer, de soirs, de parfum et d'écume', appears virtually to disappear before a representation which is not 'of anything' except the rich contrast of the 'impulsion fugace' and 'sa statuette, stricte, debout'. The movement of the dancer does not 'represent' anything; it demonstrates only the presence of an 'Idée' or 'signe'. Language, on the other hand, more aptly fitted to the ex-pression of scene or idea, is actually capable, in its moments of highest expressiveness, of attaining a mirage of movement. It is interesting that in both passages there are more static points than indications, in the sense of the words, of movement, as if Mallarmé were compensating for the movement of the mind across the words. While of course the very presence of static moments in writing, such as the 'Signe!' discussed above, creates an effect of excitement and precariousness, a probability of movement which is perhaps even more compelling than movement itself.

Ballet is not the only form of theatre which offers Mallarmé a rich and compatible figuration of suspense. In *Hamlet*, 'la pièce que je crois celle par excellence' (299), Mallarmé' finds much to tempt him:

> parce qu'Hamlet extériorise, sur des planches, ce personnage unique d'une tragédie intime et occulte, son nom même affiché exerce sur moi, sur toi qui le lis, une fascination, parente de l'angoisse. (299)

If the fascination is 'parente de l'angoisse', in considerable contrast to the delight offered by ballet, it is perhaps because in *Hamlet* Mallarmé is confronted by a play in which his own conception of theatre is in part realized, where the hero is not merely a human being conveniently transposed by costume and setting into a creature of the stage, but a figuration of the very elements of theatre. Some apprehensiveness, even 'angoisse' must accompany the idea of writing about such a master-piece. Mallarmé does not attempt any large-scale exegesis; he merely discusses the ideas of suspense and of the hero as they appear in *Hamlet*.

There are many notes in 'Le Livre' concerning the quality of suspense in drama. For example:

> Le Drame est causé par le Mystère de ce qui suit l'Identité (Idée) Soi – du Théâtre et du Héros à travers l'Hymne.[1]

[1] *Le Livre*, feuillet 4 (A).

The idea here is perhaps less striking than some of its developments:

> Le Héros dégage – l'Hymne (maternel) qui le crée.[1]

and:

> il fallait que l'hymne fut à l'état de menace de Dr. [ame].[2]

It might seem curious that Mallarmé should connect the 'Hymne', with its connotations of harmony and serenity, with the 'état de menace du drame', but the state of possibility is so rich that the quality of the 'Hymne' is not out of place.[3] The qualities of the hero that Hamlet suggests to Mallarmé are also unexpected. They are not merely concerned with the hero as the high point of the play, the dominating figure in the action:

> Le – je ne sais quel effacement subtil et fané et d'imagerie de jadis, qui manque à des maîtres-artistes aimant à représenter un fait comme il en arrive, clair, battant neuf! lui, Hamlet, étranger à tous lieux où il poind, le leur impose à ces vivants trop en relief, par l'inquiétant ou funebre envahissement de sa présence. (302)

Hamlet is not so much the dominating figure of the spectacle as the figure that restores to theatre the 'je ne sais quel effacement subtil et fané et d'imagerie de jadis', the sense of the hero's being less a product of the play than a creature of the theatre, installing 'à tous lieux où il poind' (the verb used here is a subtle gesture towards the quality that Hamlet brings to the theatre), a sense of the strangeness proper to the theatre. The strangeness, in the case of Hamlet, stems not only from the poetry of Shakespeare's language, but also from his situation *vis-à-vis* the content of the play. Hamlet is:

> *le seigneur latent qui ne peut devenir*, juvénile ombre de tous, ainsi tenant du mythe. Son solitaire drame! et qui, parfois, tant ce promeneur d'un labyrinthe de trouble et de griefs en prolonge les circuits avec le suspens d'un acte inachevé, semble le spectacle même pourquoi existent la rampe ainsi que l'espace doré quasi moral qu'elle défend, car il n'est point d'autre sujet, sachez bien: l'antagonisme de rêve chez l'homme avec les fatalités à son existence départies par le malheur. (300)

---

[1] *Ibid.*

[2] *Ibid.* feuillets 83 (B) and 84 (B).

[3] Cf. Borges's more insistent comment that 'the imminence of a revelation which does not occur is, perhaps the aesthetic phenomenon': Jorge Luis Borges, *Labyrinths*, ed. D. A. Yates and J. E. Irby (Penguin, 1970), p. 223.

148

As the Hero, or 'seigneur latent qui ne peut devenir', Hamlet might be the original anti-hero, only rescuing his reputation as hero in the last act. Yet this is not the crux of Mallarmé's appreciation of Hamlet. From the passage quoted here it is evident that Hamlet's procrastination, his inability to become what he is, a man who must murder his uncle, constitutes to Mallarmé a realization of the essential qualities of the theatre. Mallarmé ends a little dogmatically with the assertion that the subject of the play is 'l'antagonisme de rêve chez l'homme avec les fatalités à son existence départies par le malheur', but his earlier comments reveal as emphatically that it is essentially the result of this antagonism, or the 'suspens d'un acte inachevé' which captures his imagination. For if a play is basically concerned with an event which does not happen (or, as in *Hamlet*, only happens right at the end), then the substance of the play must create and sustain that sense of theatre which is produced in too facile a fashion by an excess of action and event.

In such a situation the hero, by his presence alone takes on an added emphasis. Yet:

> Comparses il le faut! car dans l'idéale peinture de la scène tout se meut *selon une réciprocité symbolique des types entre eux ou relativement à une figure seule.* (301)

The relationship between the hero and the other characters is of primary interest, for the hero certainly derives some of his impressiveness from the fact that he is now alone, where lately he was not. It is a common and traditional moment in the theatre, when the hero appears alone on the stage, fulfilling not only the stage and its décor, but also the expectations of the audience, the apparently endless mass, watching for the Type relative both to themselves and to the theatre.[1] Mallarmé notes that the power of *Hamlet* is such that it is not even necessary to dress the hero in Elizabethan style:

> Hamlet, lui, évite ce tort, dans sa traditionnelle presque nudité sombre un peu à la Goya. L'œuvre de Shakespeare est si bien façonnée selon le seul théâtre de notre esprit, prototype du reste, qu'elle s'accommode de la mise en scène de maintenant, ou s'en passe, avec indifférence. (300)

The essence of the hero, like that of the theatre itself, does not depend upon the authenticity of its trappings; it is that which strikes a chord

---

[1] Cf. Mallarmé's vivid image in the article 'Catholicisme', where we, the spectators, 'sommes circulairement le héros' (393).

in the 'seul théâtre de notre esprit, prototype du reste', which assures the spectator/reader of the presence of theatre. The position of the hero is such that he is likely to bear the weight of that assurance.

In Mallarmé's 'Rêverie' about Wagner, there are several emphatic passages about the status and effect of the hero, and, although the ideas are often interesting, they are naturally coloured by the context, by Wagner. Yet the trio formed by Hamlet, the virtual hero/heroine of ballet, and the Wagnerian hero, gives a broad impression of the characteristics of the hero. The first two testify largely to intellectual or poetic insights, and the last to a mythical tradition to which the hero belongs:

> Toujours le héros, qui foule une brume autant que notre sol, se montrera dans un lointain que comble la vapeur des plaintes, des gloires, et de la joie émises par l'instrumentation, reculé ainsi à des commencements. Il n'agit qu'entouré, à la Grecque, de la stupeur mêlée d'intimité qu'éprouve une assistance devant des mythes qui n'ont presque jamais été, tant leur instinctif passé se fond! sans cesser cependant d'y bénéficier des familiers dehors de l'individu humain. (544)

This is a great contrast to the heroic stance of Hamlet, whose fragile, sombre presence is nowhere to be found in the 'stupeur mêlée d'intimité' that characterizes the audience's reaction to Wagner's music dramas. The Wagnerian hero needs the presence of choruses, as if to form the mythical, luxuriant path of the tradition from which he springs; whereas Hamlet treads the ground of his solitary inaction. He moves, like the mime:

> dans un hymen (d'où procède le Rêve), vicieux mais sacré, entre le désir et l'accomplissement, la perpétration et son souvenir. (310)

In fact Hamlet appears to be an instance of the mime, caught, transfixed, at the point before the 'perpétration', yet already anticipating the 'souvenir'. He has thus a hold upon time – or an impunity to its ills – characteristic of all great moments of expression.

Yet the notion of the hero, taken at whatever level, does depend to a certain extent upon recognition of myth, of the kind which figures in Wagner's conception:

> les Mythes...Le Théâtre les appelle, non: pas de fixes, ni de séculaires et de notoires, mais un, dégagé de personnalité, car il compose notre aspect multiple: que, de prestiges correspondant au fonctionnement national, évoque l'Art, pour le mirer en nous.

150

Type sans dénomination préalable, pour qu'émane la surprise: son geste résume vers soi nos rêves de sites ou de paradis, qu'engouffre l'antique scène avec une prétention vide à les contenir ou à les peindre. (545)

The type of the hero, according to the Wagnerian image, is the apparition 'dégagé de personnalité', responding to the traditional need for a heroic figure, who by his grandeur and imposing qualities 'évoque l'Art, pour le mirer en nous', and also prompts belief in our 'rêves de sites ou de paradis'. The mythical, Wagnerian hero is one who has almost despotic command over time and place, one whose mysteriousness is only inherent in his appearing now, 'sans dénomination préalable, pour qu'émane la surprise', the visible presence of a long tradition. The presence of tradition is felt more strongly in the theatre, partly because its form has scarcely altered, partly because the audience, by their compliance with that form, seem to pay mass homage to the tradition:

est-ce qu'un fait spirituel, l'épanouissement de symboles ou leur préparation, nécessite endroit, pour s'y développer, autre que le fictif foyer de vision dardé par le regard d'une foule! (545)

The very fact of mass attention, reminiscent of cult worship, is theatrical. And, whatever Mallarmé's doubts about the real value of Wagner's art, there could be no doubting its impact upon audiences.

Cult-worship, however, is little more than a blind indulgence in mythical traditions, and Mallarmé is more interested in another aspect of myth:

Saint des Saints, mais mental... alors y aboutissent, dans quelque éclair suprême, d'où s'éveille la Figure que Nul n'est, chaque attitude mimique prise par elle à un rythme inclus dans la symphonie, et le délivrant! Alors viennent expirer comme aux pieds de l'incarnation, pas sans qu'un lien certain les apparente ainsi à son humanité, ces raréfactions et ces sommités naturelles que la Musique rend, arrière prolongement vibratoire de tout comme la Vie. (545)

In the case of Wagner, it is ultimately the music which saves the situation, celebrating the central figure as more than simply the high point of mythical proceedings, and delivering him, through myth, to the ultimate configuration of hero – 'la Figure que Nul n'est'. The impressiveness of the hero depends on his being a clear instance of the present, a more secret gesture of affiliation with the past, in short, a mythical being.

The Wagnerian hero, such as Mallarmé conceives him, is not unlike 'la Femme' who hovers behind the whole of 'La Dernière Mode'. The 'Figure que Nul n'est' is essential to the whole, but is forced to hold the focus of so great a range of phenomena that, although the presence is real enough, even physically there, it never appears to be anything more than the precarious central point of a number of mirages. If the hero appears a Hero, it is because the spectator can see the full panoply that surrounds him, can sense the tradition from which he springs, and can see also that to detach him from the setting would be entirely to destroy his qualities. The spectator, who cannot see the extent and the fragility of the spider's web of which he is the central point, recognizes and appreciates all the more strongly that of the hero.[1]

The phrase 'Saint des Saints, mais mental' reminds us that, despite the density and heaviness of the mythical image, Mallarmé's conception of the hero was not one which really needed the three-dimensional figure on the stage. The very fact that Hamlet is so obviously the type of the hero to Mallarmé, and for reasons pertaining largely to his presentation of a 'suspens d'un acte inachevé' (300), is indicative of a mature predilection for the figure of a hero rather than the heroism of a hero, stemming, certainly, from a 'foi de lettré en la toujours certaine et mystérieuse beauté du rôle' (300). This 'foi de lettré' is attributed to the actor Mounet-Sully, but applies equally well to Mallarmé himself. For the figure, and the figuration of a hero, Mallarmé turns to mime. Although he writes little on the subject, it is evident that little was needed to express its extraordinary power and charm. The whole of the passage entitled 'Mimique' (310) either expresses or points to the relevance of mime to the written page:

> Le silence, seul luxe après les rimes, un orchestre ne faisant avec son or, ses frôlements de pensée et de soir, qu'en détailler la signification à l'égal d'une ode tue et que c'est au poète, suscité par un défi, de traduire! le silence aux après-midi de musique; je le trouve, avec contentement, aussi, devant la réapparition toujours inédite de Pierrot ou du poignant et élégant mime Paul Margueritte. (310)

The mystical significance of music, at the point where it dissolves into

---

[1] Cf. Mallarmé's use of the spider's web in *Propos*, p. 71: '... centre de moi-même, où je me tiens comme une araignée sacrée, sur les principaux fils déjà sortis de mon esprit, et à l'aide desquels je tisserai *aux points de rencontre* de merveilleuses dentelles, que je devine, et qui existent déjà dans le sein de la Beauté'. Mallarmé's vision of 1866 was true to his writing of twenty and thirty years later.

silence, or, apparently dissolves its surroundings into silence, is more commonly appreciated than that of mime. And if music provides an intense example (inherent in the movement of the words, through 'silence' – 'frôlements de pensée' and the 'translation' made by the poet), mime provides a confirmation 'avec contentement', that the poet's intuitions concerning silence are not only vital but can also be visible. Pierrot 'tient et du visage et des gestes le fantôme blanc comme une page pas encore écrite'. His actions and expression demonstrate that silence, like the empty sheet of paper, is not necessarily something which just exists, that it is something which can be *made*, out of a progression of sympathetic gestures, of language, of music, or, as we see here, of mime. It is made in no chance way – 'l'esthétique du genre situé plus près de principes qu'aucun!' (310). In what appears to be a realm of entertainment of the most elementary kind, we find ourselves confronted by 'principes', directed by 'l'instinct simplificateur direct' (310). It is the combination of that which has the strength and simplicity of the instinctive, combined with the suggestive power of the notional world:

> Voici – 'la scène n'illustre que l'idée, pas une action effective, dans un hymen (d'où procède le Rêve), vicieux mais sacré, entre le désir et l'accomplissement, la perpétration et son souvenir: ici devançant, là remémorant, au futur, au passé, *sous une apparence fausse de présent*. Tel opère le Mime, dont le jeu se borne à une allusion perpétuelle sans briser la glace: il installe, ainsi, un milieu, pur, de fiction'. (310)

The 'milieu, pur, de fiction', signalling the theatrical, has then in Mallarmé's view its basis in a particular working of time. Hamlet, the hero 'par excellence', is chiefly characterized by his delaying, and by his consequent filling of theatrical time with the quality of his delay. The mime, 'dont le jeu se borne à une allusion perpétuelle sans briser la glace', appears never quite to arrive at whatever he is portraying; it is within reach, as music is within reach of silence even while it is being played, but never quite identifiable with it. The allusive strength of mime is not unlike that of music, offering a constant surprise in the sensation that 'something has happened although nothing appears to have happened'. The mime always seems to gesture towards some future event, or to evoke a past one, so that his presence, definitive and hypnotic as it is, seems to spread out fan-like, circling around, out from the present, while inevitably united to it.

The phenomenon of allusion, in this strength, is also the phenomenon of fiction, since what is visible never appears to be 'the real thing', but only anticipation or recollection of it.[1] Thus it is not quite the suspense of wondering 'what is going to happen'. The sensation is more subtle, playing between, on the one hand, the assertion that nothing has yet happened, and, on the other, that it has all happened before, and that we are only seeing the rich commemorative shadow of it. Gestures towards a half-apparent past, towards a half-apparent future, centre the gaze more strangely upon the present, and especially upon the space which it occupies. In bringing to a close his piece on Paul Margueritte, Mallarmé draws attention to the parallel between the silence of mime and the silence of reading, by situating that silence between the book and the reader's eyes:

> Surprise, accompagnant l'artifice d'une notation de sentiments par phrases point proférées – que, dans le seul cas, peut-être, avec authenticité, entre les feuillets et le regard règne un silence encore, condition et délice de la lecture. (310)

It is a banal fact that reading is a silent operation; less banal is the notion that language should create that silence. It is significant that the process of distillation operated by language, and by mime, and its resulting silence, do not seem entirely to leave substantiality. On the contrary, silence installs (the very homeliness of the word is emphatic) 'un milieu, pur, de fiction'. Thus it appears that the place – page or theatre stage – as much as its supersession by action and idea, is essential to dramatic expression, that in the attitude of vigil that characterizes the stage there is already a play.

The space of dance

Both mime and ballet make extraordinary use of the space of the stage, and bring to it a virtual and inner liveliness that is immediately analogous, for Mallarmé, to the virtual space created by means of language. It is naturally tempting – and the results of the temptation can be seen to a certain extent in the fragments of the 'Livre' – to believe that the virtual space can be better sensed by a more physical use of language, that is, by allowing the full resonance or impressiveness of language to come out in speech or declamation. This temptation must be discussed at greater length, but it is also important to look at

---

[1] It is worth noticing how different is this relationship with the 'real thing' from the more usual symbolic one. The fictional object is not one that represents another, real object; it has a hold upon time that the contingent object – and the fallible human – cannot have.

the effects that can be created by written language when it attempts to evoke the qualities of dance.

We have seen how Mallarmé's writing about ballet is comparable with some of his writing about language, how his own language adapts to, and in part adopts the impulse of the virtual language of dance. The sense of movement which results has two main effects: first, that of guaranteeing, paradoxically, the limits and the contained-ness of place; and second, that of suggesting, by the insistence and the clarity of the pattern of movement, a presence of 'un instrument direct d'idée' (312). The two are, of course, very closely connected. If a dancer seems by her movement to express an idea, that idea is no more than her configuration of the space in which she moves, her 'version' of it, which, by its intensity, seems of an ideal, essential nature. Similarly the 'Idée' expressed by language is only seen as such in the light of the words that precede and follow, that is, in the language 'space' that it summons.

At an immediate level, the dancer is 'la mouvante écume suprême' (322) of the theatre, yet the power of her presence goes further than that. One of the richest pieces Mallarmé wrote about the ballet, entitled 'Les Fonds dans le Ballet', contains several passages that show us how. He begins by mentioning the fact that the dancer Loïe Fuller inspired many poets:

> Relativement à la Loïe Fuller, en tant qu'elle se propage, alentour, de tissus ramenés à sa personne, par l'action d'une danse, tout a été dit, dans des articles quelques-uns des poèmes. (307)

Elsewhere Mallarmé mentions that the poet Rodenbach 'écrit aisément des phrases absolues, sur ce sujet vierge comme les mousselines et même sa clairvoyance' (311). Mallarmé's 'version' of ballet is not 'poetic' in the sense that it evokes the atmosphere of ballet, but precise and reverential in that it creates, as nearly as possible, the movement (and hence the atmosphere) of ballet:

> Au bain terrible des étoffes se pâme, radieuse, froide la figurante qui illustre maint thème giratoire où tend une trame loin épanouie, pétale et papillon géants, déferlement, tout d'ordre net et élémentaire. Sa fusion aux nuances véloces muant leur fantasmagorie oxyhydrique de crépuscule et de grotte, telles rapidités de passions, délice, deuil, colère: il faut pour les mouvoir, prismatiques, avec violence ou diluées, le vertige d'une âme comme mise à l'air par un artifice. (308)

It is Mallarmé's language too, that would create 'le vertige d'une âme comme mise à l'air par un artifice', by the breadth and variation of his images: from the geometrical 'maint thème giratoire', and later 'rapidités de passions' become 'prismatiques' (the prism, rich in suggestion, seems to hold, in geometrical form, the infinite variety and gradation of light), to the slightly 'précieux' indulgence of petal, butterfly, or 'fantasmagorie oxyhydrique de crépuscule et de grotte'. The very spread of these references, quite apart from drawing attention to language by the simple device of strangeness or exoticism, actually seems to create, as the dancer does, a space which signifies in unique fashion – the imaginative space is never the same twice, or to two different people. Thus it is the movement between extremes, populated in between by the banality of limitation – in words, as in the movement of the dancer – which creates 'une virginité de site pas songé, qu'isole, bâtira, fleurira la figure'. (308) The space in which the dancer moves seems new, virgin, because each movement, rather than defining the space, seems to re-create it, just as the movement of words, by its constant novelty of experience seems at once to open new ground and confirm the old.

The relationship of ballet to the space it uses is essential, apparently compulsive:

> La danse seule, du fait de ses évolutions, avec le mime, me paraît nécessiter un espace réel, ou la scène.

> A la rigueur un papier suffit pour évoquer toute pièce: aidé de sa personnalité multiple chacun pouvant se la jouer en dedans, ce qui n'est pas le cas quand il s'agit de pirouettes. (315)

Although a play can be thought, or virtually performed in the mind, ballet must be seen, since movement is its essence and adequate space obviously necessary. (One only has to see a ballet on a stage that is too small to understand how, in ideal conditions, ballet relates to space and appears to overcome its contingency.) One long paragraph of 'Les Fonds dans le Ballet' needs to be quoted in full to bring out the impact that the dance made on Mallarmé. His perceptions are as detailed as they are powerful:

> Quand, au lever du rideau dans une salle de gala et tout local, apparaît ainsi qu'un flocon d'où soufflé? furieux, la danseuse: le plancher évité par bonds ou dur aux pointes, acquiert une virginité de site pas songé, qu'isole, bâtira, fleurira la figure. Le décor gît, latent dans l'orchestre, trésor des imaginations; pour en sortir, par éclat, selon la vue que dispense la représentante çà et là de l'idée à la rampe. Or cette transition de sonorités aux

tissus (y a-t-il, mieux, à une gaze resemblant que la Musique!) est, uniquement, le sortilège qu'opère la Loïe Fuller, par instinct, avec l'exagération, les retraits de jupe ou d'aile, instituant un lieu. L'enchanteresse fait l'ambiance, la tire de soi et l'y rentre, par un silence palpité de crêpes de Chine. Tout à l'heure va disparaître comme dans ce cas une imbécillité, la traditionnelle plantation de décors permanents ou stables en opposition avec la mobilité chorégraphique. Châssis opaques, carton cette intrusion, au rancart! voici rendue au Ballet l'atmosphère ou rien, visions sitôt éparses que sues, leur évocation limpide. La scène libre, au gré de fictions, exhalée du jeu d'un voile avec attitudes et gestes, devient le très pur résultat. (308–9)

The effect given by the dancer is not merely made out of the contrast between movement and stillness, although this is obviously the most impressive element. It is not the fact that the dancer's movement forms an expressive whole with the dancer's stillness, but that the way in which she moves – 'le plancher évité par bonds ou dur aux pointes' – is not so much covering the floor as avoiding it. Between the leap or pirouette and the touch 'dur aux pointes' on the floor, there appears a sensation of suspense and uncertainty. The spectator feels that, in reality, the space has scarcely been used or touched, yet the intricate avoidance of it seems to render it more present than it would otherwise have been. Ambiguity, or at least a rich degree of uncertainty, is aroused by the fact that the visions of ballet are 'sitôt éparses que sues', that the dancer, rarely still, (and when still, breathtakingly and hence timelessly so) appears to 'speak' by her movements, yet it is never possible to remember the detail of her 'speech' because of its power and its transience.[1] Also, if the dancer speaks, it is unconsciously, out of the qualities of her being, and not, apparently, out of the arrangement of her potential by any outside force: 'elle paraît appelée dans l'air, s'y soutenir, du fait italien d'une moelleuse tension de sa personne' (303). It is not the choreography nor the scenery, but the 'moelleuse tension de sa personne' which communicates. The combination of extreme tension – the human body as well as the space of the stage apparently stretched as far as possible – and extreme lightness or weightlessness, generates a force which takes Mallarmé, and subsequently his reader, to a different realm of significance. If the dancer's movement is such that:

---

[1] A parallel to this can be seen in the reactions of Mallarmé's adherents to the conversation of their 'Maître'.

> La scène libre, au gré de fictions, exhalée du jeu d'un voile avec
> attitudes et gestes, devient le très pur résultat

its effect is not unlike that of language which, at its most powerful, seems
to create, not sense, but the sensation of silence, 'que c'est au poète,
suscité par un défi, de traduire!' (310). The dancer creates the 'très
pur résultat' of space, and the poet creates the equally pure space of
silence. In the case of the dancer, it is not so much the movement itself
as the relation between movement and stillness, between movement and
the space of the stage, that signifies. Similarly, in language it is not
always the content of the movement (the significance of the words)
which provides the total of the sense, but also the way in which movement at once forms an equilibrium with, and supersedes, the sense of
language.

It is not surprising then, that Mallarmé should often draw attention
to the parallel between language and dance, that he should even suggest
that the dancer can indicate the nature of the 'Idée'. In a piece about
Loïe Fuller, Mallarmé remarks that the chorus only exists:

> pour une spirituelle acrobatie ordonnant de suivre la moindre
> intention scripturale (311)

of the 'danseuse-étoile'. She, in turn, is more than just a centre-piece:

> La presque nudité, à part un rayonnement bref de jupe, soit pour
> amortir la chute ou, à l'inverse, hausser l'enlèvement des pointes,
> montre, pour tout, les jambes – sous quelque signification autre
> que personnelle, comme un instrument direct d'idée. (311–12)

The often-mentioned, imprecise 'Idée' appears here to be not the culmination of any series of perceptions or intuitions, but the last apprehensible point of a movement, given that such a point could not exist
without the seeing, however mirific and transient, of the rest of the
movement. All Mallarmé's writing about ballet stresses the ephemerality,
combined with great force, of the movement involved, while the combination creates, as it were, a need for the purity of the 'scène libre', or
ground of 'l'Idée'.

Mallarmé takes the metaphor of the dance to such lengths that it no
longer even seems to be a metaphor. It is suggestive to say that ballet is
hieroglyphic, or to say that it is 'le rendu plastique, sur la scène de la
poésie' (312), but it is also facile. It is similarly suggestive, and indeed
'précieux', to write of the dancer:

> ainsi qu'avant un pas elle invite, avec deux doigts, un pli fré-

missant de sa jupe et simule une impatience de plumes vers l'idée.
(306)

The very Mallarméan 'pli frémissant'[1] and also the 'impatience de
plumes', reminiscent of the essential 'Femme' of 'La Dernière Mode',
might appear light-hearted or at best whimsical. But this does not
apply to the passage in which Mallarmé describes the possibilities
inherent in 'reading' ballet:

> L'unique entraînement imaginatif consiste, aux heures ordinaires
> de fréquentation dans les lieux de Danse sans visée quelconque
> préalable, patiemment et passivement à se demander devant tout
> pas, chaque attitude si étranges, ces pointes et taquetés, allongés
> ou ballons. 'Que peut signifier ceci' ou mieux, d'inspiration, le
> lire. A coup sûr on opérera en pleine rêverie, mais adéquate:
> vaporeuse, nette et ample, ou restreiente, telle seulement que
> l'enferme en ses circuits ou la transporte par une fugue la
> ballerine illettrée se livrant aux jeux de sa profession. (307)

Mallarmé's reading of the 'ballerine illettrée' might appear as modest
and tactful a gesture as that of his 'reading' of the writing of others. But
the case of 'reading' ballet is, obviously, a special one. It is not as
specifically grounded as the 'reading', or transposing into one's own
language, of the attractive elements in another's work; yet it is not at all
an unspecific indulgence in the obvious qualities of the dance – 'à coup
sûr on opérera en pleine rêverie, mais *adéquate*'. The precise movements of the dancer, contained within the space of the stage, offer the
compelling illusion that there is indeed something to be 'read', something more than the story which classical ballet often uses as a starting
point. Yet it is not just the movement which Mallarmé 'reads', it is the
series of signs that the dancer creates, forming a kind of vaporous
bridge between the 'story' of the ballet, and the movement itself. The
fluctuations between obvious movement, unexpected movement, slowing down, subtle gesturing, are so great that they give the impression of
a strong directive force which somehow commands conviction that there
is indeed something to be 'read'. It may be that 'toujours une banalité
flotte entre le spectacle dansé et vous' (308), and that banality consists
largely in the rational facts of the dancer's movements and the space in
which she moves. Yet there can be no real closing of the gap between
the sensation that ballet 'means something', and the sensation of

[1] See Richard, *L'Univers Imaginaire de Mallarmé*, for discussion of
Mallarmé's predilection for 'le pli', p. 177ff.

watching it. If the spectator is 'reading' one thing, he is watching another. He is 'reading' something like this:

> A savoir que la danseuse *n'est pas une femme qui danse*, pour ces motifs juxtaposés qu'elle *n'est pas une femme*, mais une métaphore résumant un des aspects élémentaires de notre forme, glaive, coupe, fleur, etc., et *qu'elle ne danse pas*, suggérant, par le prodige de raccourcis ou d'élans, avec une écriture corporelle ce qu'il faudrait des paragraphes en prose dialoguée autant que descriptive, pour exprimer, dans la rédaction: poème dégagé de tout appareil de scribe. (304)

On the other hand, what he watches is less specific, no less convincing. For example he watches:

> cette espèce d'extatique impuissance à disparaître qui délicieusement attache aux planchers la danseuse (305)

and sees, rather than knows, that the dancer:

> livre à travers le voile dernier qui toujours reste, la nudité de tes concepts et silencieusement écrira ta vision à la façon d'un Signe, qu'elle est. (307)

The combination of the 'extatique impuissance à disparaître' and the presence of the dancer as 'Signe' together form the kind of lucid suspense which is essential to the sensation of reading.

> Oui, le suspens de la Danse, crainte contradictoire ou souhait de voir trop et pas assez, exige un prolongement transparent. (311)

Reading, at certain levels, is also a 'prolongement transparent', giving an impression of precariousness, the fear that the sensation cannot last, and involving too, in the power of its projection, the sensation that this is only anticipatory, much as the movement of the dancer, or of music, suggests that it will only be afterwards, when it has stopped, that the revelation will be complete. The end of the dance, or of the music, or of the poem, shows of course that the ultimate meaning that always seemed in view, *was* in fact revealed in the quality of the anticipation.

Language too can give a glimpse of these same qualities – most often in the young poet's aspiration, and belief that 'the best always lies further on', even that 'reality or truth itself lies further on'. Mallarmé's reading of ballet gives the valuable intuition that, rather than expecting anticipation and event to add up to significance, the reader should see that true vision must come out of movement, out of the operation of the forces of drama made visible. Language is only too efficient at operating drama; its problem is to create a moment which forms the key point without letting the presence of the operation overwhelm, and without suggesting that the drama is anything other than that of language itself. Ballet creates its 'language' out of movement and out of the ephemeral capturing of space, appearing to have for its aim no more than that capturing, not true capture, no more than a kiss – 'toute la Danse n'étant de cet acte la mystérieuse interprétation sacrée' (305). The capture is, however, as illusory as that of sense by language. It is illusory because, though it appears to be a kind of focal point, a point of significance, just as the word's rational 'capture' of sense seems to be a point of significance, in fact, as far as the overall impression is concerned, it is only a contribution in the form of a contrast, a kind of pinning down of the movement; it is what the spectator of ballet watches rather than 'reads'. Similarly, in the instance of reading, it is possible to 'read' one thing, and, at the same time, to 'watch' or sense another. There are not two kinds of writing, one where the reader moves from one point of sense to another, and one where he receives only a loose, if lucid impression. The two can operate simultaneously, as they do in the case of ballet, where, because there is not, in the usual sense, very much to read, there is a correspondingly high probability that the spectator will seek out a subject. It is natural that Mallarmé, in an age where even the theatre succumbed to the reign of 'reportage', should place great emphasis on the 'readability' of what is in fact wordless, and that he should also want to confer these qualities on language itself. It is also understandable that such language should then have a much stronger relation to space, both to the space on the page, and to the theatrical space of their absorption by the reader or their declamation by the actor. It is theatricality, or spectacle, of the kind where 'rien n'a lieu, sauf la perfection des exécutants' (305), which allows us to read the wordless and to understand that quality in reading which makes the meaning at the end of the words always less impressive than the fact of their stopping. If this is so, the most expressive situation that language can offer (expressive of its own life and potential that is) is one which has been built up in the manner in which the 'meaning' of the dance is built up. The climax of the dance, just before the end, forms a pattern that would, on its own, and out of nowhere, merely be satisfying to the eye, but which, coming after the display of movement, is supreme in expression of all that the last words of the poem would like to have for their own.

The book and the spoken word

The impact of Mallarmé's appreciation of ballet can be felt at many points throughout his writing, and especially where he writes of the 'Livre'. He found in ballet a form that *is* what it expresses, and, while recognizing that language could not consistently achieve this, Mallarmé would obviously want to make full use of any illuminating example. It is always apparent that the fragments of the 'Livre' edited by Schérer are concerned with presentation and not content,[1] indicating that, for Mallarmé, presentation could influence and even determine substance or subject. From the summary notes that do exist, it is evident that the content of the 'Livre' largely, if not wholly, involved an exploration of the theatrical form in which it was to be presented. The many diagrams showing the interplay between hero, drama, mystery, theatre and idea, demonstrate what amounts to an obsession with the qualities of theatrical form. The reader is able to sense even out of these inchoate fragments that Mallarmé is always considering language at the same time as theatre, that his endless juggling of the theatre's qualities is also a juggling of thoughts about language. Ballet appears the perfect or near-perfect silent language, manifesting rather than saying. Its example leads Mallarmé to consider what looks like the most theatrical presentation of language – the spoken word. (His equivalent experience in written form is certainly 'Un Coup de Dés' where he attempts to reproduce on paper the quality of reverberation that the spoken word can have.)

The 'feuillets' of 'le Livre' contain instructions for the 'Maître' of a gathering to read out loud, not sentences, but words or short phrases. The note on 'feuillet' 34 contains the words: 'Lect. 12 personnes. Lect. la messe.' The reference to 'la messe' is no coincidence; Mallarmé saw the readings of 'le Livre' as having the character of a ceremonial. His writing that touches on the atmosphere of religious celebration, and his predilection for, not only the tacit ceremonial of ballet and mime, but also for his 'cher mélodrame français' (323) testify to a fascination with ceremony, and a belief that the procedure of ceremony is, or could be, the sole subject of language. It is perhaps a delusion to believe that this can be effected simply, or largely by organizing the reading of 'le Livre' as a ceremonial where the 'manuscrit seul est mobile'.[2] It seems too simple, too much a solution to a situation so complex and so fruitful that it could not need – for the writer's lifetime at least – a solution.

There is a note written in 1895 which testifies to what must have been a late fascination with the expressiveness of the spoken word:

[1] As Schérer himself remarks, p. 125. [2] *Le Livre*, feuillet 52.

> Le Vers et tout écrit au fond par cela qu'issu de la parole doit se montrer à même de subir l'épreuve orale ou d'affronter la diction comme un mode de présentation extérieur et pour trouver haut et dans la foule son écho plausible, au lieu qu'effectivement il a lieu au delà du silence que traversent se raréfiant en musiques mentales ses éléments, et affecte notre sens subtil ou de rêve. (855)

Mallarmé is fascinated by the fact that what looks like the most straightforward use of language can 'affecte notre sens subtil ou de rêve'. The apparent clarity of spoken words creates its own echoing quality, seeming more physical than that of written words since it is an attempt to capture, or just see the impact of the passing words. In a much earlier note, from 1869, we find:

> C'est donc puisque la Conversation nous permet une abstraction de notre objet, le Langage, en même temps que, site du Langage, elle nous permet d'offrir son moment à la Science, dans la conversation que nous étudierons le Langage. (853)

Again it is not the substance of the spoken word but its resonance that Mallarmé finds interesting. Here we see the spoken word as an abstraction that nonetheless belongs to a place, a site. Words become detached from the speaker as soon as they are spoken; now they seem part of a human presence, now they are mere abstractions. It is thus capable of seeming more abstract than written language. In the piece 'Sur Madame Georgette Leblanc' Mallarmé writes:

> A l'encontre de la loi que le chant, pur, existe par lui, rend l'exécutant négligeable, une interprète, de très loin, revient, avec mystère, s'y adapter, plus comme instrument, ni actrice, en tant que le spectacle humain visible, ou personnage, de la Voix qui baigne une face expressive... (861)

This piece, published in 1898, suggests a broadening of Mallarmé's viewpoint. It is no longer the detached, nearly inhuman voice that expresses, but a combination of that same voice and the human dramatic presence. Another late piece, written as a 'Toast à Ses Jeunes Amis' in 1897, touches on a different, though related aspect of the spoken word:

> Sans phrase je vous remercie ému, tout ce que je dirais flotte ici, d'avoir, maintenant, par une inversion spirituelle et jeune, fait de moi l'invité si vous passez les hôtes. (865)

In the warmth and affection of the gathering, the scenario for Mallarmé's speech, there is little need for specificity, and all gestures of appreciation converge in the comment 'tout ce que dirais flotte ici'. These words suggest not a floating away but a suspension whose detail is unseen, perhaps non-existent, yet clearly dictated by the setting in which it is spoken, so that whatever language is used, it appears to echo the virtual language of the setting.

Spoken language forms a nearly physical presence, whose significance is sensed according to tone and apparent mass. There are words that float, words that fill the room, uncertain words like 'le nom soudaine-ment d'Arthur Rimbaud' which is 'bercé à la fumée de plusieurs cigarettes' (512). These different characteristics point to one, fundamental, that:

> le Verbe apparaisse derrière son moyen du langage rendu à la physique et à la physiologie, comme un principe, dégagé, adéquat au Temps et à l'Idée. (854)

Although this was written as early as 1869, its sense is not lost in the later writing, where it is evident that Mallarmé is still investigating the possibilities of 'la physique et la physiologie' of language, even if he would not, in later years, formulate his ideas in quite the same way. 'Le Verbe' would certainly be replaced by 'Le Livre', since the 'Livre', with its breadth and theatrical possibilities, seems to include all that renders it possible to read the qualities of language rather than just its sense. For the 'Livre', as it appears in the 'Autobiographie' written for Verlaine, is, in its conception, of enormous magnitude:[1]

> un livre, tout bonnement, en maints tomes, un livre qui soit un livre, architectural et prémédité, et non un recueil des inspira-tions de hasard fussent-elles merveilleuses...J'irai plus loin, je dirai: le Livre, persuadé qu'au fond il n'y en a qu'un, tenté à . son insu par quiconque a écrit, même les Génies. L'explication orphique de la Terre, qui est le seul devoir du poète et le jeu littéraire par excellence: car le rythme même du livre, alors im-personnel et vivant, jusque dans sa pagination, se juxtapose aux équations de ce rêve, ou Ode. (662–3)

When the Book grows to this order of magnitude, obviously something like the impressiveness of the spoken word, or a nearly inhuman rhetoric, seems to be demanded. The book is an artifice, like the theatre, it is

---

[1] The magnitude is well balanced in the fragments of the 'Livre' by the figures Mallarmé gives for the distribution of his work, as well as for its actual length. For details see Schérer's preface.

'architectural et prémédité', yet it is also 'l'explication orphique de la Terre'. The contrast of these two factors alone guarantees the '*jeu littéraire*', and demands too, that the dreamlike quality of its conception, and its presence, however inchoate, be expressed by the 'Ode'.

If it seems strange that so great a champion of the written word should extend his appreciation to the powers of the spoken word, it must be remembered that, in practical terms, writing is not only the best means of evolving a view of language, but is also the least 'dangerous'. Its automony is assured, and the confrontation of a notion of language with its actuality is therefore less vulnerable. The various factors involving spoken language are so uncertain that it is not surprising that the writer approaches it with greatest circumspection, if the greatest interest. Mallarmé's fascination, both with spoken poetry, or the 'Ode', and with the possibilities of his envisaged 'Séances' of language, stems from a highly developed belief in the powers of language. In a piece written (with a great sense of relief, it appears, that there should be one play or theatrical piece of writing that in some way comes up to or fulfils the potential of the theatre) about Banville's 'Le Forgeron', we read:

> La merveille d'un haut poème comme ici me semble que, naissent des conditions pour en autoriser le déploiement visible et l'interprétation, d'abord il s'y prêtera et ingénument au besoin ne remplace tout que faute de tout. J'imagine que la cause de s'assembler, dorénavant, en vue de fêtes inscrites au programme humain, ne sera pas le théâtre, borné ou incapable tout seul de répondre à de très subtils instincts, ni la musique du reste trop fuyante pour ne pas décevoir la foule; mais à soi fondant ce que ces deux isolent de vague et de brutal, l'Ode, dramatisée ou coupée savamment; ces scènes héroiques une ode à plusieurs voix. (335)

Mallarmé himself wrote 'Hérodiade', describing it as 'scènes héroiques'; while admitting the 'Après-midi d'un faune' to be '*non possible au théâtre*, mais *exigeant le théâtre*'.[1] Also his impatience with contemporary theatre makes it understandable that he should look to a slightly different area for a realization of what he saw as the essential qualities of theatre. None the less, it is clear that Mallarmé was fascinated, and tempted by the possibilities of dramatic language, by the 'déploiement visible et l'interprétation'. The use of the word 'déploiement' here,

[1] *Propos*, p. 51.

with its connotation of the unfolding newspaper, as well as the slow but confident opening of any ideal movement, shows that Mallarmé's expectations of the 'Ode' and of the spoken word in general, were quite specific: that it should in some measure fulfil the theatrical possibilities of language Mallarmé sensed in writing, that it should do justice, too, to the physical character of the book, the 'minuscule tombeau, certes, de l'âme' (379). Thus Mallarmé's expectations of the spoken word have an ultimate quality to them. They suggest that in this realm the notion of language built up in writing will now be realized. For the reader, on the other hand, the interesting and perhaps predictable revelation is that, although it is inevitable that the writer should try to reach some kind of solution, that he should want to express, not the notion, but 'the thing itself', in fact the *effect* of language that remains at a notional level is far stronger, far more alive than any prospective 'terme du chemin'. In view of the private nature of the fragments of the 'Livre', and in view of the emphasis of most of Mallarmé's writing, it seems likely that the proposals for 'le Livre' were to Mallarmé as conjectural as his musing about writing.[1] In the 'Autobiographie', we find Mallarmé admitting that one life is not enough for the completion of the 'Livre', but without the anxiety or frustration that might be expected in such a confession:

> Voici l'aveu de mon vice, mis à nu, cher ami, que mille fois j'ai rejeté, l'esprit meurtri ou las, mais cela me possède et je réussirai peut-être; non pas à faire cet ouvrage dans son ensemble (il faudrait être je ne sais qui pour cela!) mais à en montrer un fragment d'exécuté, à en faire scintiller par une place l'authenticité glorieuse, en indiquant le reste tout entier auquel ne suffit pas une vie. Prouver par les portions faites que ce livre existe, et que j'ai connu ce que je n'aurai pu accomplir. (663)

The choice is left to the needs of the reader: whether the fragments of 'Le Livre' are a plan for the 'Livre' which Mallarmé was unable to finish, or whether they form yet another delay, compiling merely the theatrical space in which language would perform, where words would be, and be what they were saying. For the nature of language – that is, what it is saying – the reader must look, not to the fragments of 'Le Livre', but to the 'Variations', where Mallarmé sets out an extraordinarily detailed and dense plot, weaving in language, the book, theatrica-

[1] That much of his writing should be a kind of blueprint for writing, and that the 'Livre', as it exists, is essentially the shell of a book, is certainly no coincidence.

lity – once again, all but the content of the book. But in the 'Variations' the quality of Mallarmé's language is such that the reader, brought under the spell of a virtual presence of the book, can sense what would be the contents, or rather, can feel that Mallarmé's language is itself the content of the book.

6

The language of literature

Even within the modest and cautious title 'Variations sur un Sujet' we can see a justification for looking at Mallarmé's contribution to the *language* of literature, rather than to literature 'tout court'. The title also calls to mind the considerable span of the other prose writings, emphasizing both its extent and its essential focusing upon 'un sujet': language. The variation-form is such that we are reminded by the intensity and, often, the difficulty of the writing, that we are not involved merely in an explanation of the qualities of language, but also in a performance of them. It would be a mistake to approach the 'Variations' with an attitude different from that which was necessary in reading, for example 'La Dernière Mode': the latter has an unexpected, hidden seriousness, and the former an unexpected, patent air of enjoyment. Just as Mallarmé was delighted that it should even be possible to understand certain qualities of language through the eyes of the 'femme du monde', so he writes with equal pleasure of those apparent commonplaces of language which contribute, unobserved, to its literary effect. Such 'apparent commonplaces' include the qualities of the printed word, its possible variation on the page; the ways in which the common currency of language can be overcome; the play between that currency and the words' own strong atmosphere, and, perhaps most importantly, the way in which the reader's special attention to literary language is found to be more vital than any amount of analysis. That special attention, furthermore, is not just to be found in the 'Variations'; it is a thread that runs through all Mallarmé's prose, and it is this indeed that assures us that the title 'Variations sur un Sujet' is no idle inspiration but a quiet gesture towards the character and content of all the prose writing. However far the variations might move, they are always held to the 'subject' by the quality of Mallarmé's language and by the attention it demands from the reader. The language of the 'Contes Indiens' or of 'La Dernière Mode' is superficially far less difficult than that of the 'Variations', yet its full effect can only be sensed by the reader who does read in the manner that more difficult writing demands. Without that special attention, amounting, as we shall see, to a fluency of movement rather than to any detailed and static knowledge that the professional 'Littérateur' might have, it is possible to read the 'Contes Indiens' as ordinary fairy tales, and 'La Dernière Mode' as a more or less ordinary fashion magazine. The 'Variations', on the other hand, without adequate reading would amount only to an intensely difficult and private working-out of a theory of literature apparently intended to exclude the creation – then necessarily separate – of a piece of literature.

The musical form of 'theme and variations' is artificial, even ingenious; it lacks the rigour and force of the more complex and 'difficult' fugue. Mallarmé's 'variations' also include moments where the intensity of the fugal form is reached, where, bypassing any need to explain or apologize, he puts his theme, so to speak, into the hands of language: 'Je dis "une fleur"', he says, and then creates, in words, the performance and finally the re-emergence of that phrase. More often, though, we see a less intense enjoyment, punctuated by moments when Mallarmé is suddenly made aware, perhaps by the very power of his own writing and its difference from even a literary norm, of a need to 'explain'. These moments of explanation can perhaps be accounted slight failures of nerve on Mallarmé's part, and an unavoidable succumbing to a degree of irritation that it should even be necessary to make public 'statements' about the nature of language. Some anger at being misunderstood is understandable in the case of Mallarmé, in that he responded so easily, so valuably, to such a variety of language situations, and yet was so often dubbed an obscure or 'ivory tower' writer, suggesting a narrowness of interest and application in every way belied by the prose works.

Hence we find a number of instances in the 'Variations' where Mallarmé is reminded, especially at points where a crucial issue is being considered, of the grave problems that face the writer as soon as he remembers the reader, unseen and potentially unseeing. Once reminded of his worst fears about the abilities of readers, Mallarmé may give a demonstration, as it were, for the benefit of unbelievers, and also in order to show that no palliative explanation can be adequate. For example, near the end of 'Le Mystère dans les Lettres', we find Mallarmé at his most unambiguous:

Je préfère, devant l'agression, rétorquer que des contemporains ne savent pas lire – (386)

Then a few lines later we read:

Lire –

  Cette pratique –

  Appuyer, selon la page, au blanc, qui l'inaugure son ingénuité,
  à soi, oublieuse même du titre qui parlerait trop haut... (386–7)

Mallarmé demonstrates here what those he aims the first at fail to do.
He does not merely tell us about the nature of reading; in reading his
words we realize that, through the structure of the syntax, through the
punctuation, we are given a paradigm of the experience. Any manual
entitled 'How to read', on the other hand, 'parlerait trop haut'.

  Similarly, in the piece entitled 'Solitude', we find a perhaps predictable, almost trite complaint about the plight of the writer in relation to the everyday world, a complaint probably prompted by Mallarmé's sensitivity to the frustrations of teaching. When given the
opportunity to expound both his language and his point of view in a
magazine article, Mallarmé writes:

  L'existence littéraire, hors une vraie, qui se passe à réveiller la
  présence, au-dedans, des accords et significations, a-t-elle lieu,
  avec le monde; que comme inconvénient – (405)

Words like these only seem to serve as support to the image of Mallarmé
the 'private' writer. But that in turn obscures what he actually makes
clear in this piece: that the writer does not disdain or consistently
escape from the real world; it is merely that his way of looking at it is so
different that it passes for escape. A seeing of the world that serves 'à
réveiller la présence, au-dedans, des accords et significations', naturally
will not come out in writing as the kind of one-to-one relationship
normally associated with seeing reality and transcribing it into words.[1]
It is important, then, for the reader of Mallarmé not only to understand
his words, but also to understand the kind of seeing that governs them.

  Another point peculiar to the 'Variations' (and, to a certain extent,
some of 'Crayonné au Théâtre') is that the reader is evidently confronted by a mature Mallarmé who, though *ready* to 'write his vision' rather
than discuss it, is still not actually doing so. His most effective prose is
still mostly writing 'about' writing, and the over-expectant reader,
hoping to find Mallarmé 'in action', will either be disappointed or conclude that the prose is merely explanation, that the 'real' writing is to
be found in the poetry. But a reading of the 'Variations' which takes
account of the revelations found in his other prose, will show that this
view does a great injustice to what Mallarmé wrote.

---

[1] See Mallarmé's comments on this kind of writing 'qui ne compte pas
littérairement', p. 384.

Mallarmé often remarks on the superiority of poetry, but his remarks by no means suggest that prose is only a runner-up. As he points out in 'La Musique et Les Lettres', the letters of the alphabet move towards 'une transfiguration en le terme surnaturel, qu'est le vers' (646), and the word 'surnaturel' obviously tends to suggest that 'le vers' is 'higher' on the scale, that it is more expressive than prose. However, it is central to this book to make clear that, in language, the 'terme surnaturel' is often less interesting, and also more illusory, than the route towards it. If Mallarmé nowhere says this explicitly it is because he saw the necessity of sustaining a delicate balance between belief in the 'terme surnaturel' (which must appear *possible*, just as Mallarmé's 'Livre' appeared possible to him) and enjoying that sounding out of language before the writer can even consider that he is in a position 'to begin'. There are many points on the scale between believing in any 'terme surnaturel' and wanting to reach it. However, the strength of any expressive use of language is such that the reader forgets the existence of either scale or aspiration, as well as the circumstance of the writing. Mallarmé's language at its best does not appear to reach any ultimate point but gives an impression of what language is like, of the impact it can make. This is often the case in his poetry as well as in his prose. For there too, language is often the 'subject' of language. Sonnets are written in homage to other writers, so that the quality of Verlaine's work, or Baudelaire's, or Wagner's, appears to form the subject of the poem, while Mallarmé's language merely supports it. Yet by using elliptical and intense language to say 'this is the substance and the greatness of what Baudelaire wrote', Mallarmé also pays tribute to what language can do. Thus if Baudelaire's poetry – and Mallarmé's – should here be the 'terme surnaturel', we are less conscious of that fact than of the effect language is having. Similarly, Mallarmé puts unusual emphasis on the presence of language by making words 'speak' the movement of the fan on which they are written. The fan is then less the subject of the poem than the circumstance which allows language its literary autonomy.

In a revealing sentence from the essay 'Magie', Mallarmé writes:

Il me gêne presque de proférer ces vérités impliquant de nets, prodigieux transferts de songe, ainsi, cursivement et à perte. (400)

Although Mallarmé is not making a general statement here, it is no injustice to him to treat it thus, for it is characteristic – in its meaning as well as in its form – of his attitude towards that which it is possible and desirable to write. The degree of 'gêne' which Mallarmé shows here is also obliquely present in much of his writing (perhaps all,

171

except where he is concerned to make criticisms of the reading public or theatre audiences). If he writes, not the substance of a book but its plan; if he outlines the necessity of a certain kind of language apparently without always performing it, it is not because he is concerned to live as a Hamlet-figure of constant, if highly expressive procrastination. It is because he perceived that the qualities of language were such that they were most expressive of their own potential when used, not to 'transfer' reality onto paper, but to transform it. Since transformation is a process and not an instantaneous happening, it is clear that 'proférer ces vérités' would have no meaning for Mallarmé, that his interest would be in sustaining or building up that impetus which would then suggest the undoubted presence of the 'vérité', much as we sense the presence of the neighbour in 'Le Nénuphar Blanc' and the 'fleur' at the end of 'Crise de Vers'.

The prevalence of Impressionist thought at the end of the nineteenth century might make it appear that Mallarmé was following, or began, the practice of 'not naming the object but suggesting it' in order to bring out more richly the suggestive qualities of that object. While this is true to a certain extent, it is not merely a whim of the writer, but a quality of language itself that makes suggestion rather than statement the most expressive form. A simple transfer of reality into language results in no intensification either of the impressiveness of that reality or of the expressiveness of language. It is because Mallarmé felt both of those so strongly that he was careful to do them justice. To give merely a suggestion or impression of reality in language was not enough. A dancer can transcend the limiting factors of the contingent situation; she does not thereby give only a vague impression. Similarly Mallarmé wants to give language its true status, which is not that of standard-bearer to reality, nor deferential impressionist, but that of a process equal to it in life and subtlety. The maturity of this point of view and its consequent possibilities for expression in language can be seen by comparing it briefly with the situation in *Igitur*. There Igitur, the hero of the creative process, prepared the scene, waits for midnight, and casts the die. Mallarmé's language is blatantly symbolic, visibly expectant of some other reality beyond the words. In the language of Mallarmé's late prose, and especially the 'Variations', the reader can virtually see a new Igitur, not casting the die and waiting for an answer, but casting the die in language of expressiveness such that it needs no answer.

If it appears over-facile to say that the way Mallarmé's prose works is itself the answer to any questions it poses, much as both problem and answer lie inherent in the language of mathematics, the proposition is to a certain extent belied, or at least rendered less simple, by the fact that it is almost impossible to sustain it at this level. The moments when Mallarmé's language simply is, and appears of itself to provide the significance, without moving in a realm of possible reference, are extremely precarious. They are the ultimate product of the variation or fugal form. Yet because they are held within a form and are not isolated in the way that a poem can appear isolated, they seem to provide an equilibrium between belief in the 'terme surnaturel' and desire to reach it. Both poetry and prose present an impression of a movement towards some still greater revelation as yet only glimpsed, but because the prose of the 'Variations' appears less intense, or less consistently intense, its movement is more compelling, and its precarious moments less precarious. After reading a poem, one is more likely to consider in an abstract manner its effect or aftermath; after reading a piece from the 'Variations', one can only consider the effect of the words by look-ing at them again. We saw in 'Les Mots Anglais' that Mallarmé con-sidered the impression of precariousness given by language to be partly the result of characteristics inherent in language, and not the result of any too hopeful bridging of the gap between language and reality. Thus any writing which reflects the qualities of language will give an im-pression similar to that of poetry and dissolve too the idea that there is more than one 'genre' in literary language.

It is true of the prose works already discussed that Mallarmé's lan-guage is at its most effective when referring to the medium being con-sidered – the writing of others, the expressiveness of theatre, of ballet – so that language moves parallel to another mode of expression, and so realizes more effectively its own potential. Writing about theatre, for example, seemed to provide a virtual 'place' for language, a notional scenario in which words could operate. When, in 'La Musique et les Lettres', Mallarmé puts the movement of language alongside that of music, we see that music provides an elaborate metaphor for language, of a kind not met hitherto, since in this instance the metaphor is such that language, so to speak, has to do all the work, there being no physical basis to which it can refer. Although it is music, or rather, the relation-ship between music and language, which is discussed, it is only language which speaks. However, if the notion is easy to state, it is less easy to demonstrate, and if Mallarmé appears over-emphatic, occasionally repetitive or obscure, and sometimes pedantic, it is because he must have realized the necessity, in the face of his own intuitions, of teaching the reader how to read things which, theoretically, he had not yet written, but which were certainly nearer completion than the author's modesty, and indeed his theory, would allow. But there is one important point that the reader of the 'Variations' must accept: that it is not merely necessary to make a map of their significance, but that one must also understand what amounts almost to an invention, on Mallarmé's part, of map-making in language.

Reality and the map of words

As a combined entry into and warning of the nature of the 'Variations', it is valuable to look back to a piece from Mallarmé's tribute to Villiers. After a few gratuitous words of introduction, there is a note in the text to say that the speaker sits down, implying that the substance of the homage rather than the fact of it is about to begin:

> Sait-on ce que c'est qu'écrire? Une ancienne et très vague mais jalouse pratique, dont gît le sens au mystère du cœur.
>
> Qui l'accomplit, intégralement, se retranche.
>
> Autant, par ouï-dire, que rien existe et soi, spécialement, au reflet de la divinité éparse: c'est, ce jeu insensé d'écrire, s'arroger en vertu d'un doute – la goutte d'encre apparentée à la nuit sublime – quelque devoir de tout recréer, avec des réminiscences, pour avérer qu'on est bien là où l'on doit être (parce que, permettez-moi d'exprimer cette appréhension, demeure une incertitude). (481)

The magnitude of Mallarmé's vision of writing is probably only equalled by its mysteriousness: a practice whose sense lies 'au mystère du cœur', formed by insight and intuition, does not seem to install the writer in the real world but cuts him off from it. Yet it is only when writing is seen in the guise of a total activity that it can, in the drastic sense Mallarmé gives here, take place at all. 'Ce jeu insensé d'écrire' takes on the appearance of an inventor's folly or a scientist's obsession. Although the example of Villiers lends itself particularly to these extreme attitudes towards writing, Mallarmé in his own way is hardly less extreme. When we read the famous comment that 'tout, au monde, existe pour aboutir à un livre' (378), it is easy to take it in a very general way, as if the world operated somehow without the writer yet mindful of his needs, arranging itself in such a way as to be compatible with the form of the book. However, the emphasis throughout Mallarmé's writing lies upon the transformation brought about by the writer's perception of the world: writing appears to be an experience rather than a vision.

Only by seeing things more intensely can we write of them at all, and whoever achieves this 'intégralement, se retranche'.

In a passage that Mallarmé uses twice, once in 'Crise de Vers', and once (the original occasion) in 'La Musique et Les Lettres', we see how words map the experience rather than the fact of things:

> A savoir s'il y a lieu d'écrire. Les monuments, la mer, la face humaine, dans leur plénitude, natifs, conservant une vertu autrement attrayante que ne les voilera une description, évocation dites, allusion, je sais, suggestion: cette terminologie quelque peu de hasard atteste la tendance, une très décisive, peut-être qu'ait subie l'art littéraire, elle le borne et l'exempte. Son sortilège, à lui, si ce n'est libérer, hors d'une poignée de poussière ou réalité sans l'enclore, au livre, même comme texte, la dispersion volatile soit l'esprit, qui n'a que faire de rien outre la musicalité de tout. (645)

Language neither captures reality, nor sets it upon a visionary pedestal. Mallarmé's terminology in this passage moves away from postulating a definitive function for language (from 'description', to 'évocation', through 'allusion' and 'suggestion'); in fact the ascending order of the terms is more important than deciding whether or not the last in the series is the 'right' one. The relation that writing can have to reality is, for Mallarmé, essentially one of liberating, not the entire full-ness of visible reality, but, 'hors d'une poignée de poussière', those volatile qualities of the imagination which certain realities can prompt. The faithfulness of language to this 'dispersion volatile' results neither in a picture nor a vision of reality, but in a sensation of 'la musicalité de tout'. If this seems as facile an escape route as any 'vision of reality', one should remember that it is only a tentative summing-up; its combination of the vague and the absolute appears less evasive when one considers other evidence of the relation between Mallarmé's perception and his language.

In the introduction to 'La Musique et Les Lettres', we find Mallarmé considering the qualities of the two English university towns, Oxford and Cambridge, and doing so with the unmistakable touch of a 'littérateur' who has temporarily taken on the guise of tourist:

> Moi-même y contredis, en ce qui est de chez nous, imbu de je ne sais quelle hostilité contre les états de raretés sanctionnés par les dehors, ou qui purement ne sont l'acte d'écrire. (637)

We do not merely see here an instance of Mallarmé's taste in landscape or townscape; we see that he prefers the grandiose or the beautiful that is less the result of a presentation than of a transformation. For, as he continues, 'il faut cette fuite – en soi'. The writer confronted by a splendid building is more dazzled than inspired; he sees nothing in operation and can only receive passively. In 'Le Livre, Instrument Spirituel' Mallarmé says that the poet lives

> antérieurement selon un pacte avec la Beauté qu'il se chargea d'apercevoir de son nécessaire et compréhensif regard, et dont il connaît les transformations. (378)

On the one hand we see the poet signing a pact with 'la Beauté', and on the other hand, in the essay 'Etalages', acknowledging the necessity, even within such a pact, of experiencing all levels, not just those whose 'états de raretés' are evident from the outside:

> Le vague ou le commun et le fruste, plutôt que les bannir, occupation! se les appliquer en tant qu'état: du moment que la très simple chose appelée âme ne consent pas fidèlement à scander son vol d'après un ébat inné ou selon la récitation de quelques vers, nouveaux ou toujours les mêmes, sus. (375)

There could be nothing more certainly experiential in tone than 'se les appliquer en tant qu'état'. If Mallarmé is to be accused of élitism, it is not on account of any rarefied view of the world. Perception here takes on the various 'états' of reality as if they were so many different suits of clothes. And, as Mallarmé points out in the essay 'Bucolique', those aspects of reality which language can successfully evoke, tend to be less grandiose, less impressive, so that language can provide or invent a grandeur not inherent in reality but only prompted by it.[1] Mallarmé writes of:

> La mer dont mieux vaudrait se taire que l'inscrire dans une parenthèse si, avec n'y entre le firmament (403)

and points out:

> Un sécurité nommée la paix des champs, à l'encontre des dissipations ou verbiages, amasse, de silence, assez pour faire transparaître en ce qu'il s'agit de ne pas dire, la grandeur. (403)

There is much that language cannot accommodate, but if it cannot

---

[1] There will thus be some danger that for readers less able to see, as well as less able to read, any grandeur or expressiveness in the words will be no more real than the Emperor's new clothes – or worse, the Emperor will only appear in his familiar garb.

entirely account for the grandeur of the natural scene, heavens as well as oceans, it can create, rather than state, a grandeur of its own.

> Abolie, la prétention, esthétiquement une erreur, quoiqu'elle régît les chefs-d'œuvre, d'inclure au papier subtil du volume autre chose que par exemple l'horreur de la forêt, ou le tonnerre muet épars au feuillage; non le bois intrinsèque et dense des arbres. (365–6)

Mallarmé's theory of language as suggestion rather than statement is not simply a perverse one. It stems from a profound interest in what language can say, in how it can best fulfil its expressive potential. Going back to 'La Musique et les Lettres', we find near the end where the reader might expect the emphasis to lie in the transcendental or ultimately expressive qualities of 'la musique et les lettres', that a different point comes across:

> Le vers va s'émouvoir de quelque balancement, terrible et suave, comme l'orchestre, aile tendue; mais avec des serres enracinées à vous. Là-bas, où que ce soit, nier l'indicible, qui ment.
>
> Un humble, mon semblable, dont le verbe occupe les lèvres, peut, selon ce moyen médiocre, pas! si consent à se joindre, en accompagnement, un écho inentendu, comminiquer, dans le vocabulaire, à toute pompe et à toute lumière; car pour chaque, sied que la vérité se révèle, comme elle est, magnifique. (653)

Although the general tenor of this is powerful and emphatic, it is not in any way transcendental. Writing does not seem to operate with a view to arriving at some new, transformed object or situation, but to give the sensation of the very process itself. The presence of language, with its 'serres enracinées à vous', serves to 'nier l'indicible, qui ment'. If the truth appears, as it does here, magnificent, it is because it is an equilibrium sustained, unstated, between the movement of the 'aile tendue' and the pull of 'des serres enracinées à vous'. The process that creates this equilibrium transcends any problems of discrimination between this or that aspect of the world. If it appears perilous or un-sayable it is because it is the result of a process, rather of two processes; it is a force best described in musical terms as melodic or harmonic –

> l'hymne, harmonie et joie, comme pur ensemble groupé dans quelque circonstance fulgurante, des relations entre tout. (378)

In all considerations relative to Mallarmé's notion of the absolute, the 'Idée' or ultimate significance of language, it should be remembered that the emphasis constantly evident in his writing is not by any means the spiritual or transcendental affair it appears to be. He was not merely obsessed by the sensation of writing and its relation to reality, he was also too involved in the virtually physical movement of language to consider in any serious way a spiritual rôle for language. Language may be 'le direct affinement' (409) of the world, but:

> En vue qu'une attirance supérieure comme d'un vide, nous avons droit, le tirant de nous par de l'ennui à l'égard des choses si elles s'établissaient solides et prépondérantes – éperdument les détache jusqu'à s'en remplir et aussi les douer de resplendissement, à travers l'espace vacant, en des fêtes à volonté et solitaires.
>
> Quant à moi, je ne demande pas moins à l'écriture et vais prouver ce postulat. (647)

Alongside the 'attirance supérieure' or sense of aspiration, we see something much clearer. The tendencies towards the metaphysical or spiritual that beset most young writers have, in Mallarmé's case, too strong a link with physical spectacle; the sacred is not the invisible but the distillation, apparently into the invisible, of the physical. The sense of involvement possible to both reader and writer makes the 'indicible' less interesting, a false or unnecessary emphasis on the qualities of language. The unsayable, in great moments of expression, always seems to be there. It is not merely a part of the reader's wordless appreciation; it is a natural, unreadable palimpsest. The strength of language in operation seems to suggest the likelihood and the desirability of that which can be conceived as absolute. No less, one might add, does a sensitive perception of reality.

It is perhaps true of the highest degree of sophistication in any realm that it relies largely upon a consciousness of very simple origins, constantly working alongside a state of distinctive complexity. Indeed the very origin of the word 'sophistication' suggests that he who practises it is performing a very conscious act, one which is by no means accessible to those who have not come so far and have not such a strong sense of the origin, or, in the case of Mallarmé, of the language:

> Un homme peut advenir, en tout oubli – jamais ne sied d'ignorer qu'exprès – de l'encombrement intellectuel chez les contemporains; afin de savoir, selon quelque recours très simple et primitif, par exemple la symphonique équation propre aux saisons, habitude de rayon et de nuée; deux remarques ou trois d'ordre analogue à ces ardeurs, à ces intempéries par où notre passion relève des divers ciels: s'il a, recréé par lui-même, pris

soin de conserver de son débarras strictement une piété aux
vingt-quatre lettres comme elles se sont, par le miracle de
l'infinité, fixées en quelque langue la sienne, puis un sens pour
leurs symétries, action, reflet, jusqu'à une transfiguration en le
terme surnaturel, qu'est le vers; il possède, ce civilisé édennique,
au-dessus d'autre bien, l'élément de félicités, une doctrine en
même temps qu'une contrée. Quand son initiative, ou la force
virtuelle des caractères divins lui enseigne de les mettre en
œuvre. (646)

Few readers – or writers – have that 'piété aux vingt-quatre lettres'
which Mallarmé has so markedly; and few achieve the equilibrium of
'ce civilisé édennique'. The substance of Mallarmé's 'paradise' is elemental, but has that tension peculiar to the elemental as sensed by a
'civilisé édennique'. Mallarmé remarks with typical concision that the
letters of the alphabet, 'par le miracle d'infinité' contain the possibility
of distillation 'en le terme surnaturel, qu'est le vers', and that, in the
miraculous simplicity of language, there lies the possibility of transformation into a sense that, although appearing to belie the original
simplicity of language, in fact balances and supports it. To have 'une
doctrine en même temps qu'une contrée' is invaluable not only in the
sense that it does away with the difference between theory and practice;
it also, as a result, endows with a powerful life and lucidity writing
which could otherwise appear 'encombrements intellectuels'. It is often
as a consequence of trying to say something basically very simple that
the original impact of the phenomenon is lost. It is certainly Mallarmé's
aim, and often his achievement, to show that words can 'talk about
themselves', and, in so doing, provide 'une doctrine en même temps
qu'une contrée'.

Clearly the vision that the 'civilisé édennique' has of the book and
of the activity of writing will be at once extraordinarily lucid and
extraordinarily *felt*. It is the combination of these two elements
which produces both the sometimes forbidding strangeness of Mallarmé's writing, and the great strength of what he says. The two
qualities – the clear-sighted, intellectual 'civilisé', and generously
imprecise, experiential 'édennique' – form, out of their apparent
differences, an impact of lucid conviction. Experience is often lucid by
the unerring power of its impact, but quite the opposite when looked
at from the viewpoint of the intellectual; while the 'civilisé' in Mallarmé
contributes another kind of lucidity, and the two together provide an
irrefutable conviction that 'le monde est fait pour aboutir à un beau
livre' (872). The book itself of course, containing both the map of

179

words and the mark of the map-maker, is an 'objet privilégié' that Mallarmé never takes for granted:

> Le Livre, où vit l'esprit satisfait, en cas de malentendu, un obligé par quelque pureté d'ébat à secouer le gros du moment. Impersonnifié, le volume, autant qu'on s'en sépare comme auteur, ne réclame approche de lecteur. Tel, sache, entre les accessoires humains, il a lieu tout seul: fait, étant. Le sens enseveli se meut et dispose, en chœur, des feuillets. (372)

Taken on their own these last phrases might merely look like a flight of fancy. Yet the previous words are abrupt and positive: 'il a lieu tout seul: fait, étant'. The book's solidity and presence are such to Mallarmé that it scarcely even stretches his imagination to see that the meaning of the book might move and 'dispose, en chœur, les feuillets'. Since no physical description is adequate, Mallarmé turns to this highly imaginative, precarious form of language. The special status of the book for Mallarmé makes such language understandable; its slightly exaggerated quality can also stand as a model for those less dramatic and more expressive moments where language confronts reality.

There is some danger, in Mallarmé's version of the book he sees, that he might lose his case by wanting too much to make it clear. In the essay 'Le Livre, Instrument Spirituel', the spiritual form of the book itself is apparently quite overlaid by the impact of its physical presence. In the passage cited above from 'L'Action Restreinte', there was a balance in Mallarmé's language between the notional and the physical. In some of his other comments on the physical nature of the book the balance is less successful, and sometimes not there at all. For example, near the end of 'Le Livre, Instrument Spirituel', we see Mallarmé 'comme le cuisinier égorgeur de volailles':

> Le reploiement vierge du livre, encore, prête à un sacrifice dont saigna la tranche rouge des anciens tomes; l'introduction d'une arme, ou coupe-papier, pour établir la prise de possession.[1] (381)

Although the tone of this is in some measure influenced by Mallarmé's dislike of most of the books that come his way 'dans le cas réel' (381), it remains clear that such dramatizing of the banal is not always successful. Of a different kind are Mallarmé's remarks about the book as a magic box, full of hidden or partly hidden treasure. These images figure often

---

[1] Cf. the more sympathetic treatment given to the cutting of pages in a 'Chronique' of 'La Dernière Mode': 'Solennités tout intimes, l'une: de placer le couteau d'ivoire dans l'ombre que font deux pages jointes d'un volume'. (718)

in Mallarmé's writing, and give a far stronger sense of the possibility the book suggests. They form a link too, with Mallarmé's fascination with often erotic images of the folded, the hidden and the glimpsed. Earlier on in the piece 'Le Livre, Instrument Spirituel', we find two comments on the nature of the book. The first is the more sober and reverent:

> Le pliage est, vis-à-vis de la feuille imprimée grande, un indice, quasi religieux: qui ne frappe pas autant que son tassement, en épaisseur, offrant le minuscule tombeau, certes, de l'âme. (379)

This is reminiscent in its certainty and lucidity of image, of the words in 'Le Livre':

> et le livre est pour ce lecteur bloc pur – transparent.[1]

Mallarmé transfers the effect of reading a book – the transparency of words' sense and sensation – into the actual appearance of the book. The difference between this metaphorical use and that of the 'butcher's sacrifice' above, is that here we see the book in the process of transformation, caught between fact and suggestion, between reality and dream. Mallarmé not only mentions the imaginative process, he makes us use it. The image of density, of settling down, suggests the simultaneous intricacy and simplicity of the soul – here roughly equivalent to the imagination – and points to the kind of comment Mallarmé makes further on, this time starting from the basis of a discussion of the qualities of newspapers:

> Jusqu'au format, oiseux: et vainement, concourt cette extraordinaire, comme un vol recueilli mais prêt à s'élargir, intervention du pliage ou du rythme, initiale cause qu'une feuille fermée, contienne un secret, le silence y demeure, précieux et des signes évocatoires succèdent, pour l'esprit à tout littérairement aboli. (379)

Here, the combination of the 'vol recueilli' and secret of 'une feuille fermée' points more clearly towards the suggestive power that the form of the book had for Mallarmé.[2] If the ideas are still 'précieux' the impact is less so, since the form of the sentence is taut, tending towards convolution, coiling up its own 'vol recueilli', and with it, doubtless, its own secret. Where 'le fond et la forme' to a certain extent coincide, the

---

[1] *Le Livre*, feuillet 43.
[2] Such suggestiveness here is reminiscent of Mallarmé's relish for the vision of the 'femme du monde' in 'La Dernière Mode', and the compatibility of her response with his own vision.

reader can feel the authenticity of Mallarmé's intuition, and can recognize that what he says about the book is being revealed in the way he says it.

The newspaper, about which Mallarmé obviously had complex feelings, does provide a spur to thoughts about the impact of book, page and letters. Entirely negative reactions can only incite over-positive defence, but Mallarmé's attitude towards newspapers is only uncertainly negative. He can be impressed by the way in which the sheer reproduction of words, a ritual of newsprint, bears a resemblance to the apparently more restricted ritual of literary words:

> Un miracle prime ce bienfait, au sens haut où les mots, originellement, se réduisant à l'emploi, doué d'infinité jusqu'à sacrer une langue, des quelque vingt lettres – leur devenir, tout y rentre pour tantôt sourdre, principe – approchant d'un rite la composition typographique.
>
> Le livre, expansion totale de la lettre, doit d'elle tirer, directement, une mobilité et spacieux, par correspondances, instituer un jeu, on ne sait, qui confirme la fiction. (380)

The extraordinary *mass* of newsprint, impressive over and above what it communicates, can offer a kind of mobility, an assurance of a place in which language and letters move, but miraculously also 'tout y rentre pour tantôt sourdre, principe'. Beyond the variations in headline typesizes, newspapers make no real use of typography as an expression in itself. In the book, on the other hand, the possibilities are, or should be according to Mallarmé, fully realized. The 'jeu' of typography equals and parallels the play and mobility of the sense of the words. Out of a banal object or a banal representation in words we perceive a fiction, an unreal level of perception. The words on the page attempt in all possible ways to do justice to the writer's conception of their expressiveness.

In black and white

Although the concept of the 'Livre' has almost cosmic proportions, there is an important counter-influence in Mallarmé's discussions of a much smaller notion, that of putting pen to paper. His consciousness of the phenomenon developed early on, though in those early stages, he had a tendency to doubt the power of language either to capture the absolute or simply to transform the white page:

> En effet, voici la phase singulière où je suis. Ma pensée, occupée

182

par la plénitude de l'Univers et distendue perdait sa fonction normale: j'ai senti des symptômes très inquiétants causés par le seul acte d'écrire.[1]

In later writings the tone of such speculations is closer to that of the poem 'Salut', written in 1893, where 'le blanc souci de notre toile' creates less anxiety than excitement. More sure, by this time, of what it is possible to communicate by the written word, Mallarmé is proportionately more free to appreciate the experience of writing, the complex instrument of book, page and word, and the ultimate, striking simplicity of their co-ordination:

> Rien de fortuit, là, où semble un hasard capter l'idée, l'appareil est l'égal: ne juger, en conséquence, ces propos – industriels ou ayant trait à une matérialité: la fabrication du livre, en l'ensemble qui s'épanouira, commence, dès une phrase. Immémorialement le poète sur la place de ces vers, dans le sonnet qui s'inscrit pour l'esprit ou sur espace pur. (380)

The dense and elliptical language appears to deal with a loftier theme than that of putting words down on paper. Mallarmé's sensitivity to the act of writing is such that he sees marking the page as a microcosm of the experience given by the whole book. The whole begins 'dès une phrase'. Naturally it is not the journalist who only covers the page with 'simple maculature' (380), but the poet who can best appreciate the sensation of writing the first words.

The very first piece in the 'Variations' begins with the words:

> Longtemps, voici du temps – je croyais – que s'exempta mon idée d'aucun accident même vrai; préférant aux hasards, puiser, dans son principe, jaillissement. (355)

The sensation of 'jaillissement', at once purposeful and merely initiatory, is fundamental to Mallarmé's impression of the contact between words and paper. It answers curiously that more familiar 'jaillissement' of thought or image, a free, spontaneous outpouring rather than a structured overture. Mallarmé wants to explore the 'principe' rather than its consequences. In practice this leads to the controlled and contained excitement of a theory on the brink, so to speak, of being proved. The word 'jaillissement' in the passage above does not realize its full expressive potential; it is held back by the punctuation and structure of the sentence. Yet neither does it look like an understatement. It suggests that the impact of the word on the page is neither

---

[1] *Propos*, p. 86.

explosive nor merely introductory, but intimates, by its control, the rich 'déroulement' that is to come.

Mallarmé can be straightforward and unambiguous on the subject of word and page:

> Je me figure par un déracinable sans doute préjugé d'écrivain, que rien ne demeurera sans être proféré; (367)

Or he can be suggestive:

> Ton acte toujours s'applique à du papier; car méditer, sans traces, devient évanescent, ni que s'exalte l'instinct en quelque geste véhément et perdu que tu cherchas. (369)

The writer's thoughts are evanescent and precarious, and language appears a means of fixing both their form – before it vanishes, untracked, into the memory – and their sense. Mallarmé believes written language versatile enough to capture the fleeting approximations of sense as we experience them. It is even, one might say, better than thought or the imagination since it can create, out of the contrast of permanent print and evanescent sense, a rich and apparently endless mobility. The belief that language can capture a fleeting sense may be gratifying, but it is limited. In 'L'Action Restreinte' Mallarmé indicates that writing is altogether more mysterious, and more significant in itself, than its simple presence on the page would seem to suggest:

> Ecrire –
> L'encrier, cristal comme une conscience, avec sa goutte, au fond, de ténèbres relative à ce que quelque chose soit: puis, écarte la lampe.
>   Tu remarquas, on n'écrit pas, lumineusement, sur champ obscur, l'alphabet des astres, seul, ainsi s'indique, ébauché ou interrompu; l'homme poursuit noir sur blanc. (370)

There is perhaps an over-ingeniousness in Mallarmé's appreciation of the black and white of writing which could detract from the authenticity of what he says here. However, in the piece which follows Mallarmé moves closer to the letter on the page to consider it alone, though in tacit relation to the sense of the words:

> Ce pli de sombre dentelle, qui retient l'infini, tissé par mille, chacun selon le fil ou prolongement ignoré son secret, assemble des entrelacs distants où dort un luxe à inventorier, stryge, nœud, feuillages et présenter.

184

Avec le rien de mystére, indispensable, qui demeure, exprimé, quelque peu. (370)

The tempo and timbre of this passage quite dispel the impression of playful ingenuity or 'préciosité' of the preceding one. The letter on the page appears in the guise of the highly Mallarméan 'pli', always richly suggestive. Here it 'retient l'infini', not only in the decisive, infinite mark of black upon white, but also in a more figurative sense, in that the shape of the letters on the page is the mysterious mark of a pattern of thought. It appears from this passage that Mallarmé found it only a delightful coincidence that the shape of letters on the page should be of the same lace-like tracery that characterizes patterns of thought, the 'luxe à inventorier'. Language seems to make no more than an inventory, by its very shape on the page, of the secrets of the 'sombre dentelle'. Yet 'le rien de mystère' that runs through thought is not entirely dispelled by this intricate parallel. The simple black on white is still mysterious, despite its being no more than an inventory of a far less knowable realm.

At the extreme end of this scale of mystery is a view borrowed from the alchemists:

Si! Avec ses vingt-quatre signes, cette Littérature exactement dénommée les Lettres, ainsi que par de multiples fusions en la figure de phrases puis le vers, système agencé comme spirituel zodiaque, implique sa doctrine propre, abstraite, ésotérique comme quelque théologie. (850)

Again, in 'Etalages', Mallarmé transforms the alphabet into a mysterious keyboard:

Avec les caractères initiaux de l'alphabet, dont chaque touche subtile correspond à une attitude de Mystère. (375)

It seems as though Mallarmé were divided between a liking for the mysterious and esoteric, and a subtle capacity for 'explaining' it in terms of simple physical facts. Both these last quotations suggest that the workings of the letters of the alphabet are obscure in the extreme, and that this is in part a contribution to their significance. But the level at which this kind of thinking operates is quite different from that at which Mallarmé 'explains' why language should appear difficult. The mysteriousness of the word on the page does not create any difficulty for the reader; if it is sensed at all it is only as an impact. What can be difficult for the reader is the way in which Mallarmé uses the arrangement and

185

spacing of words on the page as an integral part of the communication. In the intense passage about Poe which figures amongst the fragments of 'Le Livre', Mallarmé attempts to map out the play of clarity and mystery in the words of a poem:

> L'armature intellectuelle du poème se dissimule et tient – a lieu – dans l'espace qui isole les strophes et parmi le blanc du papier: significatif silence qu'il n'est pas moins beau de composer, que les vers. (872)

Again, it is easy to see such an 'explanation' of the mysteriousness of writing as dangerously over-extended, if not over-simplified. It seems facile to say that the sense, and especially the mystery of words, lie not in the black of the print but in the white of the page. Mallarmé is led to make this kind of explanation for two reasons. Always extremely conscious of the act of reading, he likes to keep the mysterious effects of language, so to speak, as far as possible on the page, so that the white spaces become coloured if not filled by the effects of the words. On the other hand, by concentrating on the white as much as on the black, Mallarmé gives his support to the theory that one sees an object more clearly by looking near it rather than at it. The reader does not, of course, look *at* the words for very long, yet his general impression is not that the black and white have coalesced into a uniform grey, but that they remain at once distinct and interwoven.[1] The black of the letters can appear mysterious although it also represents clarity and control; while the white of the page, at first clear, becomes mysterious when it accommodates the effect of the words.

When, in 'Le Livre, Instrument Spirituel', Mallarmé reflects upon the disturbing qualities of the newspaper format, he muses:

> *Mais . . .*
>
> J'entends, *peut-il cesser d'en être ainsi*; et vais, dans une échappée, car l'œuvre, seule ou préférablement, doit exemple, satisfaire au détail de la curiosité. Pourquoi – un jet de grandeur, de pensée ou d'émoi, considérable, phrase poursuivie, en gros caractère, une ligne par page à l'emplacement gradué, ne maintiendrait-il le lecteur en haleine, la durée du livre, avec appel à sa

---

[1] Mallarmé's evident liking for the writings and near-mythology of alchemy would have been well-nourished had he read the following comment by Paracelsus about the balance between the mysterious – the white of the page – and control of it: 'Know, therefore, that it is arcana alone which are strength and virtues. They are, moreover, volatile substances, without bodies; they are a chaos, clear, pellucid, and in the power of a star.' Paracelsus, *The Hermetical and Alchemical Writings*, vol. I, p. 153.

puissance d'enthousiasme: autour, menus, des groupes, secon-
dairement d'après leur importance, explicatifs ou dérivés – un
semis de fioritures. (381)

This is in effect an outline of the procedure adopted in 'Un Coup de
Dés', where the title and 'spine' – 'Un coup de dés n'abolira le hasard' –
leave an essential open-endedness. As Mallarmé says in his introduction
to the poem: 'Tout se passe, par raccourci, en hypothèse; on évite le
récit.' (455) It was inevitable that Mallarmé should have attempted a
project like 'Un Coup de Dés', yet the degree of difficulty it presents to
the reader is such as to suggest that Mallarmé neither satisfies the
criteria nor overcomes the temptations glimpsed in the passage above
from the 'Variations'. And although this is experienced as the reader's
difficulty, it has its source outside questions of the reader's competence.
It has to do with the substance of Mallarmé's own theory about the
expressiveness of language. In a note written in 1895 we see Mallarmé
considering, in an essentially private way, without intent to convince
or 'be creative', the 'hidden meaning' of words:

> *S*, dis-je, est la lettre analytique; dissolvante et disséminante, par
> excellence: je demande pardon de mettre à nu les vieux res-
> sorts sacrés qui...ou de me montrer pédant jusqu'aux fibres, j'y
> trouve l'occasion d'affirmer l'existence, en dehors de la valeur
> verbale autant que celle purement hiéroglyphique, de la parole
> ou du grimoire, d'une secrète direction confusément indiquée par
> l'orthographe et qui concourt mystérieusement au signe pur
> général qui doit marquer le vers. (855)

It is the 'secrète direction confusément indiquée par l'orthographe'
which Mallarmé sets out to explore and clarify in 'Un Coup de Dés'.
Sensing intuitively the strength and significance of the mysterious
movement that seems to hover behind both written and spoken language, Mallarmé proves his point by attempting to pin down that
movement by the artifice, far more advanced and striking than that of
punctuation and paragraphing, of *arrangement*, grading the size and
weight of type according to the relationship of meaning to the sum or
centre, that 'un coup de dés n'abolira le hasard'. There is no narrative
in the usual sense, but there is a virtual narrative in the alternating
stresses between the different typefaces, and the varying proportions of
white space. In the straightforward form of prose the reader is freer,
paradoxically, to 'read' or 'see' the 'jet de grandeur' and the 'semis de
fioritures' (381), and to sense their significance, than when they are

actually performed on the page.[1] This conclusion might seem damning to the success of any creative venture, but in fact it merely diverts creativity elsewhere. Vestiges of Mallarmé's early aspirations 'vers l'Idéal' take on a different form in the later writing. For example:

> *Autre chose*. . . ce semble que l'épars frémissement d'une page ne veuille sinon surseoir ou palpite d'impatience, à la possibilité d'autre chose. (647)

It is not necessary to make such elaborate allowance for this 'autre chose' as Mallarmé does in 'Un Coup de Dés'. Far more ordinary forms of language can suggest 'autre chose' and also relate it to the notional or attempted 'œuvre pure'.

'L'œuvre pure': expectation and experience

Mallarmé's concept of an 'œuvre pure' was not more ethereal or unattainable than another; it implied simply an experience of language in which reality is as far transformed as it may be. That poets appear propelled towards an ideal realm or expression is not just a personal taste or quirk, as we saw in 'Les Mots Anglais'; it stems from certain characteristics inherent in language:

> Les langues imparfaites en cela que plusieurs, manque la suprême: penser étant écrire sans accessoires, ni chuchotement mais tacite encore l'immortelle parole, la diversité, sur terre, des idiomes empêche personne de proférer les mots qui, sinon se trouveraient, par une frappe unique, elle-même matériellement la vérité. (363–4)

The particular quality of literary language stems from the absence of a 'perfect language', and the writer's success tends to be judged on his ability to overcome the difficulties this presents. The absence of a perfect or fully expressive language gives an order and a force to all literary attempts. And because language is not automatically capable of capturing exactly the things and resultant sensations that the author sees and feels, it becomes autonomously expressive. A poem is an idiosyncratic vision often of something quite ordinary; in attempting to give the object an individual edge of strangeness, language substitutes

---

[1] The temptation to which Mallarmé succumbs in actually producing the 'jet de grandeur' and the 'semis de fioritures' is not unlike that of Apollinaire, whose *Calligrammes* attempt to make the best of the same sort of temptation: for example, printing a poem about rain in 'rivulets' of words down the page.

its own uneven qualities for those of reality. For Mallarmé the form of
poetry is a homage paid to the absent, perfect language:

> Le souhait d'un terme de splendeur brillant, ou qu'il s'éteigne,
> inverse; quant à des alternatives lumineuses simples – *Seulement,*
> sachons, n'*existerait pas le vers*: lui, philosophiquement rémunère
> le défaut des langues, complément supérieur. (364)

Poetry may be a 'complément supérieur', but it is not a perfect language; it is merely a more rarefied and personalized use of the same imperfect language. It is also, in one sense, a reaction to the subservience
of language in most situations, an emphatic gesture of defiance to all
'reportage':

> Parler n'a trait à la réalité des choses que commercialement: en
> littérature, cela se contente d'y faire une allusion ou de dis-
> traire leur qualité qu'incorporera quelque idée.
> A cette condition s'élance le chant, qu'une joie allégée.
> Cette visée, je la dis Transposition – Structure, une autre.
> (366)

Unlike the passive language of 'commercial' exchanges, literary language
almost operates a 'prise de possession' on reality.

Such decisive relating of words to things may seem strange in view
of what Mallarmé mentions so often concerning the apt use of language
for allusion rather than statement. However, the 'Transposition' of
objects into language is, in view of the latter's imperfections, more
powerful than any reproduction could be. Not only does language
become virtually independent of reality, it also seems to forbid even the
author's presence:

> L'œuvre pure implique la disparition élocutoire du poète, qui
> cède l'initiative aux mots, par le heurt de leur inégalité mobilisés;
> ils s'allument de reflets réciproques comme une virtuelle traînée
> de feux sur des pierreries, remplaçant la respiration perceptible
> en l'ancien souffle lyrique ou la direction personnelle enthousiaste
> de la phrase. (366)

Mallarmé is nowhere more positive in stating his relationship to the
words he writes (for if he does not profess to be writing 'l'œuvre pure'
it is obvious that all his efforts tend towards it) than in this passage with
its dramatic 'abdication' of the poet. Instead of the poet's voice being
evident either in 'l'ancien souffle lyrique', or in 'la direction personnelle
enthousiaste de la phrase', he puts together words that reflect their own

qualities and not ideas or opinions or even experiences of his own. That, at any rate, would be the content of 'l'œuvre pure'. Yet Mallarmé, like other writers, does not always write 'l'œuvre pure', he also explains. Even in this dense piece there is a measure of explanation. Words move by 'le heurt de leur inégalité', they 's'allument de reflets réciproques comme une virtuelle traînée de feux sur des pierreries'. In other words, language is expressive not because it is particularly good at transmitting in precise detail the writer's vision or experience, but because it performs such tasks inadequately. Even when attempting to transmit a sense, words instead transmit, with equal and perhaps greater strength, another, anterior sense, stemming from the 'inégalité – in size upon the page, and in expressiveness to the reader.

Even without knowing what a writer meant by the phrase 'l'œuvre pure', one would expect it to have no ordinary subject, even no subject at all. Mallarmé's consciousness of the sense which language best conveys leads him to write in what looks like a provocative manner of the subject of the 'œuvre pure'.[1] The mystery that appears in Mallarmé's writing is not mystification but a very detailed observance of certain qualities of language. Yet, when forced to simplify for the needs of an interview, Mallarmé does not deny that mystery and enigma are attractive to him:

> Il doit y avoir toujours énigme en poésie, et c'est le but de la littérature, – il n'y en a pas d'autres – d'*évoquer* les objets. (869)

Mallarmé often stresses the need to distinguish the standpoint of the writer from that of other language users, not so that the writer should only be understood by a few (although this is often a consequence), but because the distillation his language operates on the real world necessitates some kind of distancing:

> Pourquoi ne la rédiger, au retour, cursive preuve ultérieurement qu'un jour de grand soleil, peut-être, j'ai perçu, dans la différance qui le sépare du travailleur, l'attitude, exceptionnelle, commise au lettré.
>
> Une élégance, la dernière, elle se renforce de la seule bravoure encore, ou devant le numéraire, persiste, ainsi que la fleur d'à-présent humaine: qui porte quelques privilèges, anonymement, de royauté. (411)

This distinctiveness of literary language – and of some literary person-

---

[1] Cf. the openly jesting manner of Mallarmé in 'Solitude': 'Attendez, par pudeur...que j'y ajoute, du moins, un peu d'obscurité.' (407)

ages too – is often forbidding to the reader. Purity becomes confused with obscurity, and obscurity with perverse privacy. There are traces in Mallarmé of the proud preservationist guarding a poetic stronghold of the last purity.[1] But this is not the limit of his views on the mystery or obscurity of literary language.

Language is, to Mallarmé, evidence of 'another world': not a detached world but a transformation of the real one. It is because it does not operate according to the rules which govern reality that it seems strange. As Mallarmé says in 'Le Mystère et les Lettres':

> Il doit y avoir quelque chose d'occulte au fond de tous, je crois décidément à quelque chose d'abscons, signifiant fermé et caché, qui habite le commun: car, sitôt cette masse jetée vers quelque trace que c'est une réalité, existant, par exemple, sur une feuille de papier, dans tel écrit – pas en soi – cela qui est obscur: elle s'agite, ouragan jaloux d'attribuer les ténèbres à quoi que ce soit, profusément, flagramment. (383)

Mallarmé here attributes to reality what many of his readers would attribute to language, although it is mere quibbling to discuss whether language or reality contributes the mystery. In either case, the result of the meeting of reality and language is, in the hands of the writer, mysterious. In the paragraphs that follow the one cited above, Mallarmé pursues a highly elliptical argument on the virtues of obscurity. Although it is chiefly an instance of Mallarmé's defence mechanisms in operation, it stands in striking complement to moments in the same essay where he actually demonstrates, as effectively as anywhere else, the kind of mysteriousness which is not merely expressive, but essential in his eyes to literary language.

As evidence of the defensiveness we find:

> Sa crédulité vis-à-vis de plusieurs qui la soulagent, en faisant affaire, bondit à l'excès: et le suppôt d'Ombre, d'eux désigné, ne placera un mot, dorénavant, qu'avec un secouement, que ç'ait été elle, l'énigme, elle ne tranche, par un coup d'éventail de ses jupes: 'Comprends pas!' – l'innocent annonçat-il se moucher. (383)

Such hypothetical – and not unlikely – attitudes in the reader, which, as Mallarmé notes further on 'implique un renoncement antérieur à juger',

---

[1] Cf. the comment in 'Sur l'Evolution Littéraire': 'Car moi, au fond, je suis un solitaire, je crois que la poésie est faite pour le faste et les pompes suprêmes d'une société constituée où aurait sa place la gloire dont les gens semblent avoir perdu la notion.' (869)

fail to take note of the true rôle of enigma in language. It is the aberration of most readers to expect a measure of comprehensibility, so to speak, at the same time as a measure of incomprehensibility, thus separating the effect of language from 'what it says'. In an obvious attack on such attitudes, Mallarmé writes:

> De pures prérogatives seraient, cette fois, à la merci des bas farceurs.
>
> Tout écrit, extérieurement à son trésor, doit, par égard envers ceux dont il emprunte, après tout, pour un objet autre, le langage, présenter, avec les mots, un sens même indifférent: on gagne de détourner l'oisif, charmé que rien ne l'y concerne, à première vue. (382)

This is obviously Mallarmé's version of 'Aristocratie, pourquoi n'énoncer le terme' (415), and shows too that there is nothing whimsical about all the references to the subject of writing. The references are not only difficult out of deference to a complex situation, but also for reasons of defensiveness. Doubtless wearied by the incomprehension of most of the public, Mallarmé would obviously prefer his language to be difficult in appearance in order to 'détourner l'oisif', so that the true reader should persevere for reasons which are not to do with the 'culling' of a sense, but with an involvement with the words on the page.

The hypothetical 'true' reader will expand his appreciation of language from what others find forbidding:

> Si tout de même, n'inquiétait je ne sais quel miroitement, en dessous, peu séparable de la surface concédée à la rétine – il attire le soupçon: les malins, entre le public, réclament de couper court, opinent, avec sérieux, que, juste, la teneur est inintelligible. (382)

The vague or obscure effect which is off-putting to many readers is here termed a 'miroitement, en dessous', a precise set of reflections and refractions which do not obscure but illuminate the sense of the words. In her own way, the 'abonnée' of 'La Dernière Mode' appreciated better this 'miroitement' than many readers of literature, since to her it was part of the effect or spectacle, not worrying and even essential. In a letter of 1868, Mallarmé wrote:

> je veux dire que le sens, s'il en a un, (mais je me consolerais du contraire grâce à la dose de poésie qu'il renferme, il me semble) est évoqué par le mirage interne des mots mêmes. En se laissant

aller à la murmure plusieurs fois, on éprouve une sensation assez cabalistique.[1]

Whereas the 'femme du monde' seemed to fulfil the suggestion of the 'miroitement, en dessous', it is the 'sensation assez cabalistique', a feeling of ritual and magic, which springs to mind in connection with the 'mirage interne des mots mêmes'. Although Mallarmé is in many ways indebted to the examples both of the fashion world and the world of ritual and alchemy, these are only images that help us understand the 'miroitement' and 'mirage'. These do not guard the sanctity of the 'œuvre pure'; they are products of it. Also, as images of mirrored light, they remind us that the 'œuvre pure' is essentially self-reflecting, transforming and drawing into its uneven play all facets of the perceived world.

Always an apt commentator on his own procedures, Mallarmé gives in 'Le Mystère dans les Lettres' a highly revealing image of 'le nuage, précieux, flottant sur l'intime gouffre de chaque pensée' (384), an image of language stretched taut over the gulf of the writer's intended sense, indicating how perilous that sense is. One might use such an image to describe the after-effect of reading. During reading, on the other hand, any perilousness meets a counter-influence:

> Dites, comme si une clarté, à jet continu; ou qu'elle ne tire d'interruptions le caractère momentané, de délivrance.
> La Musique, à sa date, est venue balayer cela –
> Au cours, seulement, du morceau, à travers des voiles feints, ceux encore quant à nous-mêmes, un sujet se dégage de leur successive stagnance amassée et dissoute avec art –
> Disposition l'habituelle. (384)

The introduction of the musical metaphor here is of the greatest importance, since it brings with it the notion of movement, and the way that contributes to the sense. We read here that 'un sujet *se dégage*'; it is so composed that:

> Une directe adaptation avec je ne sais, dans le contact, le sentiment glissé qu'un mot détonnerait, par intrusion. (385)

If words gradually shed their meaning, as the eye moves across them, much as a chrysalis eventually sheds its butterfly, they do so in an extremely precise way. Mallarmé recognizes:

> La menace de dissiper, en y touchant à même ou à part, des

---

[1] *Propos*, p. 83.

vérités qui le sont à l'état de gammes, accords posés préludant au concert: tout silence, mieux, envers un art lui-même de paroles – hors les prestiges et l'inspiration. (408)

Throughout the 'Variations' and 'La Musique et les Lettres' Mallarmé's use of musical metaphors is highly expressive, underlining the united precision and grandeur of –

un art, l'unique ou pur qu'énoncer signifie produire: il hurle ses démonstrations par la pratique. L'instant qu'en éclatera le miracle, ajouter que ce fut cela et pas autre chose, même l'infirmera: taut il n'admet de lumineuse existence sinon d'exister. (295)

This emphatic piece from 'Crayonné au Théâtre' finds no better echo than in Mallarmé's explanations of how language expresses. For these, no less than Mallarmé's poetry, have the intense impact of words whose form and content cannot be divided.

In a dense but lucid paragraph of 'Le Mystère dans les Lettres', Mallarmé expounds his vision of words themselves, considered before, or independent of the sense they express:

les mots, d'eux mêmes, s'exaltent à mainte facette reconnue la plus rare ou valant pour l'esprit, centre de suspens vibratoire; qui les perçoit indépendamment de la suite ordinaire, projetés, en parois de grotte, tant que dure leur mobilité ou principe, étant de ce qui ne se dit pas du discours: prompts tous, avant extinction, à une réciprocité de feux distante ou présentée de biais comme contingence. (386)

Words express as the pieces in a kaleidoscope express, by a succession of mental mirrors that meet in a 'centre de suspens vibratoire' that they seem to have created. Words refract and reflect so sharply that the 'centre du suspens' even becomes necessary. This says nothing of what they might represent, but emphasizes their expressive power. The reader who aims to do no more than pick out the structure of the sense here, will automatically feel too some of the words' power. The words signal by 'une réciprocité de feux distante' to one another, and, in so doing, create the mobility which Mallarmé sees as essential to their expressive task. The mobility is only virtual; it appears almost a necessary after-effect of the words' precision. It is thus at approximately the same level of half-conscious experience as the movement of reading. The reader does not usually notice, except perhaps in detective novels,

194

the movement of his own attention; he only notices it when for some reason it is alerted or stopped.

In 'La Musique et les Lettres' Mallarmé comments on the combination of the precise or geometrical in language and the imprecise effect of its movement:

> Quelque chose comme les Lettres existe-t-il; autre, (une convention fut, aux époques classiques, cela) que l'affinement, vers leur expression burinée, des notions, en tout domaine. (645)

The key words are 'notion' and 'burinée'; this much can be seen by substituting 'objet' for 'notion'. If language were able to give the 'expression burinée' of an object, there would be no task for language, since the efficacy of the expression would put all the emphasis on the object and not on the language used. To one who, like Mallarmé, saw language as an essentially creative entity, (as in the assertion: 'Les mots, d'eux-mêmes, s'exaltent à mainte facette' (386, emphasis mine)) there could be no interest in such an enterprise. On the other hand, if we think again of Mallarmé as 'civilisé édennique', it is unlikely that he would see the *notion* of anything as an entity having other than an 'expression burinée'. The 'architect' in Mallarmé is not an idle preference; the idea is fundamental to his understanding of language. A notion may have an appearance of vagueness to all but him who senses it, but the Mallarméan notion is born of a process other than that, simply, of the imagination. It is the product of the interactions of words with the imagination, of the attempt, on the part of the writer, to express not the objects of the world, but the relations between them and the sensations they offer:

> les choses existent, nous n'avons pas à les créer; nous n'avons qu'à en saisir les rapports; et ce sont les fils de ces rapports qui forment les vers et les orchestres. (871)

In the interview 'Sur l'Evolution Littéraire', Mallarmé can afford to be as straightforward as this. Elsewhere, in the 'Variations', he is no less clearsighted, perhaps less accessible, but highly expressive of the literary task of language.

The last six paragraphs of 'Crise de Vers' form a kind of credo and at the same time explain why Mallarmé is so concerned to give 'l'initiative aux mots, par le heurt de leur inégalité mobilisés' (366). The qualities of language that arise out of the interaction of words, as it were, before they signify in the normal way, show Mallarmé that words are rarely used so as to reveal their full expressiveness. We saw in 'Les Mots Anglais' how Mallarmé could find fascination and also a virtual sense in reading lists of words not put together in order to form a referential or detachable sense. He would argue that this applies to literature as well, that the special qualities of language in literature have to do with the fact that they do not merely transmit a sense:

> Narrer, enseigner, même décrire, cela va et encore qu'à chacun suffirait peut-être pour échanger la pensée humaine, de prendre ou de mettre dans la main d'autrui en silence une pièce de monnaie, l'emploi élémentaire du discours dessert l'universel *reportage* dont, le littérature exceptée, participe tout entre les genres d'écrits contemporains. (368)

That language *can* perform in this way there is no doubt. Equally there is no doubt in Mallarmé's mind that such usage adds nothing to the expressiveness of language, that the silence of an 'exchange of coin' in language is not the silence of real expressiveness, but closer to that 'spiritual zero' which is described in the essay 'Or':

> L'incapacité des chiffres, grandiloquents, à traduire, ici relève d'un cas; on cherche, avec cet indice que, si un nombre se majore et recule, vers l'improbable, il inscrit plus de zéros: signifiant que son total équivaut à rien, presque. (398)

Naturally as soon as the writer moves away from language as a kind of counting house and searches for what language can express without, so to speak, the intermediary of a straightforward transmission of sense, he arrives at something like this:

> A quoi bon la merveille de transposer un fait de nature en sa presque disparition vibratoire selon le jeu de la parole, cependant; si ce n'est pour qu'en émane, sans la gêne d'un proche ou concret rappel, la notion pure. (368)

This paragraph touches what is perhaps the heart of Mallarmé's understanding of language, and like the one that follows it, deserves a detailed appreciation.

An essential characteristic of this piece is the contrast between the physical and the intangible. The final emphasis lies, without doubt, upon the 'notion pure', but every ideal of Mallarmé's has 'des serres enracinées à vous' (653). First, Mallarmé does not talk about the objects which language transposes, but about 'un fait de nature'; second, the transformatory powers of 'le jeu de la parole' do not effect a disappearance of that 'fait de nature' in the manner of a mystic vision, but a 'presque disparition vibratoire'. It is a quality of language that the 'faits de nature' that it presents do not entirely disappear before the impetus or expressiveness of words. The words set up a series of vibrations that cause reality almost, but not quite, to disappear. It is because of this that the reader is left with the impression that what language has given us is 'la notion pure' of reality, without the disturbance of too clear-sighted a 'proche ou concret rappel'. 'La notion pure' does not cause reality to 'abdicate', but sets up a pattern of virtual, literary time, which merely sets reality on a different plane. The notion of an object is a precarious combination of the reminiscence of an object with its imminence. It is not the vague suggestion of an object; nor is it the philosophical 'absence of the object being discussed or evoked'. The written notional reality is more like the reality of a dream that one seems to see clearly enough to be convinced that it exists, but which can never be reached or verified: the sense of its presence is its only guarantee. It is the unique sense of an imminent object, and imminence cannot be re-created, or, in a way, disputed.

Hence Mallarmé's language, in more ways than one, speaks for itself:

> Je dis: une fleur! et, hors de l'oubli où ma voix relègue aucun contour, en tant que quelque chose d'autre que les calices sus, musicalement se lève, idée même et suave, l'absente de tous bouquets. (368)

It is a natural consequence of the progression of Mallarmé's thought here that his language should appear to enter the realm of the ideal. But it should be evident from preceding paragraphs that, if ideal there is, it is not quite the concerted force of absence and impossibility that it might appear to be. The 'fleur' is not absent because it is an ideal flower existing in an ideal realm, but because it is an emanation of other words, because it exists across the movement and not statically anywhere along it. It is here that the reader must remember Mallarmé's emphasis on the white of the page between the words, and the somewhat 'précieux' assertions that the meaning of the words was to be found between the words rather than within them. For example:

> Tour devient suspens, disposition, fragmentation avec alternance et vis-à-vis, concourant au rythme total, lequel serait le poème tu, aux blancs; seulement traduit, en une manière, par chaque pendentif. (367)

The 'poème tu' has an existence more real than such comments appear to allow; it exists because words, in attempting to transmit, also transform.

The degree of transformation operated by the 'littérateur' is such that language produces in its impetus the sense which it cannot state:

> Au contraire d'une fonction de numéraire facile et représentatif, comme le traite d'abord la foule, le dire, avant tout, rêve et chant, retrouve chez le Poète, par nécessité constitutive d'un art consacré aux fictions, sa virtualité. (368)

It is because language is 'avant tout rêve et chant', that the objects or realities that it best presents, even 'only' presents, are virtual ones, not with intent either to deny the qualities of reality, nor in order to give language a forbidding autonomy, but in order to grant language the expressiveness of reality itself:

> Evoquer dans une ombre exprès, l'objet tu, par des mots allusifs, jamais directs, se réduisant à du silence égal, comporte tentative proche de créer: vraisemblable dans la limite de l'idée uniquement mise en jeu par l'enchanteur de lettres jusqu'à ce que, certes, scintille, quelque illusion égale au regard. (400)

This passage, from the end of the essay 'Magie', with its progression through silence and creativity to 'quelque illusion égale au regard', shows how Mallarmé considered the 'poème tu', and the art of suggestion in language, as the only way of creating an entity *equal* in expressiveness to that which is seen and felt. It is precisely because Mallarmé felt so strongly that language could and should be both a created and a creative entity that he took such pains, and appeared to call upon such obscurity of expression, to show what it was that language could express. Language does not express a flower, but 'l'absente de tous bouquets'; it does not designate a place, but the 'élargissement du lieu par vibrations jusqu'à l'infini' (396); not an object, but an 'illusion égale au regard'. Language is not a 'numéraire facile'; it does not offer objects, but presents the emotion or sensation that objects might arouse. If this seems in a way to degrade words into something like apologetic shop assistants, regretting that they cannot show you what you have asked for, but only something 'just as good', it must be remembered that the words of poetry, for Mallarmé, essentially 'kept a shop' in which the goods offered were all of their own fabrication. It is a quality of poetry, and of the best of Mallarmé's prose, that the words one reads appear expressive in their own right, and not only because of their relationship with reality:

> Le vers qui de plusieurs vocables refait un mot total, neuf, étranger à la langue et comme incantatoire, achève cet isolement

198

de la parole: niant, d'un trait souverain, le hasard demeuré aux termes malgré l'artifice de leur retrempe alterné en le sens et la sonorité, et vous cause cette surprise de n'avoir ouï jamais tel fragment ordinaire d'élocution, en même temps que la réminiscence de l'objet nommé baigne dans une neuve atmosphère. (368)

The magical 'isolement de la parole' which language can effect does not stem entirely from the words' autonomy, but *despite* their connections (in the 'retrempe alterné en le sens et la sonorité') with reality. It is the interaction of language with reality, both that experienced by the writer and that of the word on the page and in the mind, which creates not only autonomy but also expressiveness such that 'l'objet nommé baigne dans une neuve atmosphère'; it is transformed, yet has not entirely disappeared.

It is clear from Mallarmé's exposé of the operation which makes a flower into a 'literary fact', that the flower itself, or the subject of a piece of writing, can actually be detrimental to the total effect if its presence is too strongly felt. Hence:

Attribuons à des songes, avant la lecture, dans un parterre, l'attention que sollicite quelque papillon blanc, celui-ci à la fois partout, nulle part, il s'évanouit; pas sans qu'un rien d'aigu et d'ingénu, où je réduisis le sujet, tout à l'heure ait passé et repassé, avec insistance, devant l'étonnement. (382)

According to the outline of literary expressiveness given at the end of 'Crise de Vers', this apparently light-hearted comment (from 'Le Livre' Instrument Spirituel') is in fact a serious one. Language does not need more in a subject than that it be 'un rien d'aigu et d'ingénu'. Its own iconic tendencies are such that, in order to reach its full expressiveness, it is desirable to have the slightest possible 'subject', existing only as a sort of phosphorescence arising out of the movement of the words. Such a significance, naturally, cannot be inherent in any one word, or in any phrase: it only arises out of a reading of them. The reader operates, as Mallarmé says in 'Crise de Vers' 'une euphonie fragmentée selon l'assentiment du lecteur intuitif' (363), and the substance of that 'euphonie' is then, Mallarmé would argue, essential to the subject of the writing. He nowhere says that such rhythm or harmony actually *is* the subject of the kind of writing he ideally envisages; neither does he say that it is the aim of such writing to express, in the common conception, nothing at all. Returning for a moment to the last paragraph of 'Crise de Vers', we find that it is not merely sense or sonority which achieves 'cet isolement de la parole' which is the mark of literary expression. It is the strangeness, the patterns of apparent obscurity that the reader accumulates, which deny 'le hasard' or random effect that language usually has: that such a group of words should say anything about a flower, or a tree, or a palace...Literature is distinguished from other forms of language in that it does not present objects or 'meaning' *despite* the obscurity brought about by its inadequacy. It does not rely upon the chance presentation that convention and tradition offer, but presents its objects in such a way that the patterns of obscurity actually seem to stand in place of the object, while assuring us at the same time of either our reminiscence or our anticipation of its actual existence. The apparent obscurity (in terms, at least, of what we think we see, and what we usually take language to express) is a result not only of what it is that language seems capable of saying, but also stems from the more intense seeing, both of language and of reality, on the part of the writer.

'La Musique et Les Lettres'

Certain qualities of the language which Mallarmé envisages and to some extent creates are already clear, and not the least amongst these is a distant or forbidding quality. This is so close to the quality of music, probably the most 'other-worldly' and traditionally the most expressive of the arts, that Mallarmé makes constant use of the metaphor or example of music. Although the reader cannot expect to find the answer to problems of expressiveness in language in the example of music, its witness is invaluable, especially in showing how its truths operate in prose as well as in poetry. The licence of poetry to disgress from straightforward transmission of sense is sufficiently well-known for the metaphor of music to fit without question. There is nothing unusual about describing the significance of a poem as a rhythm or melody. It is, however, a dangerous illusion that prose contains a mechanism capable of transmitting 'd'une façon univoque', and it is Mallarmé's achievement to show how prose, in its own way, can create rhythms more subtle than those of poetry.

The close relationship between music and poetry is as old as the practice of each, yet the parallel is usually seen as a loose compatibility, stemming from the most superficial characteristics of each. However there is, at the basis of the relationship, the link of our response to each. In the presence of music, we feel in the presence of something complete, yet there is no reason, or none that we can put into words,

why this is so. If the same is true of poetry it is because of the impact
that language makes and not because of its verse form. In the essay
'Crise de Vers', Mallarmé, with lucidity and some superciliousness
(especially in his comments on Hugo, 360–1), discusses the striking
situation of French poetry at the end of the nineteenth century, and
the way in which poets were gradually liberating themselves from what
could be seen as the straitjacket of the alexandrine. On the one hand,
certain poets continued to use it:

> Les fidèles à l'alexandrin, notre hexamètre, desserrent intérieure-
> ment ce mécanisme rigide et puéril de sa mesure; l'oreille,
> affranchie d'un compteur factice, connaît une jouissance à dis-
> cerner, seule, toutes les combinaisons possibles, entre eux, de
> douze timbres. (362)

This in itself is but little, although it does indicate an emergent, if
confused recognition on the part of poets that it is not the form of the
alexandrine that guarantees poetry, but the expressiveness of the words
used. On the other hand:

> Autre chose ou simplement le contraire, se décèle une mutinerie,
> exprès, en la vacance du vieux moule fatigué, quand Jules
> Laforgue, pour le début, nous initia au charme certain du vers
> faux. (362)

The reserve evident in Mallarmé's comments on these two attitudes is
not exactly critical. It merely suggests that, although such variations
on the traditional form of poetry might be 'better' than blind adherence
to that form, they do not constitute a meaningful liberation. Consider,
for example, the coolness of the comment:

> Je dirai que la réminiscence du vers strict hante ces jeux à côté et
> leur confère un profit. (362)

Interesting, even compelling, as far as the mode of analysis is concerned,
as such observations might be, they appear to defer the moment of
saying: if the alexandrine does not 'contain' poetry, is there any form
of language that does? A little later in the same essay, Mallarmé comes
closer to explaining:

> Le remarquable est que, pour la première fois, au cours de
> l'histoire littéraire d'aucun peuple, concurremment aux grandes
> orgues générales et séculaires, où s'exalte, d'après un latent
> clavier, l'orthodoxie, quiconque avec son jeu et son ouïe indivi-
> duels se peut composer un instrument, dès qu'il souffle, le frôle

ou frappe avec science; en user à part et le dédier aussi à la Langue. (363)

The significantly musical image of forming, rhythmically, an instrument not merely *of* language, but also dedicated *to* Language, brings us to a crux in Mallarmé's attitude towards the forms of literature.

Although, as Mallarmé is the first to admit, 'dans les occasions amples on obéira toujours à la tradition solennelle' (363), this is by no means fundamental to literary activity. In saying that the poet forms the instrument of language as a homage to the notion of language, 'La Langue', Mallarmé suggests that the most valuable form of language will be that which best reveals its qualities. The way in which he describes the efforts of writers to move away from traditional form is almost always connected to the image of music. The language that Mallarmé would dedicate 'to language', is one which reflects both the tradition of literature and rhythms innately sensed by the writer:

> Toute âme est une mélodie, qu'il s'agit de renouer; et pour cela, sont la flûte ou la viole de chacun.
>
> Selon moi jaillit tard une condition vraie ou la possibilité de s'exprimer non seulement, mais de se moduler, à son gré. (363)

The phrase 'qu'il s'agit de renouer', unemphatic as it is, constitutes a kind of declaration on Mallarmé's part of 'what the writer should be doing'. The image of the soul as a melody is not original, nor particularly expressive on its own; but the continuation of the sentence is more explicit. The fluidity, the precariousness of our perception and understanding must be caught or held by the equal fluidity of language, the 'flûte ou la viole' being particular or personal 'instruments' of language. This concordance of writer and writing is neither common nor easy, as is suggested in the second part of the quotation. In order to 'modulate' language as, largely unconsciously, experience and intuition 'modulate' what we see, think and write, it is necessary to learn first the limitations of different forms of 'expression'. The way in which Mallarmé writes of 'une condition vraie', and of a state in which the writer does not so much express, but modulates what he sees and what he writes, suggests above all that Mallarmé was not moving towards a facility of language which would *say* exactly what he wanted to say, but rather towards a state – 'une condition vraie' – in which the rhythms of language fitted the rhythms of perception and experience. If such designs seem as extreme and potentially as frustrating as those which figured in Mallarmé's early poetry (where the 'Azur' lay constantly out of reach), this is apparent only in summary and explanation. The substance of such assertions on Mallarmé's part is backed, in the 'Variations' and in 'La Musique et Les Lettres', by examples of writing which are both explanation and confirmation.

The beginning of 'La Musique et Les Lettres' is perhaps surprising. After a few lines of formalities, amounting to little more than an invitation to submit to the spell of 'la superstition d'une Littérature' (643), Mallarmé states, almost brusquely:

> J'apporte en effet des nouvelles. Les plus surprenantes. Même cas ne se vit encore.
>
> On a touché au vers.
>
> Les gouvernements changent: toujours la prosodie reste intacte: soit que, dans le révolutions, elle passe inaperçue ou que l'attentat ne s'impose pas avec l'opinion que ce dogme dernier puisse varier. (643–4)

The quiet, unchanging appearance of prose is one which Mallarmé almost secretly depends upon, in the sense that it is possible to express in prose certain perceptions about language that poetry, by its very form would not so much forbid as in a way distort. The very impact that a poem makes, for reasons of its density and musicality, is in some measure gratuitous, at least at first. Mallarmé wrote many variations on the theme of 'le vers est tout, dès qu'on écrit' (644), yet its presence as an ultimate, although giving it special status, does not make prose a mere introductory or explanatory mode:

> Style, versification, s'il y a cadence et c'est pourquoi toute prose d'écrivain fastueux, soustraite à ce laisser-aller en usage, orne-mentale, vaut en tant qu'un vers rompu, jouant avec ses timbres et encore les rimes dissimulées: selon un thyrse plus complexe. (644)

Prose actually appears, in this passage, to be a more 'difficult' way of achieving the effect that poetry can give. Yet in that measure of diffi-culty, which certainly exists at least because of the fact that the writer must overcome the acknowledged 'humble' function of prose, lies a necessity for a greater, or at least different, degree of involvement on the part of the reader. In reading poetry, there is some licence to 'feel' rather than to understand completely. Such a state of affairs is less easy to achieve in prose, since the reader expects a certain degree of com-prehensibility, and must learn, to borrow Mallarmé's phrase, 'selon un thyrse plus complexe', to find the harmonies which exist there, and which are often fundamental to the sense of the words, playing alternately with them and against them. Mallarmé, if over-subtly, is certainly an 'écrivain fastueux', and the show, or rather the ceremonial, lies in the movement his language achieves, and the contribution of that movement to the sense of the words.

A case in point is Mallarmé's 'explanation' of how the writer arrives at 'la notion d'un objet, échappant, qui fait défaut', and how this practice is the 'creative task' for language:

> Semblable occupation suffit, comparer les aspects et leur nombre tel qu'il frôle notre négligence: y éveillant, pour décor, l'ambiguïté de quelques figures belles, aux intersections. La totale arabesque, qui les relie, a de vertigineuses sautes en un effroi que reconnue; et d'anxieux accords. Avertissant par tel écart, au lieu de déconcerter, ou que sa similitude avec elle-même, la soustraie en la confondant. Chiffration mélodique tue, de ces motifs qui composent une logique, avec nos fibres. Quelle agonie, aussi, qu'agite la Chimère versant par ses blessures d'or l'évidence de tout l'être pareil, nulle torsion vaincue ne fausse ni ne transgresse l'omniprésente Ligne espacée de tout point à tout autre pour instituer l'idée; sinon sous le visage humain, mystérieuse en tant qu'une Harmonie est pure (647–8)

The very density of this passage makes it necessary for the reader to look for some way of discerning the author's intentions other than by simply 'understanding', one by one, the words he wrote. The reader must actually 'comparer les aspects et leur nombre tel qu'il frôle notre négligence', taking note of the 'vertigineuses sautes' and 'd'anxieux accords' in much the same way as our features perform a kind of unnoticed dumb-show when listening to, or reading something moving or exciting.[1] If this amounts to a 'chiffration mélodique tue' (a dense enough phrase in itself, with its combining of the analytical, the musical and the silent), it is nonetheless real and apprehensible to the reader. For it is the sensation of our involvement in the words we read, at the highest virtually 'avec nos fibres', that provides a guarantee not only of the sense of the words but also of their rhythm. Furthermore, whatever the splendours of 'la Chimère', the abundance of perception or imagination, and whatever distortions we make, there is no avoiding the fundamental simplicity of the relationships between things, all the more evident in written language, where word follows word with varying space and tempo 'pour instituer l'idée'. The essential point of this

---

[1] Cf. feuillet 12 (A) of 'Le Livre', for a version of Mallarmé's appreciation of the physical reaction to words.

passage, which Mallarmé himself describes a little later in the lecture as 'ce tracé...des sinueuses et mobiles variations de l'Idée' (648), is precisely the way in which language plays its rhythms one against the other, not in order to give colour or create impact, but in order to show how such a rhythm can indicate the nature of 'l'omniprésente Ligne espacée de tout point à tout autre pour instituer l'idée'.

The metaphor of music is particularly suited to the expression of such notions because of the unique combination it offers of the virtually physical, in its rhythm, impetus and impact, and the nearly transcendental and extremely fragile in its effect or 'meaning'. Naturally the absence of any 'real meaning' in music allows it a purer harmony than language can provide. Music *is* harmony; language can only create 'an effect of harmony'. It is this, doubtless, that propels the poet towards a closer relationship with the qualities of music. But Mallarmé approaches the situation in a different way, leaving aside for the most part the more gratuitous approaches to music that language can make, and operating instead a rhythm: at once in the impetus offered by the sense of the words, and also in the phrasing and placing of words. Indeed, he sets up a number of different rhythms, under the aegis of Harmony. Moving away from the image of music for a moment, it might be revealing to compare the procedure with the image of swingboats, and the way in which their apparently confused rhythms are expressive. The temptation and the question is to decide which of the moving boats has the 'right' rhythm, the answer, the true 'idea'. If you concentrate on the farthest point at the back, you choose and reject each swingboat as it reaches that point; no two arrive together. There is perpetual confusion as to which one you are concentrating on, but not a confusion in complete chaos, rather a number of juxtaposed rhythms moving so quickly that they appear virtually superimposed, while each still retains its distinctiveness. As you recognize each one, you think it to be the primary rhythm, until you notice that another has taken up the primary position, and is playing, not in opposition to, but *against* the rhythm first perceived. And so it continues, one after another, until you are only bewildered by the precision with which you have recognized and continue to recognize the rhythms as they come; until you realize that there could not have been one primary point or one primary movement, but the sense of all the points and all the rhythms as they create a pattern out of their multiplicity into a virtual, solitary rhythm.

It is this kind of multiple, rhythmic, yet *single* impression which language, in common with music, can offer, and which Mallarmé sees as the task for the writer:

Surprendre habituellement cela, le marquer, me frappe comme une obligation de qui déchaîna l'Infini; dont le rythme, parmi les touches du clavier verbal, se rend, comme sous l'interrogation d'un doigté, à l'emploi des mots, aptes, quotidiens. (648)

The opening words of this extract indicate the delicate level at which the operation takes place. The rhythm of language is neither learned nor put together; 'surprendre habituellement cela' implies a close interaction of chance and innate sensibility operating on a phenomenon which is not unfamiliar in its substance – 'des mots, aptes, quotidiens' – but which is always different in its effect. To put side by side the effect of language and the 'Harmonie' or 'Ligne' that it expresses, might seem incongruous, but Mallarmé makes clear that what we crudely term the effect of Language is of the utmost importance:

Avec véracité, qu'est-ce, les Lettres, que cette mentale poursuite, menée, en tant que le discours, afin de définir ou de faire, à l'égard de soi-même, preuve que le spectacle répond à une imaginative compréhension, il est vrai, dans l'espoir de s'y mirer. (648)

The spectacle of effect of language is so impressive that the reader, compelled partly by 'l'espoir de s'y mirer', and partly by the apparent orderliness of the words on the page, constantly makes the bridge between the effect and the meaning of words. In so doing, he is convinced not only of the 'justesse' of the words he reads, but also, in the rhythmic operation of reading, of the 'Harmonie' that orders them. The operation could be characterized as a conversation, though a tacit one, between the finite set of letters in the alphabet and the sensibility; while the 'speech' of this conversation is a rhythm (as indeed befits the overpowering sense of operation as opposed to statement). The rhythm cannot exist without involvement in the 'conversation', for because the rhythm itself has no 'meaning' it depends upon the support of the emotions. Similarly, it might be said that melody is not merely an agreeable tune, but is also the emotion that accompanies it and seems to deepen as it continues, to the extent that it seems as though there is an implicit suggestion of, and need for, melody in certain emotional states, in the same way that certain pieces of literature are so reminiscent of musical experience that they appear virtually to bring music to them, so that one might say of them, as Proust did of a church tower:

Je suis sûre que s'il jouait du piano, il ne jouerait pas *sec*.[1]

---

[1] Marcel Proust, *A La Recherche du Temps Perdu* (Paris, Gallimard, 1919), vol. I, p. 89.

The harmony of words is not simply the rhythm apprehended across a pattern of sentences, but also the emotional state to which it seems to correspond. Language is finite, both in its signs and in its standardized meanings. The gamut of emotional response, on the other hand, at least *appears* infinite, since it is based on confrontation with different patterns and different relationships which, despite the comparative limitations of each person's experience, certainly appear infinite in variation.

If music, by its emotional impact, has the 'touch of the infinite', it has also, perhaps paradoxically, a greater presence, and arouses a stronger consciousness of its appearance and disappearance, than does language. The impact of music, the most abstract of all the arts, is in fact extremely physical. The movement and 'meaning' of music can create an area of such attentiveness that one feels a virtual place has been created, not a place in which anything has happened, but a place in which anything could *now* happen. It is probably because music has such a unique hold upon time (a phenomenon which also characterizes the reader's reaction to words) that it has also such a powerful effect on place. Music not only occupies the mind, but also the place in which it is played,[1] so that there is no object which can be looked at fully without the music imposing its effect, and evaporating, almost inch by inch, the physicality of the object; or else the reverse, causing the object to appear, by comparison with the music, excessively gross and static. In either case, the effect upon the docile world is one of movement. Music does not deny the reality of the world, but transforms it in different ways, so that the real physicality of the place is transformed into a new virtual place by means of the music. Similarly, the banal physicality of language on the page is transformed by the virtual movement of rhythm by which, as Mallarmé explains, it signifies, a movement no less significant in its very appearance and disappearance than in its operation.

Going back to the beginning of the first piece in the 'Variations', we read:

> Longtemps, voici du temps – je croyais – que s'exempta mon idée d'aucun accident même vrai; préférant aux hasards, puiser, dans son principe, jaillissement. (355)

We have already seen how important this notion is to Mallarmé's appreciation of the word on the page. Music has, more than any other form of expression, the quality of 'jaillissement'. It appears to spring from nowhere because its form is related to no other form; its impetus is

---

[1] Cf. Mallarmé's atmospheric evocation in 'La Dernière Mode', p. 817.

such that one is never conscious that it has emerged in this form rather than that, only of the fact that it has emerged, and as so strong an intention that it is neither possible nor desirable, at least at first, to discern what, if anything, it intends. As Mallarmé writes in his piece about Poe:

> Eviter quelque réalité d'échafaudage demeuré autour de cette architecture spontanée et magique, n'y implique pas le manque de puissants calculs et subtils, mais on les ignore; eux-mêmes se font, mystérieux exprès. Le chant jaillit de source innée: antérieure à un concept, si purement que refléter, au dehors, mille rythmes d'images. (872)

That which appears to stem from a 'source innée', and is so structured as to appear without structure, operates according to a different mode of significance, 'antérieure à un concept'. However, this is only an appearance, created by language; there is, as Mallarmé says here, an 'architecture spontanée et magique' which contrives, as it were, to hide itself while contributing an atmosphere which then appears to stem from the purity and impetus of the 'source innée'. The 'jaillissement' is not a wild or dumb ritual; there is none of Rimbaud's 'déluge' in the 'mille rythmes d'images'. It is an architectonic world where the power and unexpectedness of the words' apparition from a 'source innée' also contribute to the sense. Also, that which has the character of 'jaillissement' with its consequent impetus and evanescence, will paradoxically put greater emphasis on that which *is* present, on the words on the page. If the compulsiveness of music, and of certain writing, is such that the end seems arbitrary or even impossible, it will also heighten our awareness that the 'whole' of the work is contained within beginning and end, and that the way in which we understand and appreciate the work is, in its turn, affected by this.

In his sketch of the relationship between music and language, Mallarmé makes it clear that one of the most important areas of 'compatibility' is that of the way in which a considerable presence of rhythm or harmony combines with a certain precariousness or evanescence. It is not the musicality of language that interests Mallarmé, but the similarities between the two modes of expression:

> Considérez, notre investigation aboutit: un échange peut, ou plutôt il doit survenir, en retour du triomphal appoint, le verbe, que coûte que coûte ou plaintivement à un moment bref accepte l'instrumentation, afin de ne demeurer les forces de la vie

208

aveugles à leur splendeur, latentes ou sans issue. Je réclame la restitution, au silence impartial, pour que l'esprit essaie à se rapatrier, de tout – chocs, glissements, les trajectoires illimitées et sûres, tel état opulent aussitôt évasif, une inaptitude délicieuse à finir, ce raccourci, ce trait – l'appareil; moins le tumulte des sonorités, transfusibles, encore, en du songe.

Les grands, de magiques écrivains, apportent une persuasion de cette conformité. (648–9)

The very great liveliness that Mallarmé envisages as a result of language accepting or borrowing a kind of musical instrumentation is outlined here with a noticeable bias. Mallarmé would like to 'repatriate' those aspects of music which testify to its extraordinary projection, and to its extraordinary fragility – 'chocs, glissements, les trajectoires illimitées et sûres, tel état opulent aussitôt évasif, une inaptitude délicieuse à finir'. The mobility – with its full language of stops, starts and pauses – that belongs to music, is also possible in words if they attempt to express, not a denotative sense, but one which can, like the full-grown butterfly, virtually detach itself from the words on the page and remain mobile, or at least give a sense of being so, without them. It is because music is abstract that it is capable of making felt more strongly than any other medium both the impossibility of maintaining its most powerful moments of expression – 'tel état opulent aussitôt évasif' – and the impossibility of stopping them – 'une inaptitude délicieuse à finir'. If language could do this, without actually evoking the 'you cannot leave me now' scene of a lovers' parting, it would succeed in doing what music does apparently without effort. It is Mallarmé's belief that this is the achievement of the greatest writers, that language transmutes the 'tumulte des sonorités...en du songe'.

Furthermore, the kind of presence that music has – precarious yet definite – once transferred to the realm of language, gives a new emphasis to the sense. Language does not merely transmute what would otherwise be the precision of its sense into 'du songe'; it creates an ambiguity, a reversibility of sense. If the presence of music is so great that, on hearing, for example a choral work in a cathedral, one is tempted to wonder whether the cathedral contains the music or whether the music contains and creates the cathedral, the effects in language are no less dramatic. Meaning in language would appear then not to be situated within each word and to be a result of each word's significance; it would hover, so to speak, between that significance and the effect or movement of reading. There appears an ambiguity between the meaning of the words and the effect of reading them, a constant reversibility which creates out of its movement not confusion but a measure of certainty.

However, if such a degree of ambiguity, or reversibility, is desirable in order for language to be fully expressive, it does also seem to deflect once more the writer's success into a different version of the early 'Azur'. In Mallarmé's maturity this was no longer seen as a problem; he might indeed have said, as Wittgenstein did, that the problem vanished before a comprehensive posing of the question.[1] If Mallarmé sees that language creates not an object but 'la notion d'un objet, échappant, qui fait défaut' (647), and recognizes that language, for all its appearance of precision rather intends a sense than states it, he is at once more humble and more ambitious in what he expects of language. He is more humble since he does not expect language to be 'the same as' reality, but to capture only a certain aspect or force of reality. He is more ambitious in the sense that language will then have to provide, in its precarious creation of what is an equivalent of reality rather than 'a piece of it', a means of assuring the reader, not exactly of its significance, but of the strength or possibility of that significance:

> Quel pivot, j'entends, dans ces contrastes, à l'intelligibilité? il faut une garantie –
> La Syntaxe – (385)

On the one hand Mallarmé feels almost obliged to pose such conventional questions, and to give such a trite-looking answer. On the other hand, he intends all the emphasis that appears in these lines. From the familiar pivot or starting point of syntax, language can make any number and variation of tangents, each appearing to aspire to 'autre chose'. Language may, as Walter Pater claims of all art, aspire to the condition of music, but significantly it does not reach it. It creates its significance by moving between the affirmations of syntax and straightforward meaning, and the effects of expressing 'la notion d'un objet' rather than the simple object itself.

If the situation is complex in appearance, it finds its resolution in the act of reading. In Mallarmé's rich evocation of the experience of reading, it is evident that the two apparently opposing poles of syntax and aspiration are essential to the expressiveness of language:

> Lire –
> Cette pratique –
> Appuyer, selon la page, au blanc, qui l'inaugure son ingénuité,

---

[1] Cf. Ludwig Wittgenstein, *Tractatus Logico-Philosophicus* (Routledge, 1922), p. 149.

à soi, oublieuse même du titre qui parlerait trop haut: et, quand s'aligna, dans une brisure, la moindre disséminée, le hasard vaincu mot par mot, indéfectiblement le blanc revient, tout à l'heure gratuit, certain maintenant, pour conclure que rien au-delà et authentiquer le silence –

Virginité qui solitairement, devant une transparence du regard adéquat, elle-même s'est comme divisée en ses fragments de candeur, l'un et l'autre, preuves nuptiales de l'Idée.

L'air ou chant sous le texte, conduisant la divination d'ici là, y applique son motif en fleuron et cul-de-lampe invisibles. (386-7)

The 'pressure' of the sensibility upon the words that the eye reads varies from word to word, or rather from space to space between the words. The structure is sensed rather than noticed by the sensitive reader (Mallarmé significantly points out 'devant une transparence du regard *adéquat*'). It lies below and contributes to the 'preuves nuptiales de l'Idée'. Mallarmé's apparently simplistic use of the white spaces between words seems appropriate when we consider that the same process is effected in the reader's mind, where a sense is built up out of the interaction between the process of reading and absorption of sense. Such a process of 'understanding' appears to be an endless movement whose continuation would theoretically bring still greater illumination. Yet the passage helps to show that it is Mallarmé's appreciation of the quality of the process which is truly important, rather than argument about 'how far to go'.

It might seem, especially when one reads the fragments of the 'Livre', that Mallarmé believed in the constant narrowing down or distilling of the art of language. But he believed even more emphatically in the *process*, visible on the page and apprehensible to the senses, of distillation. Thus it is clear that he would in no way want the art of language to distill itself into a transcendental state (if that were possible). His writing shows his appreciation that art has only a propensity to disappear, that it naturally takes the form of aspiration, and that it is in this state, and not after it has been superseded, that language is at its most expressive. It is not the equivalent of the alchemists' gold or absolute truth that Mallarmé seeks for language. The meaning of one word does not cancel out the meaning of the next, nor distill it into a significant disappearance. Language does not, according to Mallarmé's notion of it, distill its sense to vanishing point, but modifies or softens the connotation of precision that the word 'sense' has, to produce a rhythm, a significance of impetus akin to the pure energy of physics – or the pure grin of the Cheshire cat.

It is clearly in this realm of the abstract become virtually physical, or at least apprehensible as an experience, that Mallarmé's often mentioned 'Idée' belongs, and the paragraphs in 'La Musique et les Lettres' which provide a focal point to the whole lecture also testify to this:

> Alors, on possède, avec justesse, les moyens réciproques du Mystère – oublions la vieille distinction, entre la Musique et les Lettres, n'étant que le partage, voulu, pour sa rencontre ultérieure, du cas premier: l'une évocatoire de prestiges situés à ce point de l'ouïe et presque de la vision abstrait, devenu l'entendement; qui, spacieux, accorde au feuillet d'imprimerie une portée égale. (649)

Although language operates with a view to a 'rencontre ultérieure' with music, the possible transcendental effect of the relationship is modified by the point that Mallarmé makes here. Music is of an abstractness so powerful that it seems virtually real or visible. Similarly language, not in spite of but because of its tendency to give a sense of aspiration, because of its propensity for disappearance, offers a kind of 'counter-vision' much as music does, a nearly tangible presence resulting from its movement and the possibilities that it suggests. Where the fact of infinite aspiration or infinite movement would undoubtedly be so over-impressive as to be uninteresting, the *possibility* of it, as sensed in language, is both rich and expressive. It is this possibility, with its appearance of sense and structure, which leads Mallarmé to posit, predictably, the superiority of the book. If music is ecstasy, literature is the creation of it, and, if the superiority seems perverse, it is effectively vindicated in Mallarmé's defence. For example:

> Par contre, à ce tracé, il y a une minute, des sinueuses et mobiles variations de l'Idée, que l'écrit revendique de fixer, y eut-il, peut-être chez quelques-uns de vous, lieu de confronter à telles phrases une réminiscence de l'orchestre; où succède à des rentrées en l'ombre, après un remous soucieux, tout à coup l'éruptif multiple sursautement de la clarté, comme les proches irradiations d'un lever de jour: vain, si le langage, par la retrempe et l'essor purifiants du chant, n'y confère un sens. (648)

Quite apart from the richness and 'justesse' of such phrases as 'l'éruptif multiple sursautement de la clarté' which expresses exactly the combination of the complex and the simple in music, there is here an obvious conviction on Mallarmé's part that the almost excessive clarity of music is, ultimately, overshadowed by that of language, with its alternation between the words on the page and the effect of reading them:

Moyen, que plus! principe. Le tour de telle phrase ou le lac d'un distique, copiés sur notre confirmation, aident l'éclosion, en nous, d'aperçus et de correspondances. (646)

The highly Mallarméan 'éclosion' of perceptions and truths, is itself equal to, if not better than, the fact of the truth or clarity itself.[1] At least part of the charm of music lies in the fact that it has the character of a constant 'éclosion', and it is this, rather than the more obvious transcendental qualities of music, that leads Mallarmé to his 'conclusion' in 'La Musique et les Lettres':

> Je pose, à mes risques esthétiquement, cette conclusion (si, par quelque grâce, absente, toujours, d'un exposé, je vous amenai à la ratifier, ce serait l'honneur pour moi cherché ce soir): que la Musique et les Lettres sont la face alternative ici élargie vers l'obscur; scintillante là, avec certitude, d'un phénomène, le seul, je l'appelai, l'Idée.
>
> L'un des modes incline à l'autre et y disparaissant, ressort avec emprunts: deux fois, se parachève, oscillant, un genre entier. Théâtralement pour la foule qui assiste, sans conscience, à l'audition de sa grandeur: ou, l'individu requiert la lucidité, du livre explicatif et familier. (649)

Mallarmé first says that music and language are the two sides of one coin. That he does not intend this image to set up too much opposition between the two is evident from what follows. The 'ici...là' construction seems at first to make language turn 'vers l'obscur', and music be 'scintillante'. In view of Mallarmé's often-expressed delight in the 'scintillante' quality of language, it seems more likely that he intended the construction of the sentence to be looser than it might appear – having the more vague sense of the English 'here...and there' rather than 'former and latter'. And whatever the construction of the sentence, it is certain that the two qualities are not in such flagrant opposition as they appear to be; music and language can both be alternately obscure and 'scintillante'. The second paragraph of the declaration contains further evidence that for Mallarmé the 'ultimate clarity' of expression came from a combination of the qualities of music and language, with the play between light and dark, definite and indefinite, rather than from the highly abstract qualities of music alone. Language perfects its expressiveness not by imitating music but, as Mallarmé's image

[1] See Mallarmé's 'Eventail' poems for examples of his predilection for the sensation of 'éclosion', especially the 'Autre Eventail de Mademoiselle Mallarmé', p. 58.

suggests, by diving into it, and emerging 'avec emprunts', creating in its oscillation between one form and the other, 'un genre entier'. Yet whereas language presents both its own mode and that of music (in the 'instrumentation' of words on the page and in the rhythm of reading them), music only presents itself, and the audience listens 'sans conscience' to its ineffable splendour. This is the point at which Mallarmé separates himself most clearly from the realm of rapture and miracle towards which the poet traditionally moves. He installs himself at a point where such notions are only emergent, where the reader is still in a state of watching rather than a state of vision, and where he is fully aware, because of his own participation through reading, in the production of the 'imminent miracle'. It is evident then, that any problems apparently inherent in the presence of the 'Idée' only exist when the experience of reading is divided from its meaning, when the 'Idée' is seen as a point on the globe rather than a characteristic of the globe itself.

Reading: a paradox of movement

These last discriminations also give a clue to the way in which the reader must consider the ultimate significance of a piece of writing. Much of Mallarmé's prose serves to indicate, either directly or indirectly, the expressive movement of words, the

> secrète direction confusément indiquée par l'orthographe et qui concourt mystérieusement au signe pur général qui doit marquer le vers. (855)

Even in this brief reference, from a set of notes written in 1895, it is evident that the expressive movement of language is as if countered by a 'signe pur général'. It seems to amount to a paradox of movement: the expressive movement of language simultaneously contributes to, and eventually constitutes a moment without movement, a 'signe pur' or 'Idée'. The reader is able to sense that he has arrived at a literary 'meaning' by moving across the words, and yet his impression of that 'meaning' is essentially one of stillness that suggests a static and ultimately significant realm beyond the words, but one which is not detachable from the apprehension of their movement. Although language is, according to Mallarmé's writing, not definitive, but indicative of expression, it is resolved by both the doubting and the susceptible reader into some form of the static 'Idée'. The denotative habit of language is so strong that the reader expects even the word 'Ideal' to contain, more or less precisely, the poet's ideal. Mallarmé delivers a blow to traditional poetic egoism by indicating that language does not, at its most expressive, transmit an 'Ideal' or 'Idée', but that it is in the creation of the poise which *is* language, situated between reality and our perception of it, that we sense the quality to which poets give the name of ultimate.

It is thus misleading to talk of 'what a poet expresses'. Similarly we 'solve the problem' of the constantly unattained poetic ideal if we see, as Mallarmé did, the writer's task as essentially one of maintaining the poise between the *fact* of language, the 'emploi doué d'infinité jusqu'à sacrer une langue, des quelque vingt lettres' (380), and the quality of our perception. If language were only concerned to 'exhiber les choses à un imperturbable premier plan' (384), it would neither capture the quality of reality nor reveal the quality of words. If, on the other hand, the writer is concerned to 'tendre le nuage, précieux, flottant sur l'intime gouffre de chaque pensée' (384) then not only will language appear more fragile, more distinctive, but it will also convince us, in much the same way as music convinces, of whatever 'Idée' or Ideal we are concerned to find. Hence:

> Au cours, seulement, du morceau, à travers des voiles feints, ceux encore quant à nous-mêmes, un sujet se dégage de leur successive stagnance amassée et dissoute avec art. (384)

Literary language clearly does not, in Mallarmé's view, constitute a subject – such as we usually understand the word – but a progression rather, of so sure and definitive a nature that the only comparison which can be made is with music, whose poise, impetus and apparent 'significance' are of similarly indisputable strength. Indeed the poise of Mallarmé's language, and the way that poise seems to assure us of some ultimate meaning, without actually telling us what it is, can probably only be compared with that of music. The quality of 'meaning' of music is sensed across the span of initial entrance, actual performance, and aftermath. Its 'meaning' is an emanation out of this process. Similarly, the meaning or 'Idée' of language, boldly summed up by critic and poet alike, is to be found across the process of reading – 'selon l'assentiment du lecteur intuitif' (363). In the case of reading a poem, for example, it is difficult to say at precisely what point one discovers that which makes the poem whole and unforgettable – forbidding, for the moment, all but itself. Its slight presence, thus colossal in its fragility, offers an imminent farewell, it seems, in each apotheosis – how long can the poem continue for me at this level of expressiveness? Similarly, it is not

215

possible to say at what point one becomes conscious of a taking leave, resembling the manner in which one musical note can recall the flamboyance of the tune not yet extinct, but in the past, and permitting itself to be whittled slowly into silence. It is this kind of process which allows each reader to determine for himself the quality of great poetry, and it is, of course, one which is not directly referred to in the poem; it is something which necessarily arises from it, just as the quality of music appears to us in our anticipation, our listening, and our memory of it.

It is because language is, to Mallarmé, essentially this process revealing its own life and expressiveness, rather than a means of transmitting something which, when external to the words, expresses an imperfect image of reality, that it is not merely of no interest but actually an ineptitude to 'read in' a static meaning of 'Idée'. Mallarmé's language appears to move towards a notional, perhaps impossible expressiveness; but because it always has the character of a movement or operation, it is then less relevant – and indeed less easy – to remember that apparently impossible expressiveness. It is because language *is* able to reach certain heights of expressiveness that the reader is even tempted to declare what it means or to say that an ultimate has been reached. It is equally because language presents a progression towards such heights and not a mere static presence of them, that the sense or essence the reader finds there cannot be separated from the words themselves.[1] If language were a static presence and not a process, then the reader would be able to read in a meaning, and to contribute some extraneous 'essence'. This is the case with music, but one might say that the supreme quality of music is that its strength of entrance and of strangeness is such that one is not even tempted to 'read meaning into it', to associate and interpret. In such cases, we simply listen. Hence it could be said that only in lesser music, as in lesser writing (in each case an inadequate sounding of the medium), it is possible or necessary to posit a subject or essence. If a great work is suggestive, it is not suggestive of *meaning*, but of expressiveness.

The impact of Mallarmé's later prose is such that the reader feels such notions to be true. Yet even as early as 1869, we see that Mallarmé understood intuitively their possibility:

> Dans le 'Langage' expliquer le Langage, dans son jeu par rapport à l'Esprit, le *démontrer*, sans tirer de conclusions absolues (de l'Esprit).

[1] As Mallarmé pointed out in 'Les Mots Anglais', the reader, in a way, 'met en mouvement ces mots, pour qu'à plusieurs d'entre eux ils expriment un sens avec des nuances' (903).

> Dans le Langage poétique – ne montrer que la visée du Langage à devenir beau, et non à exprimer mieux que tout, le Beau – et non du Verbe à exprimer le Beau ce qui est réservé au Traité. (853)

If Mallarmé is attempting to convey 'la visée du Langage à devenir beau', rather than to convey 'Beauty' itself, then he will be complying with his own perceptions concerning the imperfections of language, its fundamental inadequacy as a 'conveyancer' of reality, and the subsequent need to seek some other means of using language to the best of its capabilities. In practice, the fact that language only imperfectly performs a 'conveyancing' of reality only adds to its expressiveness and to the reader's conviction of this, since the reader must collaborate more, partly in following the words rather than 'detaching' their meaning, and partly because the impression he has of them will be largely of his own making. If this is not actually so, it is so in effect. On the one hand, Mallarmé declares that:

> L'œuvre pure implique la disparition élocutoire du poète, qui cède l'initiative aux mots, par le heurt de leur inégalité mobilisés (366)

suggesting that the words have a life and impetus of their own, because of their 'inégalité' both in relation to each other, and in relation to reality. On the other hand, Mallarmé's evocation of the process of reading is such that it is obvious that he saw the reader as, in a sense, fulfilling the potential of the words on the page. The effect of this fulfilment would not be a definitive sense of 'Idée' discerned by the reader, but a sensation, the direct result of involvement with the words, that in such a process of involvement, resolving both the imperfections of language and the inadequacies of the reader, lay not only a certain truth about language, but also a truthful language. It is impossible to read much of the 'Variations' or 'La Musique et les Lettres' without sensing that, as you are reading, you are also following (or for your own satisfaction only, completing) the gesture that language makes towards reality:

> Les abrupts, hauts jeux d'aile, se mireront, aussi; qui les mène, perçoit une extraordinaire appropriation de la structure, limpide, aux primitives foudres de la logique. Un balbutiement, que semble la phrase, ici refoulé dans l'emploi d'incidences multiplie, se compose et s'enlève en quelque équilibre supérieur, à balancement prévu d'inversions. (386)

Hence it is of less interest, even of no interest at all, to consider Mallarmé's prose, or his poetry, according to the usual criteria of whether it forms a coherent point of view. At its best – to simplify – it merely says what it is and is what it says.

Mallarmé shows us that by writing 'le langage se réfléchissant' (851) it is possible to make a truth of what looks like a trite summary. Also, by creating a language that performs and reflects itself, Mallarmé indicates another truth. When he wrote: 'A l'égal de créer: la notion d'un objet, échappant, qui fait défaut', he was saying something precise and valid about perception as well as about language. That Mallarmé should have written more lucidly than he realized does not make him necessarily a greater writer; it shows that he intuitively understood the qualities of language. Intuition rather than analysis led him to his view of language as a creative entity, yet the great precision of his seeing helped him to arrive at 'certaines conclusions d'art extrêmes qui peuvent éclater, diamantairement, dans ce temps à jamais, en l'intégrité du Livre' (373). The density and elusiveness of much of Mallarmé's writing would have a more sympathetic reception if it were considered not merely as an exposé of language expressing its own qualities, but also as a result of the way in which Mallarmé *sees*. There is no question of such an enquiry being entirely foreign to Mallarmé's intentions or viewpoint, since so much of his writing is concerned to show the life and liveliness of words. Furthermore, underlying everything Mallarmé wrote, the reader can sense the Mallarmé who asks:

> que le bruit puisse cesser à une si faible distance pour qui coupe, en imagination, une flûte où nouer sa joie selon divers motifs celui, surtout, de se percevoir, simple, infiniment sur terre. (404–5)

It is the consequences of this last fact that are always evident. The reader must not merely read, but also live what he reads, in such a way that his involvement with the words forms a convincing version of his relationship with reality.

Without going into excessive detail beyond the scope of this study, it is not hard to see that there is a measure of compatibility amounting to more than a coincidence between what and how language expresses and what and how we see. If certain reservations have to be made, they would be of the kind: only one who sees (or writes) thus, can write (or see) thus. Despite Mallarmé's obvious belief that 'des contemporains ne savent pas lire' (386), it is probably fair to assume that what he wrote is not as inaccessible as he believed. For example, when he criticizes those writers who want to 'exhiber les choses à un imperturbable premier plan, en camelots' (384), he is criticizing them first for a lack of depth, and also for a lack of sensitivity towards a reality which is never 'à un imperturbable premier plan', but contains, as Mallarmé says, 'quelque chose d'occulte' (383). Furthermore, if language is not expressive, not literary, when it functions merely as transmittor of reality, and if, when it is at its most expressive, it appears either dense or mysterious, or both, it could also be argued that the same is true of the way we see things: that the reality of ten green bottles on the wall is less expressive than the apparent *un*reality of a mirage, or of anything partially obscured or altered by circumstance, light or distance. It is Mallarmé's extraordinary honesty in discerning what and how language expresses that leads to his being able to write according to the nature of language, rather than according to any sense extraneous to it. Similarly, a scrupulous seeing can result in an alteration of the original, often inexpressive object. Constant repetition of a word can appear to make it lose its sense, to become a strange and unaccountable shape or sound; on the other hand, constant watching of a chair appears to make it less clear and less certain. It appears less simple, less knowable than it was at first, because, in watching it, we gradually take into account what is behind it, how far away it is, how often it has been seen before, who last sat on it. In other words, we create our own version, our own seeing of the chair, around the simple one that we originally saw. Mallarmé's writing shows us that the subtlety of language is equal to the subtlety of our seeing, and also, that what we term 'subtlety' could equally well be termed inadequacy. The particular qualities of language arise out of its being unable to reproduce what we think we see; while the particular qualities of seeing arise out of our being unable to see for long the simplicity that first strikes our eyes. At the beginning of 'Le Mystère dans les Lettres', Mallarmé gives a very definite image of the way in which the reader picks out a meaning, or rather suspects a significance in what appear at first to be dense words:

> Si, tout de même, n'inquiétait je ne sais quel miroitement, en dessous, peu séparable de la surface concédée à la rétine – il attire le soupçon. (382)

Mallarmé closely associates the sense that the reader feels to exist (and hence, in Mallarmé's terms, 'understands') with the way in which his eyes run over the text. This process is not very different from the fundamental way in which we see things.

Such notions do not ultimately suggest that things, or words, are more complex in their significance to us than they at first appeared to be. They merely reveal the intuitive strength of Mallarmé's characterizations of language. Even when Mallarmé does not go as far as he did in 'Un Coup de Dés', the reader automatically 'grades' the words, applying shape and chiaroscuro to the sense he understands, as to the images he sees. Looking again at a passage like the one that appears near the end of 'Le Mystère et les Lettres', it is not hard to understand the delicate evocation of the sense and mobility of the words as appropriate also to the sense, the assurance, and the integrity of our seeing:

> Les mots, d'eux mêmes, s'exaltent à mainte facette reconnue la plus rare ou valant pour l'esprit, centre de suspens vibratoire; qui les perçoit indépendamment de la suite ordinaire, projetés, en parois de grotte, tant que dure leur mobilité ou principe, étant ce qui ne se dit pas du discours: prompts tous, avant extinction, à une réciprocité de feux distante ou présentée de biais comme contingence. (386)

As Mallarmé said in one of the fragments of the 'Livre': 'On ne prouve que quant aux autres'.[1] The parallel between modes of seeing and modes of language does not 'prove' Mallarmé to be right, nor does it justify the difficulty of his writing. But it does throw light on the origins of his attitudes, and also helps us to understand why his language has, when we read it correctly, such great power.

Once such a basis is established for understanding Mallarmé's writing, a number of problems vanish immediately. When we see a reference to 'L'Œuvre', we do not take it to mean a specific work, as yet unwritten, but merely a convenient way of expressing a conception of writing which does not depend upon the conventional formula of beginning, middle and end. Many have written of the difficulty a writer – or a painter – has with the beginning and end of what he writes. Mallarmé himself wrote: 'Il faut toujours couper le commencement et la fin de ce qu'on a écrit',[2] in an early letter to Henri Cazalis, and his intuition is borne out by what he wrote later, with its strong sense of an operation to which beginnings and endings are arbitrary and preferably pass unnoticed. Where the reader is conscious of a beginning and an end, he is less conscious of a process, and consequently his involvement is less great and the language he reads appears less autonomous. Mallarmé's tentative plans for a study of language involved, according to his notes, his 'explaining' language within language, demonstrating it, rather than analysing it (853). Even if this

---

[1] *Le Livre*, feuillet 189.   [2] *Propos*, p. 39.

READING: A PARADOX OF MOVEMENT

study was never officially completed, it is certainly set out, sometimes between the lines, sometimes manifestly, in his prose works which in fact only hold together by the thread of the concern for language. Each apparent 'subject', be it the writing of others, the world of fashion, ballet or theatre, is secondary to another, unstated subject, that of the language used. In this sense, it is apt to borrow a phrase from Wittgenstein, and say that:

> The subject does not belong to the world, but it is a limit of the world.[1]

The subject of Mallarmé's language is also its limit in the sense that its subject is its expressiveness, and the limit of that is certainly the limit of the inner world of the writer. Furthermore this is not merely so, but is seen to be so by the reader who finds the significance of what Mallarmé is saying, not at any point along the path of his writing, but as a result of reading any part of it. Each 'piece' of reading, be it poem, essay or tentative note, is thus not only its subject but also its world. The experience of reading is such that it is no longer important to know whether or not this is the 'Livre' or the 'Œuvre'. One might then interpret Mallarmé's plans for the performed 'Livre' as a late failure of nerve, an attempt to supersede all levels of former literary hierarchies, when this had already been effected, for the reader of Mallarmé if not for the author himself, in the process of reading his plans, explorations and approximations.

It is not, in a way, worthy of Mallarmé's achievement to discuss what he intended to do. Any statement of intentions seems to overshadow what has been achieved. Works completed then look like only the forces that propel the shape of the one, ultimate work which is not completed and which will take up the themes or the very best of what is already written. Mallarmé's apparent fragments gather together a sense, above all, of an instrument now ready for use, and played, not by any subsequent work, but by speculation only. In Mallarmé we see someone who knew, by the end of his life, what creativity in language was, and who knew so innately that he set it out in his works with that apparent secrecy or disjointedness that makes the reader feel as though he, now, were putting together both a sensibility and a language that were enigmatically half-buried in a series of tentatives. But, as Proust knew so well:

> Longtemps, un tel livre, on le nourrit, on fortifie ses parties faibles, on le préserve, mais ensuite c'est lui qui grandit, qui

[1] Wittgenstein, *Tractatus*, p. 117, 5.632.

désigne notre tombe, la protège contre les rumeurs et quelque peu contre l'oubli.[1]

'Le Livre' or 'L'Œuvre' itself grows out of the means adopted to create it, and thus, in no gratuitous sense, one might say that it is language that writes the book, and the anxious reader who confers upon it 'a local habitation and a name'.

[1] Marcel Proust, *A La Recherche*, vol. xv, p. 211.

CONCLUSION

It is generally considered a mark of reverence to trace the genealogy of an artist's influence, and it would certainly be possible to do this for Mallarmé. The task would, however, be laborious, for it would have to cover a great range of topics, both literary and scientific. The most curious aspect of Mallarmé's influence is that where at first its great extent might not seem to illuminate his achievement, it does prove, at the same time, both the nature and the essential character of his preoccupations. One might summarize Mallarmé's influence as that of a prompter rather than a precursor. He did not so much influence other creative writers as cause readers to consider the nature of creativity in language. Thus it is hardly surprising that writers with such diverse interests should acknowledge his importance. At the same time, there is no doubt that each facet of his influence can bring into focus the essential nature of his achievement. If he did fail, as some believe, to complete his 'Livre', this should only make us re-evaluate the word 'failure' rather than put Mallarmé into a literary 'salon des refusés'.

However, the reader anxious to know the form and historical context of Mallarmé's contribution to literature might be puzzled by the diverse faces that posterity gives his work. Perhaps it does no more than satisfy curiosity, or confirm a belief in the diversity of human interpretation, to know that Mallarmé may have unwittingly given his blessing to a whole range of linguistic sciences, or that modern advertisers – for their part probably unwittingly too – should make use of Mallarmé's understanding of layout. If we see Mallarmé through the eyes of a twentieth-century structuralist, we might be tempted to think that his entire opus has to be re-read within a structuralist frame, and that this is a correct – because rationally and easily upheld – interpretation. Or, if we see him as one who virtually fathered a whole school of poets, each one, in Mallarmé's own words, 'allant, dans son coin, jouer sur une flûte, bien à lui, les airs qu'il lui plaît' (866), then we might overlook his more lasting contribution to the understanding of literary language. Mallarmé's influence only helps us to understand his work if we see it as a multi-farious whole, rather than as a complex of interpretations or attitudes amongst which one might be the most appropriate. The apparent flexibility of what Mallarmé wrote is not necessarily either a virtue or a vice; it is a positive indication that his concern was not with any one branch of literature, but with its very basis.

Purely historical considerations also play their part in shaping Mallarmé's influence. He is essentially a solitary figure in nineteenth-century literary history. The words he writes in tribute to Poe apply much more closely to himself:

> stellaire, de foudre, projeté des desseins finis humains, très loin de nous contemporainement à qui il éclata en pierreries d'une couronne pour personne, dans maint siècle d'ici. Il est cette exception, en effet, et le cas littéraire absolu. (531)

Mallarmé's work is indeed a 'couronne pour personne' in the sense that it does not have any genuine imitators. Neither did any of his contemporaries approach either his plans or his achievements. Although, superficially, his attitudes and his writing allowed him to be taken as an adequate model for Huysmans's 'Des Esseintes', it is obvious that Mallarmé is no more a decadent literary hero than he is in any meaningful sense leader of the Symbolist school. One cannot be leader of a school without believing in its existence and its validity. Although famous in his own lifetime and playing a relatively important rôle in contemporary literature, Mallarmé was, by taste and in reality, very much a solitary figure, and his influence was largely a mythical wish-fulfilment on the part of those who admired him yet could not really understand him. With the exception of Paul Valéry, his literary descendants were not those who attended the Tuesday evenings. The guests at these merely recognized his undoubted future influence; their reverence guaranteed the extent of Mallarmé's influence rather than the form of it, since it created for Mallarmé the curious status of the distinguished writer whose name and assumed contribution to literature travel better than any understanding of what he had achieved. It might be said then, that Mallarmé achieved in his lifetime a certain notoriety which in itself prompted the interest of later generations. If Mallarmé did not have the ever-intriguing and popular press of the literary underdog – like Jarry, for example – he did present an enigma, both to those who had read his work and to those who had not. His influence – of a certain kind at least – was thus assured.

Mallarmé did have one obvious continuator in Paul Valéry. On the surface the 'œuvres' of the two writers are very similar: a few poems only, and a quantity of prose which often escapes ordinary categories. In Valéry's work the balance is even more weighted towards the prose. His poems, as he said himself, are mere exercises or 'charmes', almost the by-products of a creative mind mainly preoccupied with how it works. The vast 'cahiers' reveal a polymath as well as a poet, a man whose breadth of interest is so great that he runs the risk of being called a poet by scientists and a scientist by poets. Although he does not continue Mallarmé's explorations along radically different lines, he covers a greater area and to different ends. One might say that his conceptual understanding of Mallarmé was far beyond that of any of his contemporaries, but that his own work, though prompted partly by that understanding, extends the concepts rather than probes deeper into them. Where Mallarmé arouses admiration, Valéry stimulates thought. It would be misleading to say simply that Valéry was a more serious writer than Mallarmé, but he does invest the creative fabric of language with a scientific rigour that is, in Mallarmé's writing, sub-sumed under the creative performance. Valéry's poetry shows Mal-larmé's influence in its abstractness and its concern with form. The clarity with which ideas are conveyed in the poems as well as in the prose both indicated how well Valéry understood Mallarmé and how much they differ. Where Valéry designs and accomplishes, Mallarmé designs and performs. In Valéry the design is evident in the words, in Mallarmé it is in the less visible 'armature mystérieuse'. Thus while acknowledging Valéry's undoubted understanding of Mallarmé and also his independent accomplishment, one should recognize that the common ground is simply a fascination with creative literary language. Valéry wants to investigate how it works and what repercussions that has on the effect of writing. Mallarmé, on the other hand, works from an apparently more naïve standpoint: first seeing how the process works, and then putting both his understanding and his wonder or delight into words.

Mallarmé does not often make direct statements about his art – or at least not statements that look direct. Thus he does not invite either controversy or imitation. But this does make it all the more likely that later commentators should want to make his statements for him. Also, because the elusive quality of his writing seems to make it a truly modern 'œuvre ouverte',[1] no exegesis seems to have a definitive ring to it. Yet there is another side to the question of difficulty in Mallarmé's writing

---

[1] Cf. Umberto Eco, *L'Œuvre Ouverte*, trans. C. Roux de Bézieux (Paris, Editions du Seuil, 1965).

and the effect it has on his influence. By suggesting to the reader the presence of a problem of language, his work actually causes critical attention to re-focus upon language itself. The critic or writer is thus led to the heart of his own conception of the art. In fact, without being necessarily either inattentive or narrow-minded, he may be more likely to discover his own conception of language via words of Mallarmé's, than that of Mallarmé himself. In the case of difficult writing where the reader may fail to see any obvious coherence, yet recognizes an authentic and intense vision, it is likely that he will, in an effort to explain, supply a frame of reference of his own. Varied interpretations are thus not only probable, but also, given that something central seems to be at issue, likely to be dogmatic.

This brings us to the critical clue behind Mallarmé's influence and reputation. There is only one element which unites those who see Mallarmé as a precursor to their own fields of interest, and that is a preoccupation with language. The fact that a whole range of linguistic sciences and literary theories seem to connect with Mallarmé's work must make it seem as though Mallarmé's conceptual precocity was enormous, or else that he is being paid the wrong sort of compliment. The solution to the predicament is of course that two different and incompatible frames of reference are being confused here. For where linguistic science and much literary theory dissect and analyse, Mallarmé performs and unifies language. If his work were less unified, and less profoundly assertive of a truth about language, the spread of his influence would not have come about. His strangest contribution to posterity remains that of a creative artist who stands as a powerful example to those who want to understand, though without necessarily wanting to use, the instrument of that creativity.

It is probably safe to guess that Mallarmé would have been astounded by the influence ascribed to him, like all those writers who see their work as autonomous and beyond the temporal concerns even of literary history. Also, the kind of influence and importance his work now has, is certainly not that which he envisaged in his notion of how literature continues, develops and refines. Unlike most famous poets, Mallarmé does not have any serious imitators;[1] his influence can chiefly be seen in the realm of literary criticism. It is paradoxical that expectations should be thus reversed, though it must be said that the clarity and depth of Mallarmé's understanding of language must lend itself to

---

[1] Valéry is again the exception to the rule. Amongst the unserious imitators, Adoré Floupette – the pen name of two poets, Gabriel Vicaire and Henri Beauclair – provides an entertaining and interesting example of the opportunities for pastiche offered by Mallarmé's writing.

interpretation at a near-scientific level. Further, it is probably true that Mallarmé's clearsighted creativity is not a common quality, and that in many ways the logical side of his 'âme...à la fois logique et sensible' (690) is the more accessible. In a note of 1869, Mallarmé says:

> La Science ayant dans la Langage trouvé une confirmation d'elle-même, doit maintenant devenir une CONFIRMATION du Langage. (852)

Unfortunately this is by no means what has happened. The ultimate confirmation of Mallarmé's notion of language appears in our reading of his words. That of a linguist appears in his analysis, which is at a considerable remove from creative language. Although the aims are similar – to understand how language works, and to trace the limits of his expressive potential – in practice they are different. One might even say that an idea about language which is expressed in analytical terms cannot be the same as an idea, or better a notion, which emanates from a reading of language. In Mallarmé's writing ideas evolve out of the words' movement and expressiveness, and are sensed in the same way as the meaning or subject of a poem is sensed. That this is not merely a provocative whim on Mallarmé's part can be proved if we look at similar attitudes towards writing, but this time expressed in conceptual terms.

In his defence of 'new' criticism, 'Critique et Vérité', Roland Barthes says:

> Or, depuis près de cent ans, depuis Mallarmé sans doute, un remaniement important des lieux de notre littérature est en cours: ce qui s'échange, se pénètre et s'unifie, c'est la double fonction, poétique et critique, de l'écriture... il n'y a plus ni poètes ni romanciers: il n'y a plus qu'une écriture.[1]

This, like many other of Barthes's apt summaries, tends to lose by its very conciseness. His language does not demonstrate, it only says. The fact that what he says here appears flat and nearly meaningless shows the necessity, when writing about language, of acknowledging the quality of language. Naturally it would be impossible to ask all writers to express themselves as strictly and purely as Mallarmé did – impossible because so few writers have such a creative understanding of language – and there is obviously some value in summarizing new developments. But from Barthes's desire to publicize stems his particular use of language: on the one hand clear, and even ingenuous, and

---

[1] Roland Barthes, *Critique et Vérité* (Paris, Editions du Seuil, 1966), p. 45.

on the other, dense and conceptual. His language invites assent or dissent; itself so far from performance, it cannot take account of the quality of language. Furthermore, Barthes's understanding of the phrase 'il n'y a plus qu'une écriture', is certainly more reductive in quality than anything Mallarmé wrote. Equally it is clear that if a critic like Barthes wants to recognize precursors, then Mallarmé's must be the first name to appear. Barthes's mention of Mallarmé also shows that what we see here is not so much a question of influence as of the creating of precursors,[1] for reasons which pertain partly to a degree of self-justification, and also to a desire to give the guise of ancient or at least well-tried truth to that which might otherwise look like an unacceptable novelty.

Gérard Genette has written a sensitive and much needed essay on what he calls the 'Bonheur de Mallarmé', in which he discusses Mallarmé's attitude towards the theoretical, or rationally expressed side of language:

> Il ne pense pas, il caresse des idées, savoure des concepts, s'enivre de raisonnements. La pensée ne peut et ne doit apparaître qu'en tant qu'objet de ce que Richard appelle *rêverie de l'idée*, et comme résorbée dans le pur plaisir de son évocation.[2]

Genette's essay is chiefly an appreciation of the work done by J.-P. Richard in 'L'Univers Imaginaire de Mallarmé', but the points he makes are valid in their own right. Since Mallarmé's attitude towards the abstract was less rational than visceral, and since the merit of an idea lay largely, as Genette and Richard recognize, in its evolution and evocation, it is inappropriate to see Mallarmé's legacy in terms of ideas. Like many writers leaving an unfinished work, Mallarmé asked for the fragments of the 'Livre', posthumously named, to be burned after his death. The gesture is doubtless a classic and predictable one, but it could also have another significance. The fragments of the 'Livre' – which were not of course burned, out of deference to what was already seen as a colossal and challenging task for future exegetes – do contain ideas, often expressed in that shorthand which denotes the processes of thought rather than the unfurling of language. They do not, in Mallarmé's sense, express themselves. Hence it is possible that Mallarmé saw them as fragments that were only pre-language, and which, for this reason, should not be preserved. Most literary analysis is also pre-

---

[1] Cf. Borges's essay/myth entitled 'Kafka and his Precursors', in *Labyrinths*, pp. 234–6.
[2] Gérard Genette, *Figures* (Paris, Editions du Seuil, 1966), pp. 94–5.

language, though preferring the term 'meta-language' because of the connotations of greater status. Thus when, in another of Genette's essays, we find Mallarmé's name in a passage about structuralism, we should understand the limited importance of the reference:

> L'ambition du structuralisme ne se borne pas à compter des pieds ou à relever des répétitions de phonèmes: il doit aussi s'attaquer aux phénomènes: il doit aussi s'attaquer aux phénomènes sémantiques qui, comme on le sait depuis Mallarmé, constituent l'essentiel du langage poétique, et plus généralement aux problèmes de la sémiologie littéraire.[1]

The phrase 'since Mallarmé' is as common in literary criticism as 'since Stravinsky' in musicology. It is by no means indisputable that Mallarmé considered 'phénomènes sémantiques' to be 'l'essentiel du langage poétique'. The compliment is at once too great and not great enough. Even given that Mallarmé understood intuitively, without using the terminology, what Genette says here, it is the reverse of a tribute to his understanding or his achievement to sum up thus 'l'essentiel du langage poétique'.[2] It is a reductive crudity that would have horrified him.

The shift of attention from the ends of art to its means is not restricted to literary criticism or the linguistic sciences. It is a tendency so widespread that it would be wrong to over-stress Mallarmé's contribution, even if that may seem more important because Mallarmé was one of the first to recognize it. What is interesting is the way in which Mallarmé made his contribution. He does not inform the reader by giving him views and opinions; the challenge his language presents has the effect of making the reader notice the means of art. There is an enormous difference between this and the positive assertions of the literary critic. In order to show that the modern critic's disadvantage when compared with Mallarmé is not simply one of the non-creative writer put side by side with a creative one, we should look at the remarks of two 'new' novelists. Robbe-Grillet, in his study, *Pour un Nouveau Roman*, says this:

> Ne pourrait-on avancer au contraire que le véritable écrivain n'a rien à dire? Il a seulement une manière de dire.[3]

And Robert Pinget, in the introduction to *Le Libera*:

---

[1] *Figures*, p. 154.
[2] One might compare the breadth of the 'definition of poetry' that Mallarmé unwillingly gives in a letter to Léo d'Orfer, cf. *Propos*, p. 118.
[3] Alain Robbe-Grillet, *Pour un Nouveau Roman* (Paris, Editions de Minuit, 1963), p. 42.

Il me semble que l'intérêt de mon travail jusqu'aujourd'hui a été la recherche d'un *ton*...

Tout ce qu'on peut dire ou *signifier* ne m'intéresse pas, mais la *façon de dire*.[1]

Robbe-Grillet's words could be read as a version of the variously repeated comment that Mallarmé really writes about 'rien'. Pinget, although saying something similar, manages to sound far less negative. Both comments, however, have a defensive ring to them, or even, in the case of Robbe-Grillet, a belligerent one: a reputation for writing *new* novels is at stake. By over-emphasizing what is not as new as it looks, nor, in practice, as startling, the innovator destroys the essential equilibrium between theory and practice. The two novelists here are saying something that is compatible with Mallarmé's views on language, but it is relatively limited. When one compares the achievement of a novelist, a poet, a literary critic or a linguist with that of Mallarmé, it becomes apparent that each one echoes only a facet of his work.

Mallarmé's work has been subject to a very strong negative strain of interpretation by some critics. Amongst these, Maurice Blanchot notably sees Mallarmé as a writer set upon a course of reduction, or worse, destruction of language. The process is not necessarily an uncreative one; solitude, absence and death can be extremely positive. Yet the emphasis is misleading. It is true that Mallarmé's writing often brings the focus down to the single word on the page, or to the blank spaces between words, but equally and importantly it is expandable, from the single word outwards to the notional 'Livre'. To see Mallarmé's work as literature stripped to its skeleton[2] is to ignore that reversibility which lies at its centre. On the other hand, a writer like Robbe-Grillet, anxious to abide by an assertive knowledge that there is only a 'manière de dire', and not 'anything to say', actually restricts the potential of his writing. Therein lies the difference between working from a rationally accepted fact, and working from a powerful intuition. Perhaps the only writer able to allow for both was Proust, who might more than any other make a just claim to having continued what Mallarmé began. One could not exactly say that Mallarmé's influence is evident in Proust's work, but a genuine influence is not one that can be signalled by this or that phrase; it is essential and unobserved. One might even say that the notion of influence has little meaning in the case of a great artist, and that,

[1] Robert Pinget, *Le Libera* (Paris, Editions de Minuit, 1968), p. 3.
[2] Roland Barthes, *Degré Zéro de L'Ecriture* (Paris, Editions du Seuil, 1964), p. 12.

similarly, tracing an artist's influence pays him scant homage. Indeed there is almost a derogatory vein in the concept of an 'influential writer'. Valéry, for example, was probably more influential than truly creative. It is left to a remarkable innovator such as Joyce to claim the status of both.

However, there is an elusive justice in the legacy of Mallarmé. In the letter known as the 'Autobiographie', Mallarmé gives his famous and memorable apologia of the 'Livre':

> Quoi? c'est difficile à dire: un livre, tout bonnement, en maints tomes, un livre qui soit un livre, architectural et prémédité, et non un recueil des inspirations de hasard fussent-elles merveilleuses... J'irai plus loin, je dirai: le Livre, persuadé qu'au fond il n'y en a qu'un, tenté à son insu par quiconque a écrit, même les Génies. (662-3)

To the modern reader this must be reminiscent of the Book that figures in Borges's writing. It certainly opens yet another line of communication between Mallarmé and later writers. Further, within the same notional range of literary evolution, it is apt that Mallarmé should be seen as one of the forefathers of current language and literature studies. 'Le Livre' is not exclusive; it exists as myth or notion, and, at that level, all perspectives can theoretically be allowed for. And, if Borges's Pierre Menard could write Don Quixote word for word without re-reading the original, it is feasible that nearly a century of literary investigation should arrive, by diverse paths and intentions, at a semblance of Mallarmé's 'Livre'. The words are not those Mallarmé would have used, but the general intention is the same. Mallarmé's modesty would not allow him to consider his own work complete; nor his conception of language. However, we should read the rest of his confession of 'failure':

> Voilà l'aveu de mon vice, mis à nu, cher ami, que mille fois j'ai rejeté, l'esprit meurtri ou las, mais cela me possède et je réussirai peut-être; non pas à faire cet ouvrage dans son ensemble (il faudrait être je ne sais qui pour cela!) mais à en montrer un fragment d'exécuté, à en faire scintiller par une place l'authenticité glorieuse, en indiquant le reste tout entier auquel ne suffit pas une vie. Prouver par les portions faites que ce livre existe, et que j'ai connu ce que je n'aurai pu accomplir. (663)

No less than Mallarmé, the reader *knows* what he is not able to accomplish. The alacrity that modern critics and writers show in their desire to know and to accomplish, by means of explanation and analysis, only testifies to the breadth of what Mallarmé did achieve. If he did 'faire scintiller' a fragment of the 'Livre', one might say that he also succeeded in writing it. The study of his prose shows us that his understanding of language was such as to render irrelevant any but a notional or Borgesian Book. Only as a gesture to the common conception of literary achievement, then, must he add that one life is not enough to do justice to the potential that language has. Meanwhile the varied achievements in linguistic understanding of the last half-century form a sometimes awkward aureole around the 'fragment' that is Mallarmé's work, suggesting what we might have already guessed, that the completion of the 'Livre' would not, even if it were possible, be interesting. From one lucid tracing of the circle, we can know the sphere, or better, feel that we have made it.

BIBLIOGRAPHY

This bibliography is limited to selected secondary sources; it does not claim to be comprehensive. It also contains a number of other works found to be of use and interest.

Apollinaire, Guillaume, *Calligrammes* (Paris, Gallimard, 1966)
Barfield, Owen, *Poetic Diction* (Faber and Gwyer, 1928)
Barrault, Jean-Louis, *Réflexions sur le Théâtre* (Paris, Vautrin, 1949)
– *Nouvelles Réflexions sur le Théâtre* (Paris, Flammarion, 1959)
Barthes, Roland, *Critique et Vérité* (Paris, Editions du Seuil, 1966)
– *Essais Critiques* (Paris, Editions du Seuil, 1964)
– *S/Z* (Paris, Editions du Seuil, 1970)
Barzun, Jacques, *Berlioz and the Romantic Century* (Columbia U.P. 1969)
Baudelaire, Charles, *Œuvres, passim*
Beckett, Samuel, *Works, passim*
Beckford, William, 'Vathek,' in *Three Gothic Novels,* ed. Peter Fairclough (Penguin, 1968)
Béguin, Albert, *L'Ame Romantique et le Rêve* (Paris, José Corti, 1939)
Benjamin, Walter, *Illuminations.* trans. Harry Zohn (Jonathan Cape, 1970)
Berger, John, *Selected Essays and Articles* (Pelican Books, 1972)
Bernard, Suzanne, *Mallarmé et la Musique* (Paris, Nizet, 1959)
Blanchot, Maurice, *L'Entretien Infini* (Paris, Gallimard, 1969)
– *L'Espace Littéraire* (Paris, Gallimard, 1965)
– *Faux Pas* (Paris, Gallimard, 1955)
– *Le Livre à Venir* (Paris, Gallimard, 1959)
Block, Haskell M., *Mallarmé and the Symbolist Drama* (Wayne State U.P. 1963)
Borges, Jorge Luis, *Labyrinths* ed. D. A. Yates and J. E. Irby (Penguin, 1970)
Bray, René, *La Préciosité et les Précieux* (Paris, Albin Michel, 1948)
Broussard, Louis, *The Measure of Poe* (Norman University of Oklahoma Press, 1969)
Brown, Ivor, *A Word in Your Ear* (Jonathan Cape, 1942)
Butor, Michel, *Répertoire II* (Paris, Editions de Minuit, 1964)
Cage, John, *Silence* (Calder and Boyars, 1968)
Caillois, Roger, *Esthétique Généralisée* (Paris, Gallimard, 1962)
– *Images, Images* (Paris, José Corti, 1966)
Carlyle, Thomas, *Sartor Resartus* (Chapman and Hall, 1885–8)
Cassirer, Ernst, *Language and Myth* trans. Suzanne K. Langer (New York, Dover Books, 1953)
Cavell, Stanley, *Must We Mean What We Say?* (New York, Scribner, 1969)
Cervantes, *Don Quixote,* trans. J. M. Cohen (Penguin, 1970)
Chisholm, A. R., *Mallarmé's 'Grand Œuvre'* (Manchester U.P. 1962)
Cohn, R. G. *Mallarmé's Masterwork* (The Hague, Mouton & Co. 1966)
– *L'Œuvre de Mallarmé: Un Coup de Dés* (Paris, Librairie des Lettres, 1951)

Copland, Aaron, *Music and Imagination* (New York, New American Library, 1952)

Craig, Edward Gordon, *On the Art of the Theatre* (Heineman, 1958)

Davies, Gardner, *Vers une Explication Rationnelle du Coup de Dés* (Paris, José Corti, 1953)

Debussy, Claude, in *Three Classics in the Aesthetics of Music*. (New York, Dover Publications, 1962)

Deleuze, Gilles, *Proust et les Signes* (Paris, P.U.F. 1970)

Dewey, John, *Art as Experience* (New York, Capricorn Books, 1958)

Dujardin, Edouard, *Les Lauriers sont coupés* (Paris, Messein, 1924)

Eco, Umberto, *L'Œuvre Ouverte*, trans. C. Roux de Bézieux (Paris, Editions du Seuil, 1965)

Ehrenzweig, Anton, *The Hidden Order of Art* (Weidenfeld, 1967)

Epperson, Gordon, *The Musical Symbol* (Ames, Iowa State U.P. 1967)

Fiser, Eméric, *Le Symbole Littéraire* (Paris, José Corti, 1941)

Focillon, Henri, *The Life of Forms in Art* (New York, Wittenborn, 1948)

Foucault, Michel, *Les Mots et les Choses* (Paris, Gallimard, 1966)

Fowler, Roger, *The Languages of Literature* (Routledge, 1971)

Fowlie, Wallace, *Mallarmé* (University of Chicago Press, 1962)

Fry, Roger, *Vision and Design* (Pelican Books, 1961)

Frye, Northrop, *The Well-Tempered Critic* (Bloomington Indiana U.P. 1963)

Gellner, Ernest, *Words and Things* (Pelican Books, 1968)

Genette, Gérard, *Figures I* (Paris, Editions du Seuil, 1966)

– *Figures II* (Paris, Editions du Seuil, 1969)

– *Figures III* (Paris, Editions du Seuil, 1972)

Ghil, René, *Les Dates et les Œuvres* (Paris, Crès et Cie, 1923)

Gombrich, E. H., *Meditations on a Hobby Horse* (Phaidon, 1963)

Gourmont, Rémy de, *Le Livres des Masques* (Paris, Mercure de France, 1914)

Gregory, R. L., *Eye and Brain* (Weidenfeld, 1966)

– *The Intelligent Eye* (Weidenfeld, 1970)

Guichard, Léon, *La Musique et les Lettres en France au temps du Wagnérisme*. (Paris, P.U.F. 1963)

Hanslick, Edouard, *The Beautiful in Music* (Indianapolis, Bobbs-Merril, 1952)

Hartman, Geoffrey, H., *Beyond Formalism* (Yale U.P. 1970)

Hindemith, Paul, *A Composer's World* (Harvard U.P. 1953)

Holmyard, E. J. *Alchemy* (Pelican Books, 1968)

Hulme, T. E. *Speculations* (Routledge, 1960)

– *Further Speculations* (University of Nebraska Press, 1962)

Ives, Charles E., in *Three Classics in the Aesthetic of Music* (New York, Dover, 1962)

James, Henry, *Selected Literary Criticism*, ed. Morris Shapira (Penguin, 1963)

Josipovici, Gabriel, *The World and the Book* (Macmillan, 1971)

Joubert, Joseph, *Carnets*, vols. I and II (Paris, Gallimard, 1938)

Joyce, James, *Works, passim*

Kahn, Gustave, *Symbolistes et Décadents* (Paris, L. Vanier, 1902)

Langer, Suzanne K. *Feeling and Form* (Routledge, 1953)

– *Problems of Art* (Routledge, 1957)

Laver, James, *Costume in the Theatre* (Harrap, 1964)

– *Drama, its Costume and Décor* (London, Studio Books, 1951)

Lehmann, A. G., *The Symbolist Aesthetic in France, 1885–1895* (Oxford, Blackwell, 1968)

Lockspeiser, Edward, *Debussy* (Dent, 1944)

Mallarmé, Stéphane, *L'Amitié de Stéphane Mallarmé et de Georges Rodenbach*. (Geneva, Pierre Cailler, 1949)

– *Correspondance Mallarmé–Whistler* (Paris, Nizet, 1964)

– *Correspondance*, vol. I, 1862–71 (Paris, Gallimard, 1959)

– *Correspondance*, vol. II, 1871–85 (Paris, Gallimard, 1965)

BIBLIOGRAPHY

- *Correspondance*, vol. III, 1886–9 (Paris, Gallimard, 1969)
- *Les Gossips de Mallarmé* (Paris, Gallimard, 1962)
- *Les Noces d'Hérodiade* (Paris, Gallimard, 1959)
- *Poems*, trans. Roger Fry (Chatto & Windus, 1936)
- *Propos sur la Poésie*, ed. Henri Mondor (Paris, Editions du Rocher, 1946)
- *Œuvres Complètes* (Paris, Gallimard, 1945)
- *Recueil de 'Nursery Rhymes'* (Paris, Gallimard, 1964)
- *Stéphane Mallarmé – Francis Jammes, 1893–1897* (The Hague, A. A. M. Stols, 1940)

Mauclair, Camille, *Mallarmé Chez Lui* (Paris, Grasset, 1935)
Maupassant, Guy de, *Œuvres, passim*
Mauron, Charles, *Introduction à la Psychanalyse de Mallarmé* (Neuchâtel, La Baconnière, 1968)
- *Mallarmé l'Obscur* (Paris, Denöel, 1941)
Mercier, Alain, *Sources Esotériques et Occultes de la Poésie Symboliste* (Paris, Nizet, 1969)
Merleau-Ponty, Maurice, *L'Œil et l'Esprit* (Paris, Gallimard, 1964)
- *Signes* (Paris, Gallimard, 1954)
Meyer, Leonard B., *Music, the Arts and Ideas* (University of Chicago Press, 1962)
Michaud, Guy, *Mallarmé* (Peter Owen, 1965)
Mondor, Henri, *L'Amitié de Verlaine et Mallarmé* (Paris, Gallimard, 1940)
- *Vie De Mallarmé* (Paris, Gallimard, 1950)
- *Mallarmé Lycéen* (Paris, Gallimard, 1954)
- *Mallarmé Plus Intime* (Paris, Gallimard, 1944)
Moore, George, *Memoirs of My Dead Life* (Heinemann, 1966)
Mounin, Georges, *Avez-vous lu Char?* (Paris, Gallimard, 1946)
Newman, Ernest, *Berlioz, Romantic and Classic* (Gollancz, 1972)
Newton, Eric, *The Meaning of Beauty* (Pelican Books, 1962)
Noulet, E., *Œuvre Poétique de Stéphane Mallarmé* (Paris, Librairie Droz, 1940)
Paracelsus, *The Hermetical and Alchemical Writings*, vols I and II, trans. Arthur Edward Waite (New York University Books Inc., 1967)
Park, Ynui, *L'Idée chez Mallarmé* (Paris, Centre de Documentation Universitaire, 1966)
Pater, Walter, *Works, passim*
Paxton, Norman, *Development of Mallarmé's Prose Style* (Geneva, Droz, 1968)
Peterkiewicz, Jerzy, *The Other Side of Silence* (O.U.P., 1970)
Pinget, Robert, *Le Libera* (Paris, Editions de Minuit, 1968)
Poe, Edgar Allan, *Selected Writings* (Penguin, 1967)
Poulet, Georges, *La Distance Intérieure* (Paris, Plon, 1952)
- *L'Espace Proustien* (Paris, Gallimard, 1963)
Proust, Marcel, *Chroniques* (Paris, Gallimard, 1927)
- *Contre Sainte-Beuve* (Paris, Gallimard, 1954)
- *A La Recherche du Temps Perdu* (Paris, Gallimard, 1919)
- *Lettres à Reynaldo Hahn* (Paris, Gallimard, 1956)
Queneau, Raymond, *Exercice du Style* (Paris, Gallimard, 1947)
- *Œuvres, passim*
Rader, Melvin, (ed.), *A Modern Book of Aesthetics* (New York, Holt, 1960)
Raitt, A. W., *Life and Letters in the 19th Century* (Nelson, 1961)
- *Villiers et le Mouvement Symboliste* (Paris, José Corti, 1965)
Read, Herbert, *The Meaning of Art* (Pelican Books, 1949)
Renéville, A. Rolland de, *L'Expérience Poétique* (Paris, Gallimard, 1938)
Richard, Jean-Pierre, *L'Univers Imaginaire de Mallarmé* (Paris, Editions du Seuil, 1961)
- *Pour Un Tombeau d'Anatole* (Paris, Editions du Seuil, 1961)
Richards, I. A., *Principles of Literary Criticism* (Routledge, 1961)

Rimbaud, Arthur, *Poésies* (Paris, Classiques Garnier, 1960)

Robbe-Grillet, Alain, *Pour un Nouveau Roman* (Paris, Editions de Minuit, 1963)

Rodenbach, Georges, *L'Elite* (Paris, Bibliothèque Charpentier, 1899)

Royère, Jean, *Mallarmé* (Paris, Simon Kra, 1927)

Sartre, Jean-Paul, (introd.) *Poésie de Mallarmé* (Paris, Gallimard, 1945)

Schérer, Jacques, *L'Expression Littéraire dans l'Œuvre de Mallarmé* (Paris, Nizet, 1947)

– *Le Livre de Mallarmé* (Paris, Gallimard, 1957)

Sessions, Roger, *Questions about Music* (Harvard, 1970)

Sewell, Elizabeth, *The Structure of Poetry* (Routledge, 1951)

Sharman, Gopal, *Filigree in Sound* (Andre Deutsch, 1970)

Sollers, Philippe, *Logiques* (Paris, Editions du Seuil, 1968)

Southern, Richard, *The Seven Ages of Theatre* (Faber, 1960)

Steiner, George, *Extraterritorial* (Faber, 1972)

– *Language and Silence* (Faber, 1967)

Stevens, Wallace, *The Necessary Angel* (Faber, 1960)

Stokes, Adrian, *The Image in Form*, ed. Richard Wollheim (Penguin, 1972)

Stravinsky, Igor, *Conversations with Robert Craft* (Penguin, 1962)

– *The Poetics of Music* (O.U.P., 1947)

Symons, Arthur, *The Symbolist Movement* (Constable, 1908)

Thibaudet, Albert, *La Poésie de Stéphane Mallarmé* (Paris, Gallimard, 1926)

Valéry, Paul, *Ecrits Divers sur Stéphane Mallarmé* (Paris, Gallimard, 1958)

– *Eupalinos: L'Ame et la Danse* (O.U.P. 1967)

– *Œuvres, passim*

Villiers de l'Isle-Adam, *Axel* (Paris, Ed. du Vieux Colombier, 1960)

– *Contes Cruels* (Paris, Garnier, 1968)

– *L'Eve Future* (Paris, Club du Meilleur Livre, 1957)

– *Isis* (Paris, Crès et Cie. 1923)

– *Morgane* (Paris, Chamuel, 1894)

Wagner, Richard, *On Music and Drama* (New York, Dutton, 1964)

Walzer, Pierre-Olivier, *Essai sur Mallarmé* (Paris, Pierre Seghers, 1963)

Wheelwright, Philip, *The Burning Fountain* (Bloomington Indiana U.P. 1968)

– *Metaphor and Reality* (Bloomington Indiana U.P. 1962)

Whyte, L. L. (ed.) *Aspects of Form* (Lund Humphries, 1968)

Wilde, Oscar, *Complete Works* (Collins, 1948)

Wittgenstein, Ludwig, *Tractatus Logico-Philosophicus* (Routledge, 1922)

Wolfflin, Heinrich, *Principles of Art History*, trans. M. D. Holliger (New York, Holt, 1932)

Wollheim, Richard, *Art and its Objects* (Pelican Books, 1970)

INDEX

Poe, Edgar Allan, 2, 17n, 31–4, 40,
48, 60–4, 77, 186, 208, 224
poet, image of, 13, 29, 31–3, 86, 133
'Préciosité', 30, 99–100, 116, 120, 156,
181, 185, 197
prose
category of, 3
circumstances of, 55
constancy of, 203
of 'La Dernière Mode', 104–5
and hallucination, 105
and legend, 70
impact of, 171
movement of, 173
of a poet, 1
prose poem, 54, 55
rhythm of, 200
Proust, Marcel, 11, 137, 206, 221, 230
punctuation, 82, 170, 183, 187

Queneau, Raymond, 11

reading
adequacy of, 169–70
after-effect of, 193
and dance, 159–61
and 'La Dernière Mode', 86–7
and Maupassant, 46
and mime, 154
and painting, 74
practice of, 4, 204, 210–21 *passim*,
227
and silence, 154
Regnault, Henri, 24
Régnier, Henri de, 49, 125
religion
atmosphere of, 137–9
in 'Le Livre', 162
Richard, J.-P., 69n, 113, 159n, 228
Rimbaud, Arthur, 4, 17–21, 31, 33,
73, 208
Robbe-Grillet, Alain, 229, 230
Rodenbach, Georges, 95, 155

'Salut', 90n
Schérer, Jacques, 120n, 162n, 164n
sentence form, 82, 83
'Ses Purs Ongles', 3
Shakespeare, William, 34, 124, 148;
see also Hamlet and *Macbeth*
solitude
of artist/performer, 27–8
of writer, 33, 170, 191n
spoken language, 6, 110, 154, 162–6
Steiner, George, 117n
Sterne, Laurence, 74n

Stevens, Wallace, 20, 98
Stravinsky, Igor, 58, 60, 229
structuralism, 223, 229; *see also*
architectural quality of language
subject
of fashion, 105–8, 116
of language, 75, 171, 199, 221
of music, 193
of 'Le Nénuphar Blanc', 58–9
of painting, 52
of Poe's writing, 64
of sentence, 83
Swinburne, Algernon, 29–31, 61
symbolism
in dance, 146, 172
in language, 96–106, 154n
literary movement, 2, 13
nature of, 7
in 'Le Nénuphar Blanc', 59
syntax, 170, 210

Tailhade, Laurent, 23
Tennyson, 11, 28–31, 61
theatricality
of literature, 28–9, 134, 166–7
of theatre, 124, 127, 132
time
and literature, 45
and literary tribute, 41
and theatre, 150–3 *passim*
virtual literary, 197
and work of art, 53
and world of fashion, 87–93 *passim*
translation
of the 'Contes Indiens', 64–70
nature of, 60–2
of Poe's poetry, 62–4
task of, 54
virtual, of Ghil's writing, 25

Valéry, Paul, 224–5, 226n, 231
'Variations sur un Sujet', 5, 8, 54n,
109, 167. 168–222
Verlaine Paul, 4, 11, 13–15, 48, 164,
171
Vicaire, Gabriel, 226n
Villiers de l'Isle-Adam, 34, 38–45
passim, 47, 98, 119, 174

Wagner, Richard, 4, 27, 34–8, 48,
115, 128, 135, 150–2, 171
Whistler, James MacNeill, 61
Wilde, Oscar, 105
Wittgenstein, Ludwig, 24, 210, 221

Zola, Emile, 45, 47–8, 49